D1356101

Javier Esparza · Keijo Heljanko

Unfoldings

A Partial-Order Approach to Model Checking

 Springer

Prof. Dr. Javier Esparza
Chair for Foundations of Software
Reliability and
Theoretical Computer Science
Faculty of Computer Science
Technische Universität München
Munich, Germany
esparza@in.tum.de

Dr. Keijo Heljanko
Department of Information
and Computer Science
Helsinki University of Technology (TKK)
Finland
Keijo.Heljanko@tkk.fi

Series Editors

Prof. Dr. Wilfried Brauer
Institut für Informatik der TUM
Boltzmannstr. 3
85748 Garching, Germany
brauer@informatik.tu-muenchen.de

Prof. Dr. Grzegorz Rozenberg
Leiden Institute of Advanced
Computer Science
University of Leiden
Niels Bohrweg 1
2333 CA Leiden, The Netherlands
rozenber@liacs.nl

Prof. Dr. Juraj Hromkovič
ETH Zentrum
Department of Computer Science
Swiss Federal Institute of Technology
8092 Zürich, Switzerland
juraj.hromkovic@inf.ethz.ch

Prof. Dr. Arto Salomaa
Turku Centre of
Computer Science
Lemminkäisenkatu 14 A
20520 Turku, Finland
asalomaa@utu.fi

ISBN 978-3-540-77425-9   e-ISBN 978-3-540-77426-6

Monographs in Theoretical Computer Science. An EATCS Series. ISSN 1431-2654

Library of Congress Control Number: 2008921563

ACM Computing Classification (1998): D.2.4, F.3.1, F.1.2

Cover Design: KünkelLopka GmbH, Heidelberg

Printed on acid-free paper

9 8 7 6 5 4 3 2 1

springer.com

To Eike, who inspired all this.

To Virpi and Sara, with love.

Foreword by Ken McMillan

The design and analysis of concurrent systems has proved to be one of the most vexing practical problems in computer science. We need such systems if we want to compute at high speed and yet distribute the computation over distances too long to allow synchronizing communication to a global clock. At the speed of modern computer systems, one centimeter is already a long distance for synchronization. For this and other reasons, almost all systems that involve a computer also involve asynchronous concurrency in some way, in the form of threads or message passing algorithms or network communication protocols.

Yet designing correct concurrent systems is a daunting task. This is largely due to the problem of "interleavings". That is, the designer of a concurrent system must somehow account for the fantastic number of possible orderings of actions that can be generated by independent processes running at different speeds. This leads to unreproducible errors, occurring randomly with a frequency low enough to make testing and debugging extremely problematic, but high enough to make systems unacceptably unreliable.

One possible solution to the problem is offered by model checking. This is a fully automated verification technique that constructs a graph representing all possible states of the system and the transitions between them. This state graph can be thought of as a finite folding of an infinite "computation tree" containing all possible executions of the system. Using the state graph, we can definitively answer questions about the system's behavior posed in temporal logic, a specialized notation for specifying systems that evolve in time.

Unfortunately, because the computation tree explicitly represents all possible interleavings of concurrent actions, the size of the state graph we must construct can become intractably large, even for simple systems. Yet intuitively, one could argue that these interleavings must be mostly irrelevant. That is, if all the interleavings produced qualitatively different behavior, the system would not appear coherent to a user. Somehow, all those interleavings must fall into a small set of equivalence classes.

Unfoldings provide one way to exploit this observation. An unfolding is a mathematical structure that explicitly represents concurrency and causal dependence between events, and also the points where a choice occurs between qualitatively different behaviors. Like a computation tree, it captures at once all possible behaviors of a system, and we need only examine a finite part of it to answer certain questions about the system. However, unlike a computation tree, it does not make interleavings explicit, and so it can be exponentially more concise. Over the last fifteen years, research on unfoldings has led to practical tools that can be used to analyze concurrent systems without falling victim to the interleaving problem.

Javier Esparza and Keijo Heljanko have been leading exponents of this line of research. Here, they present an accessible elementary account of the most important results in the area. They develop, in an incremental fashion, all of the basic theoretical machinery needed to use unfoldings for the verification of temporal properties of concurrent systems. The book brings together material from disparate sources into a coherent framework, with an admirable balance of generality with intuition. Examples are provided for all the important concepts using the simple Petri net formalism, while the theory is developed for a more general synchronized transition system model. The mathematical background required is only elementary set theory, with all necessary definitions provided.

For those interested in model checking, this book should provide a clear overview of one of the major streams of thought in dealing with concurrency and the interleaving problem, and an excellent point of entry to the research literature. Those with a background in concurrency theory may be interested to see an algorithmic application of this theory to solve a practical problem. Since concurrent systems occur in many fields (biological systems such as gene regulatory networks come to mind) this work may even find readers outside computer science. In any event, bringing this material together into a single accessible volume is certain to create a wider appreciation for and understanding of unfoldings and their applications.

Berkeley, October 2007   *Ken McMillan*

Preface

Model checking is a very popular technique for the automatic verification of systems, widely applied by the hardware industry and already receiving considerable attention from software companies. It is based on the (possibly exhaustive) exploration of the states reached by the system along all its executions.

Model checking is very successful in finding bugs in concurrent systems. These systems are notoriously hard to design correctly, mostly because of the inherent uncertainty about the order in which components working in parallel execute actions. Since n independent actions can occur in $n!$ different orders, humans easily overlook some of them, often the one causing a bug. On the contrary, model checking exhaustively examines all execution orders. Unfortunately, naive model checking techniques can only be applied to very small systems. The number of reachable states grows so quickly, that even a modern computer fails to explore them all in reasonable time.

In this book we show that concurrency theory, the study of mathematical formalisms for the description and analysis of concurrent systems, helps to solve this problem. Unfoldings are one of these formalisms, belonging to the class of so-called *true concurrency* models. They were introduced in the early 1980s as a mathematical model of causality. Our reason for studying them is far more pragmatic: unfoldings of highly concurrent systems are often far smaller and can be explored much faster than the state space.

Being at the crossroads of automatic verification and concurrency theory, this book is addressed to researchers and graduate students working in either of these two fields. It is self-contained, although some previous exposure to models of concurrent systems, like communicating automata or Petri nets, can help to understand the material.

We are grateful to Ken McMillan for initiating the unfolding technique in his PhD thesis, and for agreeing to write the Foreword. Our appreciation goes to Eike Best, Ilkka Niemelä, and Leo Ojala for their guidance when we started work on this topic. We thank Pradeep Kanade, Victor Khomenko, Maciej Koutny, Stephan Melzer, Stefan Römer, Claus Schröter, Stefan Schwoon, and

Walter Vogler, the coauthors of our work on the unfolding technique, for their ideas and efforts. We are indebted to Burkhard Graves, Stefan Melzer, Stefan Römer, Patrik Simons, Stefan Schwoon, Claus Schröter, and Frank Wallner for implementing prototypes and other tools that very much helped to test and refine the ideas of the book. Some of them were integrated in the PEP tool, a project led by Eike Best, and coordinated by Bernd Grahlmann and Christian Stehno, and others in the Model Checking Kit, coordinated by Claus Schröter and Stefan Schwoon. We thank them for their support. Thomas Chatain, Stefan Kiefer, Victor Khomenko, Kari Kähkönen, Beatriz Sánchez, Stefan Schwoon, and Walter Vogler provided us with valuable comments on various drafts, for which we express our gratitude. We thank Wilfried Brauer for his continuous support and his help in finding a publisher, and Ronan Nugent, from Springer, for his smooth handling of the publication process.

München, Germany and Espoo, Finland,   *Javier Esparza*
October 2007   *Keijo Heljanko*

Contents

1

Introduction

State space methods are the most popular approach to the automatic verification of concurrent systems. In their basic form, these methods explore the *transition system* associated with the concurrent system. Loosely speaking, the transition system is a graph having the reachable states of the system as nodes, and an edge from a state s to another state s' whenever the system can make a move from s to s'. In the worst case, state space methods need to explore all nodes and transitions of the transition system.

The main problem of transition systems as a basis for state space methods is the well-known *state explosion* problem. Imagine a concurrent system consisting of n sequential subsystems, communicating in some way, and assume further that each of these subsystems can be in one out of m possible states. The global state of the concurrent system is given by the local states of its components, and so the system may have up to m^n reachable states; in fact, this bound is already reached by the rather uninteresting system whose components run independently of each other, without communicating at all. So very small concurrent systems may generate very large transition systems. As a consequence, naive state space methods may have huge time and space requirements even for very small and simple systems.

The unfolding method is a technique for alleviating the state explosion problem. It uses results of the theory of *true concurrency* to replace transition systems by special partially ordered graphs. While these graphs contain full information about the reachable states of the system, their nodes are not reachable states themselves. In particular, the number of nodes of the graph does not grow linearly in the number of reachable states. Since its introduction by McMillan in [84, 85, 86], the unfolding technique has attracted considerable attention. It has been further analyzed and improved [88, 39, 71, 41, 73], parallelized [61, 110], distributed [8], and extended from the initial algorithms, which only allowed us to check the reachability of a state or the existence of a deadlock, to algorithms for (almost) arbitrary properties expressible in Linear Temporal Logic (LTL) [28, 35, 37]. Initially developed, as we shall see below, for systems modeled as "plain" Petri nets, it has been extended to high-level Petri nets [72, 110], symmetrical Petri nets [29], unbounded Petri nets [2], nets with read arcs [121], time Petri nets [43, 21, 22], products of transition systems [39], automata communicating through queues [83], networks of timed automata [16, 19], process algebras [80], and graph grammars [7]. It has been implemented in several tools [110, 111, 61, 78, 89, 51, 58, 37] and applied, among other problems, to conformance checking [87], analysis and synthesis of asynchronous circuits [74, 76, 75], monitoring and diagnosis of discrete event systems [10, 9, 20], and analysis of asynchronous communication protocols [83].

The goal of this book is to provide a gentle introduction to the basics of the unfolding method, and in particular to give a detailed account of an unfolding-based algorithm for model checking concurrent systems against properties specified as formulas of Linear Temporal Logic (LTL)[1], one of the most popular specification formalisms in the area of automatic verification. Our intended audience is researchers working on automatic verification, and in particular those interested in grasping the algorithmic ideas behind the method, more than the details of true concurrency semantics.

An important question when planning the book was which formalism to choose as system model. The unfolding method requires a formalism having a notion of concurrent components; in particular, the formalism should allow us to determine for each action of the system which components participate in the action and which ones remain idle. For historical reasons, most papers on the unfolding method use Petri nets. We decided to deviate from this tradition and use *synchronous products of labeled transition systems* (*products* for short), introduced by Arnold in [4]. Loosely speaking, in this formalism sequential components are modeled as transition systems (one could also say as finite automata). Components may execute joint actions by means of a very general synchronization mechanism, containing as special cases the mechanisms of process algebras like Milner's Calculus of Communicating Systems (CCS) [90] and Hoare's Communicating Sequential Processes (CSP) [64]. There were three main reasons for choosing products. First, an automata-based model makes clear that the unfolding method is applicable not only to Petri nets. The unfolding method is not tied to a particular formalism, although its details may depend on the formalism to which it is applied. Second, products provide some more information than Petri nets about the structure of the system, and at a certain point in the book (Chap. 4) we exploit this information to obtain some interesting results. Finally (and this is our main reason), products of transition systems contain transition systems as a particular case. Since a transition system is a product of n transition systems for $n = 1$, we can present verification procedures for products by first exhibiting a procedure for the case $n = 1$, and then generalizing it to arbitrary n. This approach is very suitable for describing and discussing the problems raised by

---

[1] For the so-called stuttering-invariant fragment of LTL, see Chap. 8 for details.

distributed systems, and their solutions. Moreover, the case $n = 1$ is usually simple, and provides a gentle first approximation to the general case.

The reader may now wonder whether the book covers the unfolding method for Petri nets. The answer is yes and no. It covers unfolding methods for so-called *1-bounded* Petri nets (for definition of 1-bounded nets, see, e.g., [30]). Readers interested in unfolding techniques for more general net classes will find numerous pointers to the literature.

Structure of the Book

Chapter 2 introduces transition systems and their products as formal models of sequential and concurrent systems, respectively. As mentioned above, this makes sequential systems a special case of concurrent systems: they correspond to the tuples of transition systems of dimension 1, i.e., having only one component.

Chapter 3 presents the unfolding of a product as a generalization of the well-known unfolding of a transition system (or just a graph) into a tree. In particular, it explains why unfolding a product can be faster than constructing and representing its state space as a transition system. The chapter also introduces the notion of *search procedure*, and lists the three basic verification problems that must be solved in order to provide a model checking algorithm for LTL properties: the *executability*, *repeated executability*, and *livelock* problems.

These three problems are studied in Chaps. 4, 6, and 7, respectively. All these chapters have the same structure: First, a search procedure is presented that solves the problem for transition systems, i.e., for products of dimension 1; the correctness of the procedure is proved, and its complexity is determined. Then, this procedure is generalized to a search procedure for the general case.

The executability problem is the most important of the three. In particular, it is the only problem that needs to be solved in order to answer reachability questions and safety properties. Chapter 5 studies it in more detail, and presents a number of important results which are not directly relevant for the model checking procedure.

Chapter 8 introduces the model checking problem and presents a solution based on the procedures obtained in the previous chapters.

Chapter 9 summarizes the results of the book and provides references to papers studying experimental questions, extensions of the unfolding method, and implementations.

2

Transition Systems and Products

In this chapter we introduce transition systems as a formal model of sequential systems, and synchronous products of transition systems as a model of concurrent systems.

2.1 Transition Systems

A *transition system* is a tuple $\mathcal{A} = \langle S, T, \alpha, \beta, is \rangle$, where

- S is a set of *states*,
- T is a set of *transitions*,
- $\alpha : T \to S$ associates with each transition its *source* state,
- $\beta : T \to S$ associates with each transition its *target* state, and
- $is \in S$ is the *initial state*.

Graphically, states are represented by circles, and a transition t with s and s' as source and target states is represented by an arrow leading from s to s' and labeled by t. We mark the initial state is with a small wedge.

Example 2.1. Figure 2.1 shows a transition system $\mathcal{A} = \langle S, T, \alpha, \beta, is \rangle$ where $S = \{s_1, s_2, s_3, s_4\}$, $T = \{t_1, t_2, t_3, t_4, t_5\}$, and $is = s_1$. We have for instance $\alpha(t_1) = s_1$ and $\beta(t_1) = s_2$.

We call a finite or infinite sequence of transitions a *transition word* or just a *word*. Given a transition t, we call the triple $\langle \alpha(t), t, \beta(t) \rangle$ a *step* of $\mathcal{A}$. A state s *enables* a transition t if there is a state s' such that $\langle s, t, s' \rangle$ is a step. A (possibly empty) transition word $t_1 t_2 \ldots t_k$ is a *computation* of $\mathcal{A}$ if there is a sequence $s_0 s_1 \ldots s_k$ of states such that $\langle s_{i-1}, t_i, s_i \rangle$ is a step for every $i \in \{1, \ldots, k\}$;[1] we say that the computation starts at s_0 and leads to s_k. A computation is a *history* if $s_0 = is$, i.e., if it can be executed from the initial state. An infinite word $t_1 t_2 \ldots$ is an *infinite computation* of $\mathcal{A}$ if there

---

[1] Notice that there is at most one such sequence of states.

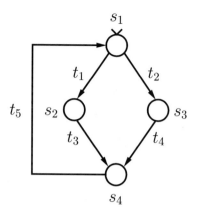

Fig. 2.1. A transition system

is an infinite sequence $s_0, s_1, \ldots$ of states such that $\langle s_{i-1}, t_i, s_i \rangle$ is a step for every $i \geq 1$, and an *infinite history* if moreover $s_0 = is$.

If h is a history leading to a state s and c is a computation that can be executed from s, then hc is also a history. We then say that h *can be extended by* c.

2.2 Products of Transition Systems

Let $\mathcal{A}_1, \ldots, \mathcal{A}_n$ be transition systems, where $\mathcal{A}_i = \langle S_i, T_i, \alpha_i, \beta_i, is_i \rangle$. A *synchronization constraint* **T** is a subset of the set

$$(T_1 \cup \{\epsilon\}) \times \cdots \times (T_n \cup \{\epsilon\}) \setminus \{\langle \epsilon, \ldots, \epsilon \rangle\}$$

where ϵ is an special symbol intended to denote inaction (idling). The elements of **T** are called *global transitions*. If $\mathbf{t} = \langle t_1, \ldots, t_n \rangle$ and $t_i \neq \epsilon$, then we say that $\mathcal{A}_i$ *participates* in $\mathbf{t}$.[2] The tuple $\mathbf{A} = \langle \mathcal{A}_1, \ldots, \mathcal{A}_n, \mathbf{T} \rangle$ is called the *product* of $\mathcal{A}_1, \ldots, \mathcal{A}_n$ under **T**. $\mathcal{A}_1, \ldots, \mathcal{A}_n$ are the *components* of **A**.

Intuitively, a global transition $\mathbf{t} = \langle t_1, \ldots t_n \rangle$ models a possible move of $\mathcal{A}_1, \ldots, \mathcal{A}_n$. If $t_i = \epsilon$, then $\mathbf{t}$ can occur without $\mathcal{A}_i$ even "noticing".

Example 2.2. Figure 2.2 shows a product of transition systems with two components and seven global transitions. The first component participates in five of them, and the second component in four.

A *global state* of **A** is a tuple $\mathbf{s} = \langle s_1, \ldots, s_n \rangle$, where $s_i \in S_i$ for every $i \in \{1, \ldots, n\}$. The *initial global state* is the tuple $\mathbf{is} = \langle is_1, \ldots, is_n \rangle$.

---

[2] This is the reason why $\langle \epsilon, \ldots, \epsilon \rangle$ is excluded from the set of global transitions: at least one component must participate in every global transition.

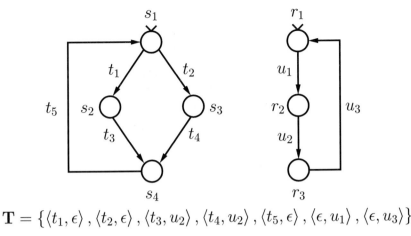

$$\mathbf{T} = \{\langle t_1, \epsilon\rangle, \langle t_2, \epsilon\rangle, \langle t_3, u_2\rangle, \langle t_4, u_2\rangle, \langle t_5, \epsilon\rangle, \langle \epsilon, u_1\rangle, \langle \epsilon, u_3\rangle\}$$

Fig. 2.2. A product of transition systems

A *step* of $\mathbf{A}$ is a triple $\langle\mathbf{s}, \mathbf{t}, \mathbf{s}'\rangle$, where $\mathbf{s} = \langle s_1, \ldots, s_n\rangle$ and $\mathbf{s}' = \langle s_1', \ldots, s_n'\rangle$ are global states and $\mathbf{t} = \langle t_1, \ldots, t_n\rangle$ is a global transition satisfying the following conditions for all $i \in \{1, \ldots, n\}$:

- if $t_i \neq \epsilon$, then $s_i' = \beta_i(t_i)$ and $s_i = \alpha(t_i)$; and
- if $t_i = \epsilon$, then $s_i' = s_i$.

We say that $\mathbf{s}$ *enables* $\mathbf{t}$ if there is a global state $\mathbf{s}'$ such that $\langle\mathbf{s}, \mathbf{t}, \mathbf{s}'\rangle$ is a step.

Once the notion of a step has been defined, we can easily lift the definitions of word, computation, and history to products. We call a finite or an infinite sequence of global transitions a *global transition word*. A (possibly empty) global transition word $\mathbf{t}_1 \ldots \mathbf{t}_k$ is a *global computation* if there is a sequence $\mathbf{s}_0, \mathbf{s}_1, \ldots, \mathbf{s}_k$ of global states such that $\langle\mathbf{s}_{i-1}, \mathbf{t}_i, \mathbf{s}_i\rangle$ is a step for every $i \in \{1, \ldots, k\}$; we say that the global computation can be executed from $\mathbf{s}_0$ and leads to $\mathbf{s}_k$. A global computation is a *global history* if one can take $\mathbf{s}_0 = \mathbf{is}$, i.e., if it can be executed from the initial global state.[3] An infinite global transition word $\mathbf{t}_1\mathbf{t}_2 \ldots$ is an *infinite global computation* if there is an infinite sequence $\mathbf{s}_0\mathbf{s}_1 \ldots$ of global states such that $\langle\mathbf{s}_{i-1}, \mathbf{t}_i, \mathbf{s}_i\rangle$ is a step for every $i \geq 1$.

Example 2.3. Consider the product of Fig. 2.2. The initial global state is $\langle s_1, r_1\rangle$. The global transition word $\langle t_1, \epsilon\rangle \langle \epsilon, u_1\rangle \langle t_3, u_2\rangle$ is a global computation, because of the following three steps:

$$\langle\langle s_1, r_1\rangle, \langle t_1, \epsilon\rangle, \langle s_2, r_1\rangle\rangle,$$
$$\langle\langle s_2, r_1\rangle, \langle \epsilon, u_1\rangle, \langle s_2, r_2\rangle\rangle, \text{ and}$$
$$\langle\langle s_2, r_2\rangle, \langle t_3, u_2\rangle, \langle s_4, r_3\rangle\rangle.$$

---

[3] Notice that, contrary to the case of a computation of a single component, a global computation can be executed from more than one global state.

The computation leads from $\langle s_1, r_1 \rangle$ to $\langle s_4, r_3 \rangle$ and so it is also a global history. The sequence $\langle t_1, \epsilon \rangle \langle t_3, u_1 \rangle$ is not a global computation, because $\langle t_3, u_1 \rangle$ is not a global transition.

If there is no risk of confusion (and this is usually the case, because global states and transitions are always written using boldface or explicitly as tuples) we shorten global word, global computation, global history, etc., to transition word, computation, history, etc..

2.3 Petri Net Representation of Products

A product of transition systems can be represented in different ways. The obvious first possibility is as a tuple of transition systems together with the synchronization constraint. However, when the transition systems are represented graphically as graphs, the global behavior of the system can be difficult to visualize, because the local transitions corresponding to a global transition may be far apart. For small products, a good alternative is to represent them as Petri nets.

A *net* is a triple (P, T, F), where P and T are disjoint sets of *places* and *net transitions* (or just *transitions* when there is no risk of their confusion with the transitions of a transition system) and $F \subseteq (P \times T) \cup (T \times P)$ is the *flow relation*. The elements of F are called *arcs*. Places and transitions are called *nodes*. Graphically, a place is represented by a circle, a transition by a box, and an arc (x, y) by an edge leading from x to y. If $(x, y) \in F$ then x is an *input node* of y and y is an *output node* of x. Notice that the input and output nodes of a place are transitions and those of a transition are places. The sets of input and output nodes of x are denoted by ${}^\bullet x$ and $x^\bullet$, respectively.

A set of places is called a *marking*. A marking is graphically represented by putting a *token* (a black dot) within each of the circles representing its places. A *Petri net* is a tuple $\mathcal{N} = (P, T, F, M_0)$ where (P, T, F) is a net and M_0 is a marking of $\mathcal{N}$ called the *initial marking*.

Example 2.4. Figure 2.3 shows the graphical representation of the Petri net (P, T, F, M_0) where

- $P = \{p_1, p_2, p_3, p_4\}$,
- $T = \{t_1, t_2, t_3\}$,
- $F = \{(p_1, t_2), (p_2, t_2), (p_3, t_1), (p_4, t_3), (t_1, p_1), (t_2, p_3), (t_2, p_4), (t_3, p_2)\}$, and
- $M_0 = \{p_1, p_2\}$.

We have for instance, ${}^\bullet t_2 = \{p_1, p_2\}$ and $t_2{}^\bullet = \{p_3, p_4\}$.

A marking M *enables* a net transition t if it marks every input place of t, i.e., if ${}^\bullet t \subseteq M$. If t is enabled by M then it can *occur* or *fire*, and its occurrence leads to a new marking $M' = (M \setminus {}^\bullet t) \cup t^\bullet$. Graphically, M' is obtained from M by removing one token from each input place and adding one token to

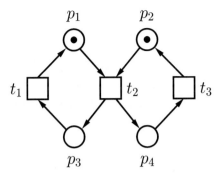

Fig. 2.3. A Petri net

each output place. An *occurrence sequence* is a sequence of transitions that can occur from the initial marking in the order specified by the sequence. We say that the sequence leads from the initial marking to the marking obtained after firing all transitions of the sequence. A marking is *reachable* if some occurrence sequence leads to it.

Example 2.5. The initial marking of the Petri net of Fig. 2.3 enables only transition t_2. After firing t_2 we obtain the marking $\{p_3, p_4\}$. The reachable markings are $\{p_1, p_2\}$, $\{p_1, p_4\}$, $\{p_3, p_2\}$, and $\{p_3, p_4\}$.

The *Petri net representation* of a product $\mathbf{A} = \langle \mathcal{A}_1, \ldots, \mathcal{A}_n, \mathbf{T} \rangle$ of transition systems $\mathcal{A}_i = \langle S_i, T_i, \alpha_i, \beta_i, is_i \rangle$ is the Petri net (P, T, F, M_0) given by:

- $P = S_1 \cup \ldots \cup S_n$,[4]
- $T = \mathbf{T}$,
- $F = \{(s, \mathbf{t}) \mid t_i \neq \epsilon \text{ and } s = \alpha_i(t_i) \text{ for some } i \in \{1, \ldots, n\}\} \cup$
  $\{(\mathbf{t}, s) \mid t_i \neq \epsilon \text{ and } s = \beta_i(t_i) \text{ for some } i \in \{1, \ldots, n\}\}$,
  where t_i denotes the i-th component of $\mathbf{t} \in \mathbf{T}$; and
- $M_0 = \{is_1, \ldots, is_n\}$.

So, loosely speaking, the Petri net representation of a product $\mathbf{A}$ has the local states of $\mathbf{A}$ as places and the global transitions of $\mathbf{A}$ as net transitions. The arcs are determined by the source and target relations of the product's components, and the initial marking by the initial states of the components.

Example 2.6. Figure 2.4 shows the Petri net representation of the product of transition systems of Fig. 2.2. We use the following convention: all nodes of the net corresponding to the states of the transition system on the left of Fig. 2.2 are white, all nodes corresponding to the transition system on the right of Fig. 2.2 are dark grey, and all joint transitions are light grey. We have
${}^\bullet \langle t_2, \epsilon \rangle = \{s_1\}$, $\langle t_2, \epsilon \rangle^\bullet = \{s_3\}$, ${}^\bullet \langle t_4, u_2 \rangle = \{s_3, r_2\}$ and $\langle t_4, u_2 \rangle^\bullet = \{s_4, r_3\}$.

---

[4] We assume that the S_i's are pairwise disjoint.

Notation 1. *Since every global transition of a product yields a net transition in the corresponding Petri net, we can transfer the $\bullet$-notation to global transitions. Given* $\mathbf{t} = \langle t_1, \ldots, t_n \rangle \in \mathbf{T}$ *with* $t_i \in T_i \cup \{\epsilon\}$, *we have*

$$\bullet\mathbf{t} = \{\alpha_i(t_i) \mid t_i \neq \epsilon\} \quad and \quad \mathbf{t}^\bullet = \{\beta(t_i) \mid t_i \neq \epsilon\}.$$

It is easy to see that the semantics of a product coincides with its semantics as a Petri net, in the following sense: A sequence $\mathbf{t}_1\mathbf{t}_2 \ldots \mathbf{t}_k$ is a global history of a product $\mathbf{A}$ if and only if it is an occurrence sequence of its associated Petri net. The advantage of the Petri net representation is that it helps to visualize the product's behavior, at least for small nets. For instance, a look at Fig. 2.4 shows that $\langle \epsilon, u_1 \rangle \langle t_2, \epsilon \rangle \langle t_4, u_2 \rangle \langle t_5, \epsilon \rangle$ is an occurrence sequence, but it is considerably more difficult for the human eye to determine from Fig. 2.2 that the same sequence is a history of the product. It becomes even more difficult for products with three or four components, of which we will exhibit a few in the next chapters.

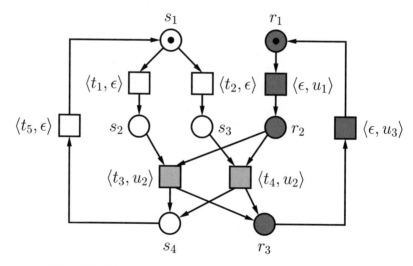

Fig. 2.4. Petri net representation of the product of Fig. 2.2

2.4 Interleaving Representation of Products

In the interleaving semantics we identify a product of transition systems with one single transition system whose states and transitions are the global states and the steps of the product, respectively.

Formally, the *interleaving semantics* of a product $\mathbf{A} = \langle \mathcal{A}_1, \ldots, \mathcal{A}_n, \mathbf{T} \rangle$ is the transition system $\mathcal{T}_\mathbf{A} = \langle S, T, \alpha, \beta, is \rangle$, where

- S is the set of global states of $\mathbf{A}$,
- T is the set of steps $\langle \mathbf{s}, \mathbf{t}, \mathbf{s}' \rangle$ of $\mathbf{A}$,
- for every step $\langle \mathbf{s}, \mathbf{t}, \mathbf{s}' \rangle \in T$: $\alpha(\langle \mathbf{s}, \mathbf{t}, \mathbf{s}' \rangle) = \mathbf{s}$ and $\beta(\langle \mathbf{s}, \mathbf{t}, \mathbf{s}' \rangle) = \mathbf{s}'$; and
- $is = \mathbf{is}$.

Observe that $|S| = \prod_{i=1}^{n} |S_i|$, and so the interleaving semantics of $\mathbf{A}$ can be exponentially larger than $\mathbf{A}$, even if we consider only the states that are reachable from the initial state. Figure 2.5 shows the interleaving semantics of the product of Fig. 2.2.

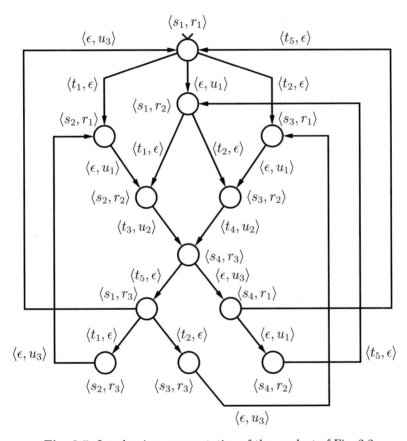

Fig. 2.5. Interleaving representation of the product of Fig. 2.2

As was the case with the Petri net representation, a product is completely determined by its interleaving semantics: The local states can be extracted from the global states, and the global transitions from the steps. Since each transition of each component appears in some global transition by assumption, this allows us to get all transitions of all components.[5]

Bibliographical Notes

As mentioned in the introduction, *synchronous products of labeled transition systems* were introduced by Arnold in [4]. In this model, the synchronization of the transition systems is described by means of an explicit enumeration of the global transitions. While this makes the model very general, when modelling systems the explicit enumeration is usually impractical, because the list of global transitions becomes very large. For instance, the description of Peterson's mutual exclusion algorithm for two processes takes more than one page in [4]. In process algebras like CSP [64] and CCS [90], the set of global transitions is described implicitly. For instance, the CSP synchronization model can be easily adapted to our transition system framework. Given a product $\mathbf{A} = \langle \mathcal{A}_1, \ldots, \mathcal{A}_n, \mathbf{T} \rangle$, we assign to each component $\mathcal{A}_i$ an alphabet Σ_i of *actions*, and label each transition with an action (different transitions may be labeled by the same action). For each action $a \in \bigcup_{i=1}^{n} \Sigma_i$, we define a set of global transitions as follows: a tuple $\langle t_1, \ldots, t_n \rangle$ belongs to the set if for every $i \in \{1, \ldots, n\}$ either $a \notin \Sigma_i$ and $t_i = \epsilon$, or $a \in \Sigma_i$, $t_i \neq \epsilon$, and t_i is labeled by a. So, loosely speaking, a tuple is a global transition for action a if and only if *all* components having a in their alphabets participate in it with a-labeled local transitions. In this way the set of global transitions is implicitly defined by the alphabets of the components and by the transition labels.

Petri nets were introduced in C.A. Petri's dissertation [101, 102]. The particular variant of Petri nets considered here is very close to Elementary Net Systems (see for instance [108]).

---

[5] Note that if we restrict ourselves to the global states reachable from the initial state, only the local transitions which are executable as a part of some global transition enabled in some reachable global state can be recovered, and similarly for the local states of each of the components.

3

Unfolding Products

A transition system $\mathcal{A} = \langle S, T, \alpha, \beta, is \rangle$ can be "unfolded" into a tree. Intuitively, the unfolding can be seen as the "limit" of the construction that starts with the tree having one single node labeled by is, and iteratively extends it as follows: If a node of the current tree enables a transition t, then we add a new edge to the tree labeled by t, and leading to a new node labeled by $\beta(t)$ (to be precise, we only add the edge and the node if they have not been added before). If the transition system has a cycle, then its unfolding is an infinite tree.[1]

Example 3.1. Figure 3.1(**a**) shows the transition system of Fig. 2.1, while Fig. 3.1(**b**) is its unfolding as a transition system, more precisely an initial part of it. For the Petri net presentation of the same unfolding, take a peek at Fig. 3.4 on p. 21. In the rest of the book we will use the Petri net representation in order to make the notation between unfoldings of a single transition system (a product of dimension 1) and a product of transition systems identical.

Notice that we can also look at the unfolding as a *labeled transition system*, i.e., as a transition system whose states and transitions carry labels. The states of the unfolding are the nodes of the tree, and they are labeled with states of the original transition system; the transitions of the unfolding are the edges of the tree, and they are labeled with transitions of the original transition system. Many states (potentially infinitely many) of the unfolding can be labeled with the same state of the original transition system: they correspond to different *visits* to the state. For instance, the unfolding of Fig. 3.1(**b**) contains infinitely many visits to s_1. Similarly with transitions: a transition of the unfolding corresponds to a particular *occurrence* of a transition of the original transition system. In a textual representation the states and transitions of the unfolding would be assigned unique names (for instance, the states labeled by s_1 could be given the names $s_{11}, s_{12}, s_{13}, \ldots$), which are not shown in the graphical representation.

---

[1] These infinite trees are often referred to as *computation trees* in the literature.

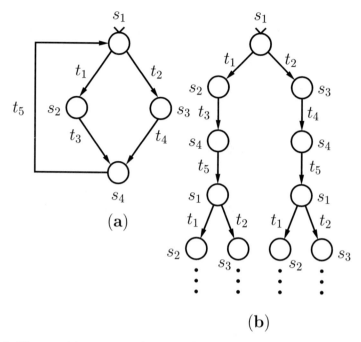

(a)

(b)

Fig. 3.1. The transition system of Fig. 2.1 (a) and its unfolding (b) as a transition system

We now address the question of how to unfold a product. The answer is easy if we take the interleaving representation of products as defined in Sect. 2.4: The unfolding of a product **A** can be defined as the unfolding of the transition system $T_\mathbf{A}$. However, in this book we investigate a different notion of unfolding, which corresponds to taking the Petri net representation of products. In Sect. 3.1 we introduce, first intuitively and then formally, the notion of *branching processes*, and the notion of *the unfolding* of a product as the "largest" branching process. In Sect. 3.2 we present some basic properties of branching processes. Section 3.3 explains why unfolding-based verification can be more efficient than verification based on the interleaving representation of products. Section 3.4 discusses the algorithmic problem of computing the unfolding. Section 3.5 introduces the notion of a search procedure for solving a verification problem. Finally, Sect. 3.6 sets the plan for the next chapters.

3.1 Branching Processes and Unfoldings

The unfolding of a transition system is a labeled transition system, and in the same way the unfolding of a product (represented by a Petri net) is going to be a *labeled* Petri net, more precisely a Petri net whose places and transitions are labeled with places and transitions of the original net. When unfolding a transition system $\mathcal{A}$ we start with one node, labeled with the initial state of $\mathcal{A}$. In the same way, when unfolding a product **A**, we start with one *place* for each component, labeled with the initial state of the component. The net $\mathcal{N}_0$ of Fig. 3.2 corresponds to this initial step for the product of Fig. 2.4 on p. 10. We use in Fig. 3.2 the same node coloring convention as in Fig. 2.4.

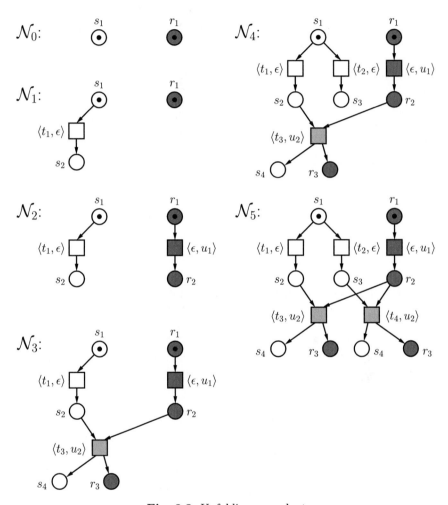

Fig. 3.2. Unfolding a product

When unfolding a transition system $\mathcal{A}$, we proceed as follows: If in the current tree a state enables a transition t then we add a new transition labeled with t and a new state labeled with $\beta(t)$. When unfolding a product **A**, we proceed similarly: If in the current Petri net a reachable *marking* enables a *global* transition **t**, then we add a new net transition labeled with **t** and new places labeled with the states of $\mathbf{t}^\bullet$. After this we connect the transition **t** to the set of places $^\bullet\mathbf{t}$ as its preset and to the freshly generated places of $\mathbf{t}^\bullet$ as its postset. The nets $\mathcal{N}_1, \ldots, \mathcal{N}_5$ of Fig. 3.2 are constructed in this way. Notice that we always add a new transition and new places, even if the current Petri net already contains transitions and places carrying the same labels. For instance, we go from $\mathcal{N}_4$ to $\mathcal{N}_5$ by adding a new transition labeled by $\langle t_4, u_2 \rangle$ and two new places labeled by s_4 and r_3, even though $\mathcal{N}_3$ already contains two places with these labels.

Figure 3.3 on shows the unfolding of the product of Fig. 2.4 on p. 10. Places and transitions are labeled with the names of local states and global transitions of the product. For convenience we use the notation where a transition t_i from the first component denotes the global transition $\langle t_i, \epsilon \rangle$ in all the figures to follow and similarly a transition t_j from the second component denotes $\langle \epsilon, t_j \rangle$. The numbering of the transitions suggests a possible order in which they could have been added, starting from the initial Petri net $\mathcal{N}_0$. Notice that this ordering is different from the one followed in Fig. 3.2, just to know that different orderings are possible.

Convention 1. *In order to avoid confusion, it is convenient to use different names for the transitions of a transition system or product of transition systems, and for the transitions of its unfolding. We call the transitions of an unfolding* events. *An event corresponds to a particular* occurrence *of a transition. In the figures we use the natural numbers* $1, 2, 3, \ldots$ *as event names.*

Formal Definition of Unfolding of a Product

In this section we introduce a class of Petri nets called *branching processes*, and define the unfolding of a product as a particular branching process. Before giving the formal definition (Def. 3.5) we need some preliminaries.

Loosely speaking, a branching process will be either a Petri net containing no events (corresponding to the Petri net $\mathcal{N}_0$ in the example of Fig. 3.2), or the result of extending a branching process with an event (this is how the Petri nets $\mathcal{N}_1, \ldots, \mathcal{N}_5$ in the same example are constructed), or the *union* of a (possibly infinite) set of branching processes. Before defining unions, let us informally explain their role. We use them to generate branching processes with an infinite number of events. In particular, the unfolding of Fig. 3.3 will be the union of *all* the branching processes that can be generated by repeatedly extending $\mathcal{N}_0$, one event at a time, in all possible ways. Intuitively, we can imagine that the sequence $\mathcal{N}_0, \mathcal{N}_1, \ldots, \mathcal{N}_5$ is extended with infinitely many more processes, each one containing one more event than its predecessor, ensuring that every event that can be added is eventually added. While the union of $\mathcal{N}_0, \mathcal{N}_1, \ldots, \mathcal{N}_i$ will always be equal to $\mathcal{N}_i$, the union of all the elements of the sequence produces a new infinite Petri net, namely the one of Fig. 3.3.

Unions of Petri nets are defined component-wise:

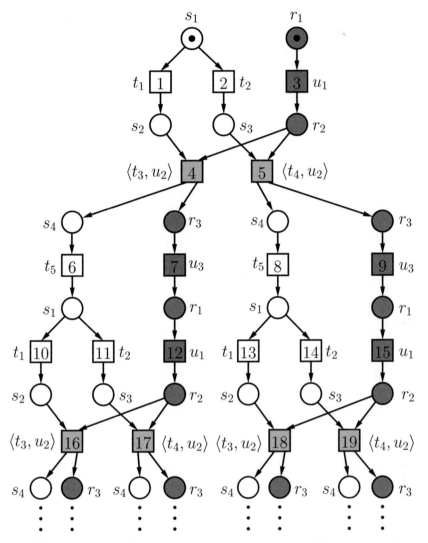

Fig. 3.3. The unfolding of the product represented in Fig. 2.4 on p. 10

Definition 3.2. *The* union $\bigcup N$ *of a (finite or infinite) set N of Petri nets is defined as the Petri net*

$$\bigcup N = \left(\bigcup_{(P,E,F,M_0) \in N} P, \ \bigcup_{(P,E,F,M_0) \in N} E, \ \bigcup_{(P,E,F,M_0) \in N} F, \ \bigcup_{(P,E,F,M_0) \in N} M_0 \right).$$

Unions, however, must be handled with some care. Unless the *names* of the nodes are well chosen, they can generate "wrong" nets that do not correspond at all to the intuition behind the unfolding process. For instance, take two "copies" of the net $\mathcal{N}_0$, but giving the places of the second copy different names than those of the first copy. The union of the two nets is a net with four places, which no longer correspond to our intuition of a branching process. More generally, the union of two isomorphic branching processes, i.e., of two identical branching processes up to renaming of the nodes, may not be isomorphic to any of them. So, even though we are not interested in the names of the nodes per se, we have to worry about them to guarantee that unions work the way they should.

We solve this problem by introducing a canonical way of naming nodes. Loosely speaking, an event labeled by a global transition $\mathbf{t} \in \mathbf{T}$ is given the name $(\mathbf{t}, X)$, where X is the set containing the names of the input places of the event. Similarly, a place labeled by a local state $s \in S_i$ is given the name $(s, \{x\})$, where x is the name of the unique input event of the place. We say that $(\mathbf{t}, X)$ and $(s, \{x\})$ are the *canonical names* of the nodes.

Formally, given a product $\mathbf{A} = \langle \mathcal{A}_1, \ldots, \mathcal{A}_n, \mathbf{T} \rangle$ we define the set $\mathcal{C}$ of *canonical names* as the smallest set satisfying the following property: if $x \in S_1 \cup \ldots \cup S_n \cup \mathbf{T}$ and X is a finite subset of $\mathcal{C}$, then $(x, X) \in \mathcal{C}$. We call x the *label* of (x, X), and say that (x, X) is *labeled* by x. Notice that $\mathcal{C}$ is nonempty, because $(x, \emptyset)$ belongs to $\mathcal{C}$ for every $x \in S_1 \cup \ldots \cup S_n \cup \mathbf{T}$.

Example 3.3. The two places of $\mathcal{N}_0$ in Fig. 3.2 are given the names $(s_1, \emptyset)$ and $(r_1, \emptyset)$. In $\mathcal{N}_1$ these places get the same names. The name of the unique event of $\mathcal{N}_1$ is $(\langle t_1, \epsilon \rangle, \{(s_1, \emptyset)\})$, and the name of its output place is $(s_2, \{(\langle t_1, \epsilon \rangle, \{(s_1, \emptyset)\})\})$.

We can now define $\mathcal{C}$-Petri nets as the Petri nets whose places and transitions are taken from the set $\mathcal{C}$, and in which a place carries a token if and only if it has no predecessors.

Definition 3.4. *A $\mathcal{C}$-Petri net is a Petri net (P, E, F, M_0) such that:*

(1) $P \cup E \subseteq \mathcal{C}$,
(2) if $(x, X) \in P \cup E$, then $X = {}^\bullet(x, X)$; and
(3) for every $(x, X) \in P$, $(x, X) \in M_0$ if and only if $X = \emptyset$.

By (2), in a $\mathcal{C}$-Petri net the preset of a node is part of the name of the node. Therefore, the set of arcs of a $\mathcal{C}$-Petri net is completely determined by its set of places and events. By (3), the same is true of the initial marking of the net. This fact is used in the definition of branching processes:

Definition 3.5. *The set of branching processes of a product $\mathbf{A}$ is the smallest set of $\mathcal{C}$-Petri nets satisfying the following conditions:*

(1) Let $Is = \{(is_1, \emptyset), \ldots, (is_n, \emptyset)\}$, where $\{is_1, \ldots, is_n\}$ is the set of initial states of the components of $\mathbf{A}$. The $\mathcal{C}$-Petri net having Is as set of places and no events is a branching process of $\mathbf{A}$.

(2) Let $\mathcal{N}$ be a branching process of $\mathbf{A}$ such that some reachable marking of $\mathcal{N}$ enables a global transition $\mathbf{t}$. Let M be the set containing the places of the marking that are labeled by $^\bullet\mathbf{t}$. The $\mathcal{C}$-Petri net obtained by adding to $\mathcal{N}$ the event $(\mathbf{t}, M)$ and one place $(s, \{(\mathbf{t}, M)\})$ for every $s \in \mathbf{t}^\bullet$ is also a branching process of $\mathcal{N}$. We call the event $(\mathbf{t}, M)$ a possible extension of $\mathcal{N}$.

(3) If B is a (finite or infinite) set of branching processes of $\mathbf{A}$, then so is $\bigcup B$.

The union of all branching processes of $\mathbf{A}$ is called the unfolding of $\mathbf{A}$. We say that every branching process is a prefix of the unfolding.

Example 3.6. Let us see how the step from $\mathcal{N}_1$ to $\mathcal{N}_2$ in Fig. 3.2 matches this definition. The reachable marking that puts a token on the places marked by s_1 and r_1 enables the transition $\mathbf{t} = \langle \epsilon, u_1 \rangle$. We have $^\bullet\mathbf{t} = \{r_1\}$, and so $\mathcal{N}_1$ can be extended with a new event labeled by $\langle \epsilon, u_1 \rangle$. Since $\langle \epsilon, u_1 \rangle$ has r_2 as only output place, we also add a new place labeled by r_2. More precisely, the names of the new event and the new place are

$$(\langle \epsilon, u_1 \rangle, \{(r_1, \emptyset)\}) \quad \text{and} \quad (r_2, \{(\langle \epsilon, u_1 \rangle, \{(r_1, \emptyset)\})\}).$$

It can be easily checked that if the places and events of the six Petri nets of Fig. 3.2 are given their canonical names, then the union of all six nets is equal to $\mathcal{N}_5$.

At this point the reader may be worried by the length and complexity of the canonical names. Actually, there is no reason to worry. Canonical names are just a mathematical tool allowing us to define the infinite branching processes of a product and reason about them. The algorithms of the next chapters only compute *finite prefixes* of the unfoldings, and the names of their places and events can be chosen arbitrarily; the canonical names need not be used. As a matter of fact, the canonical names will never be used again in this book.

Fundamental Property of Unfoldings

Intuitively, the unfolding of a product exhibits "the same behavior" as the product. We formalize this idea by defining the steps of an unfolding and arguing that the steps of a product and the steps of its unfolding are very tightly related.

Given two markings M, M' and an event e of the unfolding of a product $\mathbf{A}$, we say that the triple $\langle M, e, M' \rangle$ is a *step* if M enables e and the occurrence of e leads from M to M'. To formulate our proposition we still need some notation. Given a node x (place or event) of the unfolding, we denote the label of x by $\lambda(x)$. Furthermore, given a set X of nodes we define $\lambda(X) = \{\lambda(x) \mid x \in X\}$.

Proposition 3.7. *Let $\mathbf{s}$ be a reachable state of $\mathbf{A}$, and let M be a reachable marking of the unfolding of $\mathbf{A}$ such that $\lambda(M) = \mathbf{s}$.*[2]

---

[2] More precisely, such that $\mathbf{s} = \langle s_1, \ldots, s_n \rangle$ and $\lambda(M) = \{s_1, \ldots s_n\}$, i.e., we abuse language and identify the tuple $\langle s_1, \ldots, s_n \rangle$ and the set $\{s_1, \ldots s_n\}$.

(a) If $\langle M, e, M' \rangle$ is a step of the unfolding, then there is a step $\langle \mathbf{s}, \mathbf{t}, \mathbf{s}' \rangle$ of $\mathbf{A}$ such that $\lambda(e) = \mathbf{t}$, and $\lambda(M') = \mathbf{s}'$.

(b) If $\langle \mathbf{s}, \mathbf{t}, \mathbf{s}' \rangle$ is a step of $\mathbf{A}$, then there is a step $\langle M, e, M' \rangle$ of the unfolding such that $\lambda(e) = \mathbf{t}$, and $\lambda(M') = \mathbf{s}'$.

It is not difficult to give a formal proof of this proposition, but the proof is tedious and uninteresting. For this reason, we only present an example.

Example 3.8. Let p_{10}, p_7 be the input places of the events 10 and 7 in Fig. 3.3 on p. 17, respectively. The marking $\{p_{10}, p_7\}$ is reachable . Furthermore, the triple $\langle \{p_{10}, p_7\}, 10, \{p'_{10}, p_7\} \rangle$, where p'_{10} is the output place of event 10, is a step. We have $\lambda(\{p_{10}, p_7\}) = \langle s_1, r_3 \rangle$, $\lambda(10) = \langle t_1, \epsilon \rangle$, and $\lambda(\{p'_{10}, p_7\}) = \langle s_2, r_3 \rangle$. As guaranteed by part (a) of Prop. 3.7, the triple $\langle \langle s_1, r_3 \rangle, \langle t_1, \epsilon \rangle, \langle s_2, r_3 \rangle \rangle$ is a step of the product of Fig. 2.4 on p. 10.

For the converse, consider the global state $\langle s_1, r_3 \rangle$. The three possible steps from this state are

$$\langle \, \langle s_1, r_3 \rangle, \langle t_1, \epsilon \rangle, \langle s_2, r_3 \rangle \, \rangle,$$
$$\langle \, \langle s_1, r_3 \rangle, \langle t_2, \epsilon \rangle, \langle s_3, r_3 \rangle \, \rangle, \text{ and}$$
$$\langle \, \langle s_1, r_3 \rangle, \langle \epsilon, u_3 \rangle, \langle s_1, r_1 \rangle \, \rangle.$$

Since $\lambda(\{p_{10}, p_7\}) = \langle s_1, r_3 \rangle$, by Prop. 3.7(b) the unfolding must have three corresponding steps from the marking $\{p_{10}, p_7\}$, and indeed this is the case as shown by

$$\langle \, \langle p_{10}, p_7 \rangle, 10, \langle p'_{10}, p_7 \rangle \, \rangle,$$
$$\langle \, \langle p_{10}, p_7 \rangle, 11, \langle p'_{11}, p_7 \rangle \, \rangle, \text{ and}$$
$$\langle \, \langle p_{10}, p_7 \rangle, \ 7, \langle p_{10}, p'_7 \rangle \, \rangle,$$

where p'_7 and p'_{11} denote the output places of the events 7 and 11, respectively.

In particular, Prop. 3.7 implies the existence of a very tight relation between the histories of a product $\mathbf{A}$ and the occurrence sequences of its unfolding. In order to formulate this result, we extend the labeling function λ to sequences of events. Given a finite or infinite sequence $\sigma = e_0 \, e_1 \, e_2 \, \ldots$, we define $\lambda(\sigma) = \lambda(e_0) \, \lambda(e_1) \, \lambda(e_2) \, \ldots$.

Corollary 3.9. *(a) If σ is a (finite or infinite) occurrence sequence of the unfolding, then $\lambda(\sigma)$ is a history of $\mathbf{A}$.*

(b) If $\mathbf{h}$ is a history of $\mathbf{A}$, then some occurrence sequence of the unfolding satisfies $\lambda(\sigma) = \mathbf{h}$.

Proof. (a) Let $\sigma = e_0 \, e_1 \, e_2 \, \ldots$. Since σ is an occurrence sequence there are markings $M_0, M_1, M_2 \ldots$ such that M_0 is the initial marking of the unfolding and $\langle M_i, e_i, M_{i+1} \rangle$ is a step for every index $i \geq 0$ in the sequence. By the definition of the unfolding, $\lambda(M_0)$ is the initial state of $\mathbf{A}$; by Prop. 3.7, $\langle \lambda(M_i), \lambda(e_i), \lambda(M_{i+1}) \rangle$ is a step of $\mathbf{A}$. It follows that $\lambda(\sigma)$ is a history of $\mathbf{A}$.

(b) The argument is analogous. $\square$

Products with Only One Component

A transition system can be seen as a degenerate product of transition systems with only one component. In the rest of the book we look at transition systems this way, and speak of the branching processes and the unfolding of a transition system. Figure 3.4(**a**) shows a transition system and Fig. 3.4(**b**) its unfolding as a branching process. Observe that the branching processes and the unfolding of a transition system are trees. In particular, the events always have one single input and one single output place.

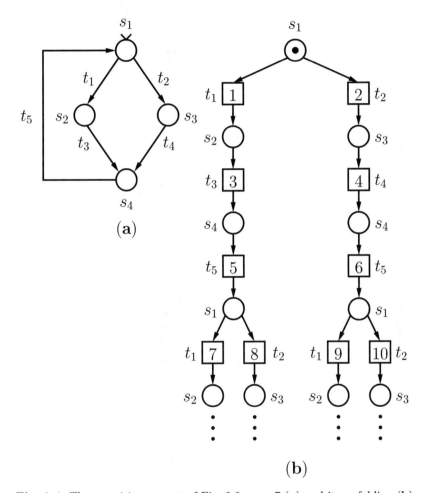

Fig. 3.4. The transition system of Fig. 2.2 on p. 7 (**a**) and its unfolding (**b**)

3.2 Some Properties of Branching Processes

We list some properties of branching processes. They can all be easily proved by structural induction on the definition of branching processes, and in most cases we only sketch their proofs.

3.2.1 Branching Processes Are Synchronizations of Trees

A branching process of a transition system is a tree. Intuitively, a branching process of a product can be seen as a synchronization of trees. We formalize this idea.

Definition 3.10. *A place of an unfolding is an i-place if it is labeled by a state of the ith component. The i-root is the unique i-place having no input events. An event is an i-event if it is labeled by a global transition $\langle t_1, \ldots, t_n \rangle$ such that $t_i \neq \epsilon$. In other words, an event is an i-event if the ith component participates in the global transition it is labeled with.*

It follows that an i-place can only be a j-place if $j = i$; on the contrary, an event can be an i-event and a j-event even for $i \neq j$ if both $\mathcal{A}_i$ and $\mathcal{A}_j$ participate in the transition it is labeled with.

Proposition 3.11. *Let $\mathcal{N}$ be a branching process of $\mathbf{A}$. Then:*

(1) $\mathcal{N}$ has no cycles, i.e., no (nonempty) path of arcs leads from a node to itself.

(2) For every $i \in \{1, \ldots n\}$, every reachable marking of $\mathcal{N}$ puts a token in exactly one i-place.

(3) The set of i-nodes of the branching process $\mathcal{N}$ forms a tree with the i-root as root. Moreover, the tree only branches at places, i.e., if a node of the tree has more than one child, then it is a place.

(4) A place of $\mathcal{N}$ can get marked at most once (i.e., if along an occurrence sequence it becomes marked and then unmarked, then it never becomes marked again), and an event of $\mathcal{N}$ can occur at most once in an occurrence sequence.

Proof. (1) The branching process without events has no cycles, and the two operations that produce new branching processes preserve this property.

(2) The property holds for the branching process without events. By Def. 3.5 every event of a branching process has an input i-place if and only if it has an output i-place, and therefore its firing preserves the property.

(3) By (1) it suffices to prove that every i-node has at most one i-predecessor. This holds for the branching process without events. By Def. 3.5, every i-event has exactly one input i-place, and every i-place has exactly one input i-event with the exception of the i-root, which has none.

(4) Let e be an event of $\mathcal{N}$, and let p be one of its input places. Let i be the unique component index such that p is an i-place and let p' be the unique

output i-place of e. Assume that e occurs in some occurrence sequence. Right after the occurrence of e the place p' is marked. By (2) and (3), every subsequent marking puts a token at some i-place $p'' \geq p$. By (1), $p'' \neq p$, and so the place p never becomes marked again, and e never occurs again.   □

Example 3.12. In Fig. 3.3 on p. 17, the 1-nodes are represented in white and the 2-nodes in dark grey. The events that are both 1-events and 2-events are in light grey. The tree of 1-nodes is the one formed by the white and light grey nodes, and the tree of 2-nodes the one formed by the dark grey and light grey nodes.

3.2.2 Causality, Conflict, and Concurrency

Two events of the unfolding of a transition system are either connected by a path of net arcs or not. For instance, events 1 and 5 of Fig. 3.4 are connected by a path, while events 3 and 4 are not. In the first case, the event at the end of the path can only occur *after* the one at the beginning of the path has occurred; we say that the events are *causally related*. In the second case, no occurrence sequence of the unfolding contains both events, and so we say that the events are in *conflict*.

Consider now events 1 and 3 of the unfolding shown in Fig. 3.3 on p. 17. Event 1 is certainly not a cause of event 3, and vice versa. Moreover, they are not in conflict, since the sequence 1 3 is an occurrence sequence of the unfolding. We need to introduce a third category of *concurrent* nodes.

Definition 3.13. *Let x and y be two nodes of an unfolding.*

- *We say that x is a* causal predecessor *of y, denoted by $x < y$, if there is a (non-empty) path of arcs from x to y; as usual we denote by $x \leq y$ that either $x < y$ or $x = y$; two nodes x and y are* causally related *if $x \leq y$ or $x \geq y$.*
- *We say that x and y are in* conflict, *denoted by $x \# y$, if there is a place z, different from x and y, from which one can reach x and y, exiting z by different arcs.*
- *We say that x and y are* concurrent, *denoted by x co y, if x and y are neither causally related nor in conflict.*

The following proposition shows that a set of places of an unfolding can be simultaneously marked if and only if its elements are pairwise concurrent.

Proposition 3.14. *Let $\mathcal{N}$ be a branching process of $\mathbf{A}$ and let P be a set of places of $\mathcal{N}$. There is a reachable marking M of $\mathcal{N}$ such that $P \subseteq M$ if and only if the places of P are pairwise concurrent.*

Proof. ($\Rightarrow$): We prove the contrapositive. Assume that two places $p, p' \in P$ are not concurrent. Then they are either causally related or in conflict. In the first case, assume w.l.o.g. that $p \leq p'$ holds. Then there is a path (possibly consisting of just one node) starting at some place of $\mathcal{N}$ carrying one token, continuing to p, and ending at p'. Since places have exactly one input event, the occurrence of an event does not change the total number of tokens marking the places of the path, and so at any reachable marking exactly one place of this path is marked. So p and p' can never be simultaneously marked. Assume now that p and p' are in conflict. Then there is a path starting at some place of $\mathcal{N}$ carrying one token, continuing to a place p'', different from p and p', and branching into two paths leading from p'' to p and p', respectively. Again, the occurrence of an event does not change the total number of tokens in the places of this structure (the path leading to p'' plus the two branches leading to p and p'), and so at any reachable marking exactly one place of the structure is marked. So p and p' can never be simultaneously marked.

($\Leftarrow$): Observe first that the property holds for the branching process without events (all its places are pairwise concurrent, and they all belong to the initial marking). Assume now that $\mathcal{N}$ is obtained by extending a branching process $\mathcal{N}'$ with a new event e. Let P' be the subset of places of P that belong to $\mathcal{N}'$. If $P' = P$, then the property holds by induction hypothesis. Otherwise, $P \setminus P'$ is a nonempty subset of $e^\bullet$. Since the places of P' are pairwise concurrent, so are the places of the set $P' \cup \{{}^\bullet e\}$ (it is easy to see that no two places of this set are causally related or in conflict). By induction hypothesis, some reachable marking M' of $\mathcal{N}'$ satisfies $P' \cup \{{}^\bullet e\} \subseteq M'$. Then, the marking M obtained from M' by firing e satisfies $P \subseteq M$, and we are done. Finally, assume that $\mathcal{N}$ is the union of a sequence of branching processes. In this case, some element of the union already contains all places of P, and the property holds by induction hypothesis.   □

We can now show that any pair of nodes of an unfolding belongs to exactly one of the causal, conflict, and concurrency relations.

Proposition 3.15. *(1) For every two nodes x, y of a branching process exactly one of the following holds: (a) x and y are causally related, (b) x and y are in conflict, (c) x and y are concurrent.*

(2) If x and y are causally related and $x \neq y$, then either $x < y$ or $y < x$, but not both.

Proof. (1) By definition, two nodes are concurrent if and only if they are neither causally related nor in conflict. So it suffices to show that no two nodes x, y can be both causally related and in conflict. Consider two cases:

- $x = y$. Then x and y are causally related, and so we have to show that $x \# x$ does not hold, i.e., that x is not in self-conflict. Observe first that, since a place of a branching process has at most one input event, a place is in self-conflict if and only if its input event is in self-conflict. So it suffices to show that no event is in self-conflict. We proceed by structural induction. For the branching process without events there is nothing to show. Assume now that no event of a branching process $\mathcal{N}$ is in self-conflict, and let e be a possible extension of $\mathcal{N}$. By the definition of conflict, $e\#e$ can only be the case if there exist two places $p_1, p_2 \in {}^\bullet e$ such that $p_1 \# p_2$. But, by the definition of a branching process, some reachable marking of $\mathcal{N}$ contains both p_1 and p_2, and so by Prop. 3.14 p_1 and p_2 are concurrent. It follows that p_1 and p_2 are not in conflict. Finally, it is easy to see that if no event of a set of branching processes is in self-conflict, then no event of their union is in self-conflict.

- $x \neq y$. If $x < y$ and $x \# y$, then there is a path leading from x to y, and a place z and two paths leaving z through different arcs and leading to x and y. So $y \# y$, contradicting (1). The case $x > y$ and $x \# y$ is symmetric.

(2) If $x < y$ and $y < x$, then $\mathcal{N}$ has a cycle, contradicting Prop. 3.11(1). $\square$

Example 3.16. In the unfolding of Fig. 3.3 on p. 17, the output place of event 4 labeled by s_4 and the output place of event 12 labeled by r_2 are concurrent, and indeed they can be simultaneously marked by letting the events 1, 3, 4, 7, and 12 occur in this order.

3.2.3 Configurations

A *realization* of a set of events is an occurrence sequence of the branching process in which each event of the set occurs exactly once, and no other events occur. A set of events can have zero, one, or more realizations. For instance, the sets $\{1,2\}$ and $\{4,6\}$ in Fig. 3.3 on p. 17 have no realizations (for the latter, recall that occurrence sequences start at the initial marking, which enables neither event 4 nor event 6), and the set $\{1,3,4,7\}$ has two realizations, namely the sequences 1 3 4 7 and 3 1 4 7.

Definition 3.17. *A set of events of an unfolding is a* configuration *if it has at least one realization.*

The following proposition characterizes the configurations of a branching process:

Proposition 3.18. *Let $\mathcal{N}$ be a branching process of a product $\mathbf{A}$ and let E be a set of events of $\mathcal{N}$.*

(1) E is a configuration if and only if it is causally closed, *i.e., if $e \in E$ and $e' < e$ then $e' \in E$, and* conflict-free, *i.e., no two events of E are in conflict.*

(2) All the realizations of a finite configuration lead to the same reachable marking of $\mathcal{N}$.

Proof. (1) The "only if" direction is easy. For the "if" direction we proceed by induction on the size of E. If $|E| = 0$, then the empty sequence is a realization, and we are done. If $|E| > 0$, let e be a maximal event of E w.r.t. the causality relation. Then $E \setminus \{e\}$ is also a configuration, and by induction hypothesis it has a realization σ. It follows immediately from the occurrence rule for Petri nets that the sequence σe is a realization of E, and we are done.

(2) It is easy to see that the marking reached by any realization of a given finite configuration E is the one putting a token in the places p of $\mathcal{N}$ such that ${}^\bullet p \subseteq E$ and $p^\bullet \cap E = \emptyset$. $\square$

Example 3.19. In Fig. 3.3 on p. 17, $\{1, 3, 4, 6\}$ is a configuration, and $\{1, 4\}$ (not causally closed) or $\{1, 2\}$ (not conflict-free) are not. The configuration $\{1, 3, 4, 6\}$ has two realizations, namely $1\,3\,4\,6$ and $3\,1\,4\,6$. Both lead to the same marking.

3.3 Verification Using Unfoldings

Transition systems are used to represent the semantics of dynamic systems, like programs or digital circuits. For instance, a sequential program can be assigned a transition system whose states are tuples containing the current value of the program counter and the current values of the program variables. The unfolding of the transition system can be seen as a data structure representing the system's computations, and so all the computations of the program. Given a question about the system, like "does some computation execute the transition t?", we can try to compute an answer by exploring the unfolding: we compute larger and larger portions of it, until an event labeled by t is found, or until somehow we are able to conclude that no future event will be labeled by t.

In the same way, the unfolding of a product can be seen as a data structure representing the product's global computations, each global computation corresponding to an occurrence sequence of the unfolding. Given the question "does some computation execute the global transition $\mathbf{t}$?", we can compute an answer by exploring the unfolding until an event labeled by $\mathbf{t}$ is found, or until we can somehow conclude that no such event can be ever added (how to conclude this is explained in the coming chapters). It is important to observe that only a *finite* prefix of the unfolding is explored.

This is the approach we study in this book. Notice that it differs from the conventional model checking approach, which consists of exploring not the product's unfolding, but its interleaving semantics. In order to give a first impression of why the new approach could be superior to the conventional one, consider the product of transition systems of Fig. 3.5. We wish to know if the global transition $\mathbf{c} = \langle c_0, \dots, c_4 \rangle$ is executable.

The Petri net representation of the product is shown in Fig. 3.6. Its unfolding is shown in Fig. 3.7. In this case, the unfolding is finite, and the finite prefix that needs to be explored in order to decide the executability of $\mathbf{c}$ is

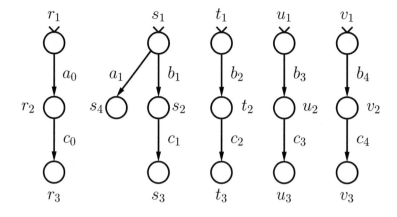

$$\mathbf{T} = \{\mathbf{a} = \langle a_0, a_1, \epsilon, \epsilon, \epsilon \rangle, \mathbf{b_1} = \langle \epsilon, b_1, \epsilon, \epsilon, \epsilon \rangle,$$
$$\mathbf{b_2} = \langle \epsilon, \epsilon, b_2, \epsilon, \epsilon \rangle, \mathbf{b_3} = \langle \epsilon, \epsilon, \epsilon, b_3, \epsilon \rangle,$$
$$\mathbf{b_4} = \langle \epsilon, \epsilon, \epsilon, \epsilon, b_4 \rangle, \mathbf{c} = \langle c_0, c_1, c_2, c_3, c_4 \rangle\}$$

Fig. 3.5. Product of transition systems

the unfolding itself. The transition $\mathbf{c}$ is not executable, because otherwise the unfolding would contain at least one event labeled by it.

If we choose the interleaving representation, then in order to find out that $\mathbf{c}$ is not executable we need to explore the whole transition system associated with the product. The important point is that the unfolding of Fig. 3.7 is more compact. The transition system has 24 global states and 40 transitions, while the unfolding has 11 places and five events. If these numbers do not look very impressive, we can always extend the system by adding new "copies" of the three components on the right of Fig. 3.5. For a product with a total of n components the unfolding contains $2n + 1$ places and n events, while the transition system has $3 \cdot 2^{n-2}$ global states and even more global transitions. Notice also that, since the transition $\mathbf{c}$ is not executable, state space exploration based on the interleaving semantics will need to compute all the global states of the product in order to decide if the property holds.

Summarizing, the prefix of the unfolding of a product that needs to be explored can be much more compact than the unfolding of its associated transition system, and this is the fact we try to exploit.[3]

---

[3] See Bibliographical Notes at the end of the chapter for alternative approaches to exploiting concurrency.

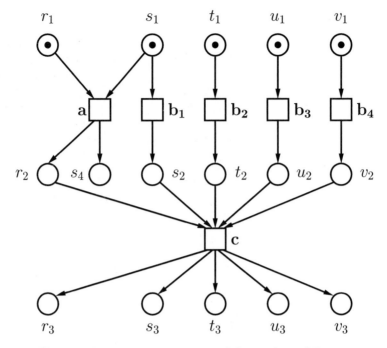

Fig. 3.6. Petri net representation of the product of Fig. 3.5

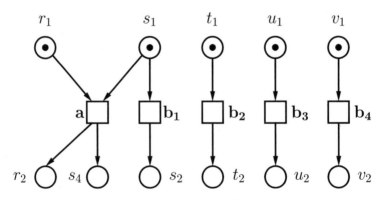

Fig. 3.7. The unfolding of the product of Fig. 3.5

3.4 Constructing the Unfolding of a Product

Exploring the unfolding of a product corresponds to generating larger and larger branching processes, each one the result of adding a new event to the previous one. The question is how to *compute* the events that can extend the current branching process. More concretely: Given a finite branching process

$\mathcal{N}$ of a product $\mathbf{A}$ and a global transition $\mathbf{t}$, how can we decide whether $\mathcal{N}$ can be extended with an event labeled by $\mathbf{t}$?

Let $^\bullet\mathbf{t} = \{s_1, \ldots, s_k\}$. Then k is the number of components of the product that participate in $\mathbf{t}$. We call this number the *synchronization degree* of $\mathbf{t}$. By the definition of branching processes, we have to decide if $\mathcal{N}$ has a reachable marking that puts a token on places $p_1, \ldots, p_k$ labeled by $s_1, \ldots, s_k$, respectively. For this, we proceed as follows:

(1) We consider all the sets $\{p_1, \ldots, p_k\}$ of places of $\mathcal{N}$ such that for $i \in \{1, \ldots, k\}$ the place p_i is labeled by s_i. Let us call them the *candidates*.
(2) For each candidate $\{p_1, \ldots, p_k\}$, we decide if some reachable marking M satisfies $\{p_1, \ldots, p_k\} \subseteq M$. We say that the candidate is *reachable*.

The complexity of the procedure is the product of the number of candidates and the time needed to check if a candidate is reachable. The number of candidates is $O((n/k)^k)$ for a branching process with n places. Checking the reachability of a candidate involves solving a reachability problem for a Petri net, which is known to be computationally expensive. Fortunately, branching processes are a very special class of nets, and for them the reachability problem is far easier than in the general case. By Prop. 3.14, a candidate is reachable if and only if its places are pairwise concurrent. There are several possible algorithmic solutions to checking pairwise concurrency, exhibiting a typical trade-off between time and space. We present two of them.

Memory-Intensive Approach

We assume that not only $\mathcal{N}$ but also the concurrency relation (i.e., the pairs (x, y) of nodes such that x *co* y) is part of the input. In this case, using an adequate data structure, e.g., a hash table, we can check the concurrency of two places in $O(1)$ time. Since a candidate contains k places, its reachability can be checked in $O(k^2)$ time. Since there are $O((n/k)^k)$ candidates, this approach takes $O(n^k/k^{k-2})$ time. However, $O(n^2)$ memory is needed to store the concurrency relation. Moreover, when extending a branching process with a new place the concurrency relation needs to be updated. The following proposition, whose proof follows easily from the definitions, shows that the update can be carried out in $O(n)$ time.

Proposition 3.20. *Let $\mathcal{N}'$ be a branching process obtained by extending a branching process $\mathcal{N}$ with an event e according to Def. 3.5. Let co and co' denote the concurrency relations of $\mathcal{N}$ and $\mathcal{N}'$, respectively, and let p_1, p_2 be distinct places of $\mathcal{N}'$. We have p_1 co' p_2 if and only if:*

- p_1 *and* p_2 *are places of* $\mathcal{N}$ *and* p_1 *co* p_2*, or*
- p_1 *and* p_2 *are output places of* e*, or*
- *one of* p_1, p_2 *is an output place of* e *and the other one is a place of* $\mathcal{N}$ *in co-relation with every input place of* e*.*

Memory-Light Approach

Assume now that $\mathcal{N}$ is the only input, and that it is stored using a data structure that implements the following operation: given a node x of $\mathcal{N}$ (place or event), the operation returns its set of input nodes. In order to determine if two places p and p' are concurrent, we first make repeated use of this operation to compute the set $C(p)$ of causal predecessors of p, i.e., the set of nodes x such that $x < p$. If p' belongs to this set, then we have $p' < p$, and so p and p' are not concurrent. Otherwise, we compute the set $C(p')$. If it contains p, then $p < p'$. If not, then we check if the set $C(p) \cap C(p')$ contains some place p'' having two output events $e \in C(p) \setminus C(p')$ and $e' \in C(p') \setminus C(p)$. If so, then p and p' are in conflict; otherwise they are concurrent. This procedure can be easily generalized to decide if the places of a set $\{p_1, \ldots, p_k\}$ are pairwise concurrent. We go through a loop that executes (at most) k iterations. We use a variable C, which after i iterations stores the set $C(p_1) \cup \ldots \cup C(p_i)$ (the initial value of C is the empty set). In the ith iteration we compute $C(p_i)$ and check whether it contains any of $p_1, \ldots, p_k$. If so, p_i is causally related to at least one of $p_1, \ldots, p_k$, and we stop. If not, we check whether $C \cap C(p_i)$ contains some place having two output events $e \in C \setminus C(p_i)$ and $e' \in C(p_i) \setminus C$. If so, p_i is in conflict with at least one of $p_1, \ldots, p_{i-1}$, and we stop. If not, we add $C(p_i)$ to C, and continue with the next iteration. Using adequate data structures the procedure runs in $O(n)$ time.

Since checking the reachability of a candidate takes $O(n)$ time, and there are $O((n/k)^k)$ candidates, we need $O(n^{k+1}/k^k)$ time.

The exponential complexity in k of the two approaches is less worrisome than it might seem at first sight. Recall that k is the synchronization degree of the transition $\mathbf{t}$. Products modelling real systems rarely have transitions of high synchronization degree. The reason is that the execution of a global transition requires the consensus of its participants, and consensus among a large number of processes is difficult to implement.

In particular, the global transitions of systems in which components are organized in an array or in a ring (think of the well-known dining philosophers example) have degree at most 3, because in these systems a component can only synchronize with its two neighbors[4]. In the case of systems whose components are arranged in a hypercube, the degree grows logarithmically in the number of components.

A Lower Bound

Even if the exponential dependency in k is not so crucial, we can still ask whether some other algorithm avoids it. The following proposition shows that this is unlikely, because it would imply P=NP.

---

[4] In fact, the degree is usually 2, because it is rarely the case that a component synchronizes with its two neighbors *simultaneously*.

Proposition 3.21. *Let $\mathcal{N}$ be a branching process of a product $\mathbf{A}$, and let $\mathbf{t}$ be a global transition of $\mathbf{A}$. Deciding whether $\mathcal{N}$ can be extended with an event labeled by $\mathbf{t}$ is NP-complete.*

Proof. For membership in NP we guess a global transition $\mathbf{t}$ and a set of places of the unfolding $M = \{p_1, \ldots, p_k\}$ labeled by ${}^\bullet \mathbf{t} = \{s_1, \ldots, s_k\}$, and check in polynomial time, using the procedure sketched above, that its input places are pairwise concurrent. After this we still need to check in polynomial time that no event exists in the unfolding labeled with $\mathbf{t}$ and having preset M to ensure the event is a proper extension of the unfolding.

We prove NP-hardness by a reduction from CNF-3SAT formula over variables $x_1, x_2, \ldots, x_n$. A literal is either a variable x_i or its negation $\overline{x}_i$. Let $F = C_1 \wedge C_2 \wedge \ldots \wedge C_m$ be a CNF-3SAT formula, where each conjunct C_j is a disjunction of at most three literals. We construct in polynomial time a product $\mathbf{F}$ of transition systems defined as follows:

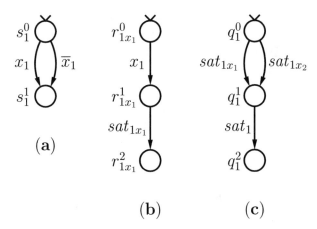

(a)

(b)   (c)

Fig. 3.8. Transition systems $\mathcal{X}_1$ (a), $\mathcal{C}_{1x_1}$ (b), and $\mathcal{E}_1$ (c) for $F = (x_1 \vee x_2) \wedge \overline{x}_1$

- For each variable x_i, let $\mathcal{X}_i$ be the transition system having two states s_i^0, s_i^1, with s_i^0 as initial state, and two transitions $x_i, \overline{x}_i$ both leading from s_i^0 to s_i^1.
  Intuitively these transitions select the truth value of x_i to be either true or false.
- For each clause C_j and each literal l of C_j, let $\mathcal{C}_{jl}$ be the transition system having three states $r_{jl}^0, r_{jl}^1, r_{jl}^2$, with r_{jl}^0 as initial state, a transition l leading from r_{jl}^0 to r_{jl}^1, and a transition sat_{jl} leading from r_{jl}^1 to r_{jl}^2
  Intuitively, $\mathcal{C}_{jl}$ moves from r_{jl}^0 to r_{jl}^1 when the literal l is set to true. It is then willing to execute transition sat_{jl}, signalling that the clause C_j is satisfied by the assignment because it contains literal l, and l has been set to true.

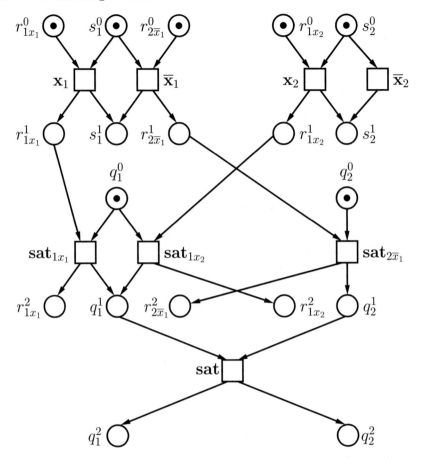

Fig. 3.9. Petri net representation of the product $\mathbf{F}$ for $F = (x_1 \vee x_2) \wedge \overline{x}_1$

- For each clause C_j, let $\mathcal{E}_j$ be the transition system having three states q_j^0, q_j^1, q_j^2, with q_j^0 as initial state, a transition sat_{jl} leading from q_j^0 to q_j^1 for every literal l of C_j, and a transition sat_j leading from q_j^1 to q_j^2.
  Intuitively the transitions from q_j^0 model all the possible ways of satisfying the clause C_j. The transition sat_j leading from q_j^1 to q_j^2 signals that the clause C_j has been satisfied.

The set of global transitions contains:

- Two transitions $\mathbf{x}_i, \overline{\mathbf{x}}_i$ for every variable x_i. The components of the tuple $\mathbf{x}_i$ corresponding to the transition system $\mathcal{X}_i$ and to all the transition systems $\mathcal{C}_{jl}$ such that $l = x_i$ are the local transitions x_i; all other components are equal to ϵ. The global transition $\overline{\mathbf{x}}_i$ is defined similarly.

- A transition $\mathbf{sat}_{jl}$ for every clause C_j and every literal l of C_j. The components of the tuple $\mathbf{sat}_{jl}$ corresponding to the transition systems C_{jl} and $\mathcal{E}_j$ are the local transitions sat_{jl}; all other components are equal to ϵ.
- A transition $\mathbf{sat}$. For every $j \in \{1, \ldots, m\}$ the component of the tuple $\mathbf{sat}$ corresponding to $\mathcal{E}_j$ is the local transition sat_j; all other components are equal to ϵ.

Intuitively, the execution of the transition $\mathbf{x}_i$ and $\overline{\mathbf{x}}_i$ corresponds to setting x_i to true or false, respectively. After $\mathbf{x}_i$ or $\overline{\mathbf{x}}_i$ has occurred for each variable, an assignment has been chosen, and the transition system C_{jl} is in state r_{jl}^1 if and only if this assignment makes the clause C_j true. Those transition systems that have reached r_{jl}^1 are willing to execute sat_{jl}. It follows that the transition system $\mathcal{E}_j$ can move to state q_j^1 if and only if the assignment makes the clause C_j true. So $\mathbf{sat}$ can occur if and only if the assignment makes all clauses true, i.e., if F is satisfiable.

Consider now the prefix of the unfolding of $\mathbf{F}$ obtained by removing from the full unfolding all events labeled by $\mathbf{sat}$. This prefix can be easily constructed in polynomial time in the size of $\mathbf{F}$ because all global transitions (except for $\mathbf{sat}$) have a bounded synchronization degree. The prefix can be extended with an event labeled by $\mathbf{sat}$ if and only if the formula F is satisfiable. $\qquad\square$

Example 3.22. Consider the formula $F = (x_1 \vee x_2) \wedge \overline{x}_1$. We have $C_1 = x_1 \vee x_2$ and $C_2 = \overline{x}_1$. Figure 3.8 shows some of the components of the product $\mathbf{F}$, namely the transition systems $\mathcal{X}_1$, C_{1x_1}, and $\mathcal{E}_1$.

Figure 3.9 shows the Petri net representation of the product $\mathbf{F}$. For clarity, some places which are not connected to any net transition have been omitted.

3.5 Search Procedures

In this book we consider verification questions of the form: "Does the system have a (possibly infinite) history satisfying a given property?" Our computational approach consists of computing larger and larger prefixes of the unfolding, until we have enough information to answer the question. The prefixes are generated by *search procedures*.

A search procedure consists of a *search scheme* and a *search strategy*. The search strategy determines, given the current prefix of the unfolding, which event should be added to it next. Notice that a strategy may be nondeterministic, i.e., it may decide that any element out of the set of possible extensions should be added next. Depth-first and breadth-first are typical strategies for transition systems. The search scheme depends on the property we are interested in. It determines which leaves of the prefix need not be explored further, and whether the search is successful. More precisely, a search scheme consists of two parts:

```
procedure unfold(product A) {
    N := unique branching process of A without events;
    T := ∅; S := ∅; X := Ext(N,T);
    while (X ≠ ∅) {
        choose an event e ∈ X according to the search strategy;
        extend N with e;
        if e is a terminal according to the search scheme then {
            T := T ∪ {e};
            if e is successful according to the search scheme then {
                S := S ∪ {e}; /* A successful terminal found */
            };
        };
        X := Ext(N,T);
    };
    return ⟨N,T,S⟩;
};
```

Fig. 3.10. Pseudo-code of the unfolding procedure

- A *termination condition* determining which leaves of the current prefix are *terminals*, i.e., nodes whose causal successors need not to be explored.[5]
- A *success condition* determining which terminals are *successful*, i.e., terminals proving that the property holds.

Once a search strategy and a search scheme have been fixed, the search procedure generates a prefix of the unfolding according to the pseudo-code of Fig. 3.10. T is a program variable containing the set of terminal events of the current prefix N, while S is the variable containing the set of successful terminals of N. $Ext(N,T)$ denotes the set of events that can be added to N according to Def. 3.5 on p. 18 and have no causal predecessor in the set of terminal events T. The search procedure terminates if and when $Ext(N,T)$ is empty, i.e., when each leaf of the current prefix is either a terminal or has no successors. (In practice, the procedure can also terminate whenever it finds a successful terminal, but for the analysis it is more convenient to consider this definition.) Given a product A and a terminating search procedure P, the *final prefix* is the prefix generated by P on input A after termination. The final prefix is *successful* if it contains at least one successful terminal. Given a property ϕ, a terminating procedure P is *complete* if the final prefix it generates is successful for every product A satisfying ϕ, and *sound* if every product A such that the final prefix is successful satisfies ϕ.

Remark 3.23. There is an important difference between the prefixes generated by search procedures in the transition system case and in the product case. In the transition system case, if an event is not a terminal, then all its successor events belong to the final prefix. This is no longer true in the case of products.

---

[5] Terminals are often called *cut-offs* in the literature.

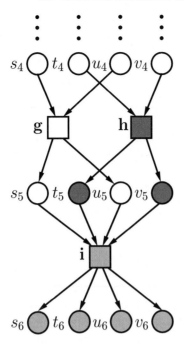

Fig. 3.11. A particularity of branching processes in the product case

The reason is that, since in the case of products events may have several input places, a successor of an event e may have a predecessor $e' \neq e$ that is a terminal. In this case, the successor will not be explored because of e', even though e may not be a terminal itself. This situation is illustrated in Fig. 3.11. The figure shows a fragment of a prefix that will appear in the next chapter. Assume that the event labeled by **h** is a terminal, but the event labeled by **g** is not. Event **i** is a successor of event **g**, but does not belong to the final prefix, because it is also a successor of event **h**.

3.6 Goals and Milestones for Next Chapters

The ultimate goal of this book is to present a search procedure for model checking a product **A** against arbitrary properties expressed in Linear Temporal Logic (LTL), a popular specification language.[6] The search procedure is presented in Chap. 8. It is based on search procedures for three central verification problems which are also interesting on their own:

---

[6] For the reader familiar with LTL we must be more precise: our model checker will only work for the fragment of LTL that does not contain the next time operator X.

- **The executability problem**: Given a set $\mathbf{G} \subseteq \mathbf{T}$ of global transitions, can some transition of $\mathbf{G}$ ever be executed, i.e., is there a global history whose last event is labeled by an element of $\mathbf{G}$?
- **The repeated executability problem**: Given a set $\mathbf{R} \subseteq \mathbf{T}$ of global transitions, can some transition of $\mathbf{R}$ be executed infinitely often, i.e., is there an infinite global history containing infinitely many events labeled by transitions of $\mathbf{R}$?
- **The livelock problem**: Given a partitioning of the global transitions into *visible* and *invisible*, and given a set $\mathbf{L} \subseteq \mathbf{T}$ of visible transitions, is there an infinite global history in which a transition of $\mathbf{L}$ occurs, followed by an infinite sequence of invisible transitions?

In the next chapters we present search procedures for these problems. The chapters follow the same systematic approach. First, we design a search procedure for transition systems, i.e., for products with $n = 1$ components, and then we generalize it to the general case $n \geq 1$. This allows us to expose the parts of the search procedure that are necessary for the cases in which $n > 1$. Since in the interleaving representation products are reduced to transition systems, our search procedures for the case $n = 1$ can be seen as solutions to our three problems in which the interleaving representation instead of the Petri net representation is used.

Before closing the chapter, we establish the computational complexity of the three problems above. We assume that the reader is familiar with basic notions of complexity theory, and only sketch the proof.

Theorem 3.24. *The executability, repeated executability, and livelock problems are PSPACE-complete for products.*

Proof. (Sketch.) We only consider the executability problem, since the proof for the other two problems is similar. To prove membership in PSPACE we observe first that, since NPSPACE=PSPACE by Savitch's theorem (see, e.g., [98]), it suffices to provide a nondeterministic algorithm for the problem using only polynomial space. The algorithm uses a variable $\mathbf{v}$ to store one global state; initially, $\mathbf{v} = \mathbf{is}$. While $\mathbf{v} \neq \mathbf{s}$, the algorithm repeatedly selects a global transition $\mathbf{t}$ enabled at $\mathbf{v}$, computes the global state $\mathbf{s}'$ such that $\langle \mathbf{v}, \mathbf{t}, \mathbf{s}' \rangle$, and sets $\mathbf{v} := \mathbf{s}'$. If at some point $\mathbf{v} = \mathbf{s}$, the algorithm stops and outputs the result "reachable". Obviously, the algorithm only needs linear space.

PSPACE-hardness is proved by reduction from the following problem: given a polynomially space-bounded Turing machine M and an input x, does M accept x? We assume w.l.o.g. that M has one single accepting state q_f.

Let $p(n)$ be the polynomial limiting the number of tape cells that M uses on an input of length n. We construct a product $\mathbf{A} = \langle \mathcal{A}_Q, \mathcal{A}_1, \ldots, \mathcal{A}_{p(|x|)}, \mathbf{T} \rangle$. The component $\mathcal{A}_Q$ contains one state s_q for each control state q of M. The intended meaning of s_q is that the machine M is currently in state q. For every $i \in \{1, \ldots, p(|x|)\}$ and for every tape symbol a of M, the component $\mathcal{A}_i$ contains two states $s_{\langle a,0 \rangle}$ and $s_{\langle a,1 \rangle}$. The intended meaning of $s_{\langle a,0 \rangle}$ is:

the ith tape cell currently contains the symbol a, and the head of M is not reading the cell. The intended meaning of $s_{\langle a,1 \rangle}$ is: the ith tape cell currently contains the symbol a, and the head of M is reading the cell. The initial states of the component are chosen according to the initial configuration of M: the initial state of $\mathcal{A}_Q$ is s_{q_0}, where q_0 is the initial state of M; the initial state of component $\mathcal{A}_1$ is $s_{\langle x_1,1 \rangle}$, where x_1 is the first letter of the input x; and so on. The transitions of the components and the synchronization vector $\mathbf{T}$ are chosen so that the execution of a global transition of $\mathbf{A}$ corresponds to a move of M. Additionally, the component $\mathcal{A}_q$ has a transition t_f with s_{q_f} as both source and target state, and $\mathbf{T}$ contains a synchronization vector $\mathbf{t}_f = \langle t_f, \epsilon, \ldots, \epsilon \rangle$.

Clearly, M halts for input x if and only if the instance of the executability problem for $\mathbf{A}$ given by $\mathbf{G} = \{\mathbf{t}_f\}$ has a positive answer. $\qquad\square$

Bibliographical Notes

Definition 3.5 (branching processes and unfolding of a product of transition systems) can be traced back to [103], where Petri introduced *nonsequential processes* as a truly concurrent semantics of Petri nets.[7] A nonsequential process, also called a *causal net* or an *occurrence net* in the literature, describes a *partial run* of a Petri net. It contains information about the events that have occurred, their causal relationship, and which events occurred independently of each other. The theory of nonsequential processes has been extensively studied already early on by Goltz, Reisig, Best, Devillers, and Fernández, among others [49, 11, 13].

A Petri net may have many different nonsequential processes. Loosely speaking, each of them corresponds to a different way of solving a *conflict*, i.e., a situation in which two different transitions are enabled at a marking, but letting one occur disables the other. The unfolding of a Petri net was introduced by Nielsen, Plotkin, and Winskel in [93] (see also Sects. 3.1 and 3.3 of [123]) as a way of describing all possible full runs (the "full branching run" of the net) by means of a single object. In [94, 95] Nielsen, Rozenberg, and Thiagarajan gave axiomatic and categorical definitions of the unfoldings of Elementary Net Systems, a class of Petri nets very close to ours, and studied their properties. Unfoldings constituted the initial inspiration for Winskel's theory of event structures [123, 124].

In [32], Engelfriet observed that nonsequential processes described partial runs and the unfolding described the unique full branching run of a Petri

---

[7] A semantics is truly concurrent if it distinguishes between a system in which two fully independent subsystems execute two actions, say a and b, and a system which nondeterministically chooses between executing the sequence $a\,b$ or the sequence $b\,a$.

net, but no objects had been defined to describe "partial branching runs". He introduced *branching processes* for this purpose. Engelfriet's definition is axiomatic, i.e., it defines branching processes as the set of Petri nets satisfying a number of conditions. Definition 3.5 is more operational and combines the definitions given by Esparza and Römer in [39] and by Khomenko, Koutny, and Vogler in [73].

The theory of nonsequential processes and branching processes has been extended to more general classes of Petri nets, like high-level Petri nets [72], Petri nets with inhibitor arcs, and Petri nets with read arcs (see for instance [67, 6, 121, 77]).

The idea that unfoldings can be interesting not only semantically but also from an algorithmic point of view is due to McMillan. In [84] he presented an algorithm to check deadlock-freedom of Petri nets based on the explicit construction of a prefix of the unfolding, and conducted experiments showing that the approach alleviated the state explosion problem in the verification of asynchronous hardware systems. McMillan's work will be discussed in more detail in the Bibliographical Notes of the next chapter. An earlier paper by Best and Esparza [12] already used the theory of nonsequential processes to obtain a polynomial model checking algorithm for Petri nets without conflicts, but this class of nets had very limited expressive power. McMillan was the first to convincingly apply the unfolding technique to verification problems.

Exploiting the concurrency of the system in order to alleviate the state explosion problem is also the idea behind *partial-order reduction* techniques. However, the approach is different. Given a product of transition systems, the unfolding technique explores the unfolding of the Petri net representation instead of the interleaving representation. Partial-order reduction techniques explore the interleaving representation, but exploit information about the concurrency of the system in order to *reduce* the set of global states that need to be explored. For this, given a global state, the techniques compute a subset of the set of transitions leaving it, the *reduced* set, and only explore the transitions of this set. The literature contains different proposals for the computation of reduced sets: Valmari's *stubborn* sets [115, 116], Peled's *ample* sets [99], and Wolper and Godefroid's *sleep* sets [48, 125, 47] are based on similar principles. Valmari's survey paper on the state explosion problem [118] presents all of them. Finally, *local first search* is still another partial-order reduction technique, due to Niebert, Huhn, Zennou, and Lugiez [91], based on a different principle.

The problem of computing the events that can be added to a given branching process was studied by Esparza and Römer in [39] (see also [107]). Khomenko and Koutny improved the algorithms in [70]. McMillan had already in his thesis [85] shown NP-hardness of deadlock detection using the unfolding as input. The NP-hardness of possible extensions calculation has been later discussed in detail by Heljanko, Esparza, and Schröter [56, 42]. For the PSPACE-hardness reduction details, see the survey of Esparza [34], where a polynomially space-bounded Turing machine is mapped to a 1-bounded Petri net, a model that can be easily simulated by products of polynomial size. See also the work of Heljanko [59] extending some of the results to finite prefixes.

The terminology we use for search procedures (terminals, successful terminal, soundness, and completeness) is inspired by the terminology of tableau systems for logics. In particular, we have been influenced by the work of Stirling, Bradfield, and Walker on tableau methods for the μ-calculus [113, 17].

4

Search Procedures for the Executability Problem

The executability problem consists of deciding if a product can execute any transition out of a given set of global transitions. It is a fundamental problem, and many others can be easily reduced to it.

4.1 Search Strategies for Transition Systems

We fix a transition system $\mathcal{A} = \langle S, T, \alpha, \beta, is \rangle$ and a set $G \subseteq T$ of *goal transitions*. We wish to solve the problem of whether some history of $\mathcal{A}$ executes some transition of G by means of a finite, sound, and complete search procedure. It is not difficult to see that such procedures exist; for instance depth-first or breadth-first search will do the job. However, we wish to prove a stronger result, namely the existence of a search *scheme* that leads to a terminating, sound, and complete search procedure *for every search strategy*. In this section we formalize the notion of strategy, and in the next one we proceed to define the search scheme.

To define search strategies, it is convenient to define the notion of *order*:

Definition 4.1. *An* order *is a relation that is both irreflexive and transitive.*

Orders are often called strict partial orders in the literature but we use the term *order* for brevity.

Recall that, loosely speaking, a search strategy determines, given the current prefix, which of its possible extensions should be added to it next. So, in full generality, a search strategy can be defined as a priority relation or as an order between branching processes. Assume the current branching process is $\mathcal{N}$ with possible extensions $e_1, \dots e_k$, and for every $i \in \{1, \dots, k\}$ let $\mathcal{N}_i$ be the result of adding e_i to $\mathcal{N}$. Then the event e_j such that $\mathcal{N}_j$ has the highest priority among $\mathcal{N}_1, \dots, \mathcal{N}_k$ is the one selected to extend $\mathcal{N}$. In terms of orders, we select an event e_j such that $\mathcal{N}_j$ is minimal according to the order.

Given two events e_1, e_2, there can be many different branching processes having e_1 and e_2 as possible extensions. For some of them the priority relation may prefer e_1 to e_2, while for others it may be the other way round. Such strategies can be called "context-dependent", since the choice between e_1 and e_2 does not only depend on e_1 and e_2 themselves, but also on their context. For simplicity, we restrict our attention to "context-free" strategies in which the choice between e_1 and e_2 depends only on the events themselves.

Notice that, from a computational point of view, it does not make sense to define strategies as priority relations (i.e., orders) *on events*. The reason is that the events are what the search procedure has to compute, and so the procedure does not know them in advance. To solve this problem we introduce the notion of an event's history.

Definition 4.2. *Let e be an event of the unfolding of $\mathcal{A}$, and let $e_1 e_2 \ldots e_m$ be the unique occurrence sequence of the unfolding and ending with e, i.e., $e_m = e$. The* history *of e, denoted by $H(e)$, is the computation $t_1 t_2 \ldots t_m$, where t_i is the label of e_i. We call the events $e_1, \ldots, e_{m-1}$ the* causal predecessors *of e_m. We denote by $e' < e$ that e' is a causal predecessor of e. The* state reached *by $H(e)$, denoted by $St(e)$, is defined as $\beta(e)$, i.e., as the state reached after executing e.*

Example 4.3. In the unfolding of Fig. 3.4 on p. 21 the history of event 7 is $H(7) = t_1 t_3 t_5 t_1$, and the state reached by $H(7)$ is $St(7) = s_2$. The causal predecessors of event 7 are the events 1, 3, and 5. We have, for instance, $H(7) = H(3) t_5 t_1$.

The following proposition is obvious:

Proposition 4.4. *An event is characterized by its history, i.e., $e = e'$ holds if and only if $H(e) = H(e')$.*

This proposition allows us to define strategies as orders on the set of all words, i.e., as orders $\prec \subseteq T^* \times T^*$. Since histories are words and events are characterized by their histories, every order on words induces an order on events. Moreover, since the set T is part of the input to the search procedure, it makes perfect computational sense to define a strategy like "choose among the possible extensions to the current prefix anyone having a shortest history".

Abusing notation, the order on events induced by an order $\prec$ on words is also denoted by $\prec$. The order need not be total (i.e., there may be distinct events e, e' such that neither $e \prec e'$ nor $e' \prec e$ holds). However, we require that $\prec$ *refines* the prefix order on T^*, i.e., for every $w, w' \in T^*$, if w is a proper prefix of w', then $w \prec w'$.[1] The reason is that if $H(e)$ is a proper prefix of $H(e')$ then e' can only be added to the unfolding after e, and so e' should have lower priority than e.

---

[1] Intuitively, we refine a given order by ordering pairs of elements that are currently unordered. For instance, if x and y are unordered, we can refine by declaring that x is smaller than y (or vice versa).

Definition 4.5. *A* search strategy *on* T^* *is an order on* T^* *that refines the* prefix order.

Notice that e is a causal predecessor of e' if and only if $H(e)$ is a proper prefix of $H(e')$. Therefore, if $e < e'$ then $H(e) \prec H(e')$ and so $e \prec e'$. We say that a search strategy *refines the causal order* on events.

4.2 Search Scheme for Transition Systems

We are ready to present a search scheme for the executability problem that is sound and complete for every search strategy. A search scheme is determined by its terminals and successful terminals, which we now define. The definition of terminals may look circular at first sight (terminals are defined in terms of the auxiliary notion of feasible events, and vice versa) but, as we shall see, it is not.

Definition 4.6. *Let* $\prec$ *be a search strategy. An event* e *is* feasible *if no event* $e' < e$ *is a terminal. A feasible event* e *is a* terminal *if either*

(a) it is labeled with a transition of G, *or*
(b) there is a feasible event $e' \prec e$, *called the* companion *of* e, *such that* $St(e') = St(e)$.

A terminal is successful *if it is of type (a). The* $\prec$*-final prefix is the prefix of the unfolding of* $\mathcal{A}$ *containing the feasible events.*

The intuition behind the definition of a terminal is very simple: If we add an event labeled by a goal transition $g \in G$, then the history of the event ends with the execution of g and so, since g is executable, the search can terminate successfully; this explains type (a) terminals. The idea behind type (b) terminals is that if two events lead to places labeled with the same state of $\mathcal{A}$, then the two subtrees of the unfolding rooted at these places are isomorphic, and so it suffices to explore only one of them. We explore the subtree of the smallest event w.r.t. the strategy $\prec$.

Example 4.7. Fig. 4.1 shows a transition system. Let $G = \{t_5\}$, and consider the strategy $\prec_1$ defined as follows: $e \prec_1 e'$ if $H(e)$ is lexicographically smaller than $H(e')$. The $\prec_1$-final prefix is shown in Fig. 4.2(**a**). Events 3 and 5 are terminals of type (b) with events 1 and 2 as companions, respectively. Event 4 is a successful terminal. Observe that $\prec_1$ is a total order, and therefore the search procedure is deterministic. The numbering of the events corresponds to the order in which they are added by the procedure.

Consider now the strategy $\prec_2$ defined by: $e \prec_2 e'$ if $|H(e)| < |H(e')|$. The $\prec_2$-final prefix s shown in Fig. 4.2(**b**). Events 3 and 4 are terminals of type (b) with events 1 and 2 as companions, respectively. Event 5 is a successful terminal. Since $\prec_2$ is not total, the search procedure is nondeterministic. The

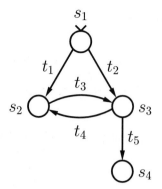

Fig. 4.1. A transition system

numbering of the events corresponds to a possible order in which the procedure may add them. The procedure might also have added the events in, say, order 2 1 5 3 4.

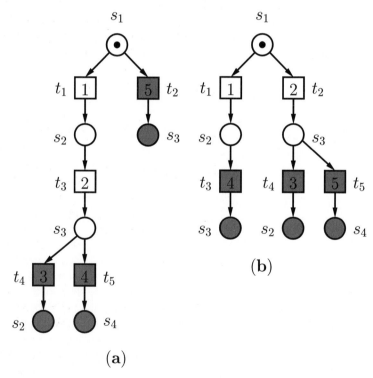

Fig. 4.2. Final prefixes for $G = \{t_5\}$ and two different strategies: $\prec_1$ **(a)** and $\prec_2$ **(b)**

In order to prove that the set of terminal events is well-defined we need a lemma.

Lemma 4.8. *Let $\prec$ be an arbitrary search strategy, and let (F, T) be a pair of sets of events satisfying the conditions of Def. 4.6 for the sets of feasible and terminal events, respectively. Then for every feasible event $e \in F$ the history $H(e)$ has length at most $|S| + 1$.*

Proof. Assume that e is a feasible event such that the length of $H(e)$ is larger than $|S| + 1$. Then, by the pigeonhole principle, there are two events $e_1 < e_2 < e$ such that $St(e_1) = St(e_2)$. Since $e \in F$, no event $e' < e$ belongs to T, and so the same holds for e_1 and e_2. It follows $e_1, e_2 \in F$. Since $e_1 < e_2$ and the search strategy $\prec$ refines the causal order, we have $e_1 \prec e_2$, and, by condition (b), $e_2 \in T$. Since $e_2 < e$, the event e cannot be feasible, contradicting the assumption.   □

A direct corollary of the proof above is that for all non-terminal events e the length of $H(e)$ is at most $|S|$.

Proposition 4.9. *The search scheme of Def. 4.6 is well-defined for every strategy $\prec$, i.e., there is a unique set of feasible events and a unique set of terminal events satisfying the conditions of the definition. Moreover, the $\prec$-final prefix is finite.*

Proof. Let (F_1, T_1) and (F_2, T_2) be two pairs of sets of events satisfying the conditions of Def. 4.6 on the feasible and terminal events. Since there are only finitely many histories of length at most $|S| + 1$, it follows from Lemma 4.8 that the sets F_1 and F_2 are finite. We prove $F_1 = F_2$, which implies $T_1 = T_2$. Assume $F_1 \neq F_2$, and let e be a $\prec$-minimal event satisfying $e \in (F_1 \setminus F_2) \cup (F_2 \setminus F_1)$ (this event exists because F_1 and F_2 are finite). Assume w.l.o.g. that $e \in F_1 \setminus F_2$. By the definition of a terminal there is an event $e' < e$ such that $e' \in T_2 \setminus T_1$. The event e' cannot be of type (a) because the definition of a terminal of type (a) only depends on the transition that labels e', and so if $e' \in T_2$ then it must also be the case that $e' \in T_1$. So e' is of type (b). By the definition of a terminal event of type (b), e' has a companion $e'' \prec e'$ in F_2, and moreover $e'' \notin F_1$ (if $e'' \in F_1$ then we would also have $e'' \in T_1$). So $e'' \in F_2 \setminus F_1$ and $e'' \prec e' < e$, giving $e'' \prec e$ and thus contradicting the $\prec$-minimality of e.

Since the $\prec$-final prefix contains the feasible events, and there are only finitely many of them, the prefix is finite.   □

Notice that the $\prec$-final prefix is exactly the prefix generated by the algorithm of Fig. 3.10 on p. 34 with $\prec$ as search strategy (in both cases the unfolding is "cut-off" at the terminal events). Since this prefix is finite, the algorithm terminates. Notice also that even though the algorithm itself is nondeterministic, it can be shown that the $\prec$-final prefix (where all isomorphic prefixes are considered equivalent) will always be generated by it for all different nondeterministic choices the algorithm makes.

The soundness of the scheme for every strategy is also easy to prove:

Proposition 4.10. *The search scheme of Def. 4.6 is sound for every strategy.*

Proof. If the final prefix is successful then it contains a terminal e labeled by a goal transition g, and so $H(e)$ is a history containing g. Thus, g is executable. $\square$

We now show that the search scheme is also complete *for every search strategy*. We present the proof in detail, because all the completeness proofs in the rest of the book reuse the same argumentation. It proceeds by contradiction: it is assumed that the product satisfies the property, but the final prefix is not successful. First, a set of *witnesses* is defined; these are the events of the unfolding "witnessing" that the property holds, i.e., if the search algorithm would have explored any of them then the search would have been successful. Second, an order on witnesses is defined; it is shown that the order has at least one minimal element e_m, and, using the assumption that the search was not successful, a new event e'_m is constructed. Third, it is shown that e'_m must be smaller than e_m w.r.t. the order on witnesses, contradicting the minimality of e_m.

Theorem 4.11. *The search scheme of Def. 4.6 is complete for every strategy.*

Proof. Let $\prec$ be an arbitrary search strategy. Assume that some goal transition $g \in G$ is executable, but no terminal of the $\prec$-final prefix is successful. We derive a contradiction in three steps.

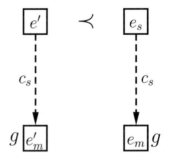

Fig. 4.3. Illustration of the proof of Thm. 4.11

Witnesses. Let an event of the unfolding of $\mathcal{A}$ be a *witness* if it is labeled with g. Since g is executable, the unfolding of $\mathcal{A}$ contains witnesses. However, no witness is feasible, because otherwise it would be a successful terminal. So for every witness e there is an unsuccessful terminal $e_s < e$. We call e_s the *spoiler* of e. (see Fig. 4.3).

Minimal witnesses. Let e be a witness and let e_s be its spoiler. Since $e_s < e$, some computation c satisfies $H(e_s)c = H(e)$. Let $l(e)$ denote the (finite) length of c. We define an order $\ll$ on witnesses as follows: $e \ll e'$ if either $l(e) < l(e')$ or $l(e) = l(e')$ and $e_s \prec e'_s$.

We claim that $\ll$ is well-founded. Assume this is not the case. Then there is an infinite decreasing chain of witnesses $e_w^1 \gg e_w^2 \gg e_w^3 \ldots$, and because $l(e_w^i)$ can only decrease a finite number of times, we must from some index j onwards have an infinite decreasing chain of spoilers $e_s^j \succ e_s^{j+1} \succ e_s^{j+2} \ldots$. Thus, since spoilers are terminals, the set of terminals must be infinite. So the $\prec$-final prefix is infinite, contradicting Prop. 4.9. This proves the claim.

Since $\ll$ is well-founded, there is at least one $\ll$-minimal witness e_m. Let e_s be the spoiler of e_m and let c_s be the unique computation satisfying $H(e_m) = H(e_s)c_s$. Notice that, since e_m is labeled by g, the computation c_s ends with g. Since e_s is an unsuccessful terminal, it has a companion $e' \prec e_s$ such that $St(e') = St(e_s)$. Since $St(e') = St(e_s)$, both $H(e_s)c_s$ and $H(e')c_s$ are histories of $\mathcal{A}$. Let e'_m be the event having $H(e')c_s$ as history, i.e., $H(e'_m) = H(e')c_s$. Since c_s ends with g, the event e'_m is also labeled by g, like e_m. So e'_m is a witness, and has a spoiler e'_s. Let c'_s be the computation satisfying $H(e'_m) = H(e'_s)c'_s$.

Contradiction. Since $H(e'_s)c'_s = H(e'_m) = H(e')c_s$, we have $e' < e'_m$ and $e'_s < e'_m$. So there are three possible cases:

- $e'_s < e'$. Then, since e'_s is a spoiler and spoilers are terminals, e' is not feasible, contradicting our assumption that e' is the companion of e_s, which according to Def. 4.6 requires e' to be feasible.
- $e'_s = e'$. Then, since $H(e'_s)c'_s = H(e'_m) = H(e')c_s$, we have $c_s = c'_s$. Moreover, since $e'_s = e'$ and $e' \prec e_s$ we have $e'_s \prec e_s$. This implies $e'_m \ll e_m$, contradicting the minimality of e_m.
- $e' < e'_s$. Then, since $H(e'_s)c'_s = H(e'_m) = H(e')c_s$, the computation c'_s is shorter than c_s, and so $e'_m \ll e_m$, contradicting the minimality of e_m.

$\square$

The next example shows that the size of the final prefix depends on the choice of strategy. In the worst case, the final prefix can be exponentially larger than the transition system.

Example 4.12. Consider the transition system of Fig. 4.4 with $G = \emptyset$. If we choose $\prec$ as the prefix order on histories, then the final prefix is the complete unfolding, shown in the same figure on the right. The same happens if we define $e \prec e' \Leftrightarrow |H(e)| < |H(e')|$, i.e., if e has priority on e' when $H(e)$ is shorter than $H(e')$. In this case, since all histories reaching a state have the same length, no event is a terminal. If the transition system of Fig. 4.4 is extended with more "diamonds", the size of the final prefix grows exponentially in the number of "diamonds".

Now define: $e \prec e'$ if and only if $H(e)$ is lexicographically smaller than $H(e')$, where we assume that the order of the transitions as the basis of the lexicographic order is just the alphabetical order of the transition labels. In this case, the event of the unfolding labeled by d and the leftmost events labeled by h and l are terminals. The final prefix has now linear size in the number of "diamonds".

One way to make the final prefix smaller is to require the strategy $\prec$ to be a total order.

Theorem 4.13. *If $\prec$ is a total order on T^*, then the $\prec$-final prefix of Def. 4.6 has at most $|S|$ feasible non-terminal events.*

Proof. If $\prec$ is total, then, by condition (b) in the definition of a terminal, we have $St(e) \neq St(e')$ for any two feasible non-terminal events e and e'. So the final prefix contains at most as many non-terminal events as there are states in $\mathcal{A}$. □

4.3 Search Strategies for Products

We fix a product $\mathbf{A} = \langle \mathcal{A}_1, \ldots, \mathcal{A}_n, \mathbf{T} \rangle$ of transition systems, where $\mathcal{A}_i = \langle S_i, T_i, \alpha_i, \beta_i, is_i \rangle$, and a set of goal global transitions $\mathbf{G} \subseteq \mathbf{T}$. We wish to solve the problem of whether some global history of $\mathbf{A}$ executes some transition of $\mathbf{G}$. Our goal is to generalize Def. 4.6 to a search scheme for an arbitrary product of transition systems.

In this section we generalize the notion of a search strategy to products. Recall that, intuitively, a search strategy determines the order in which new events are added when constructing the unfolding. In the transition system case we modeled strategies as order relations on T^*. This was possible because an event was uniquely determined by its history, and so an order on T^* induced an order on events. However, in the case of products, an event does not have a unique history, as illustrated by the example below.

Example 4.14. Consider event 10 in the unfolding of Fig. 3.3 on p. 17. Recall that this is the unfolding of the product of Fig. 2.2 on p. 7. Many occurrence sequences of events contain this event, and all of them correspond to histories of the product. Here are some examples:

Event sequence	History
1 3 4 7 6 12 10	$\langle t_1, \epsilon \rangle$ $\langle \epsilon, u_1 \rangle$ $\langle t_3, u_2 \rangle$ $\langle \epsilon, u_3 \rangle$ $\langle t_5, \epsilon \rangle$ $\langle \epsilon, u_1 \rangle$ $\langle t_1, \epsilon \rangle$
1 3 4 6 10	$\langle t_1, \epsilon \rangle$ $\langle \epsilon, u_1 \rangle$ $\langle t_3, u_2 \rangle$ $\langle t_5, \epsilon \rangle$ $\langle t_1, \epsilon \rangle$
3 1 4 6 10	$\langle \epsilon, u_1 \rangle$ $\langle t_1, \epsilon \rangle$ $\langle t_3, u_2 \rangle$ $\langle t_5, \epsilon \rangle$ $\langle t_1, \epsilon \rangle$
1 3 4 6 10 7	$\langle t_1, \epsilon \rangle$ $\langle \epsilon, u_1 \rangle$ $\langle t_3, u_2 \rangle$ $\langle t_5, \epsilon \rangle$ $\langle t_1, \epsilon \rangle$ $\langle \epsilon, u_3 \rangle$

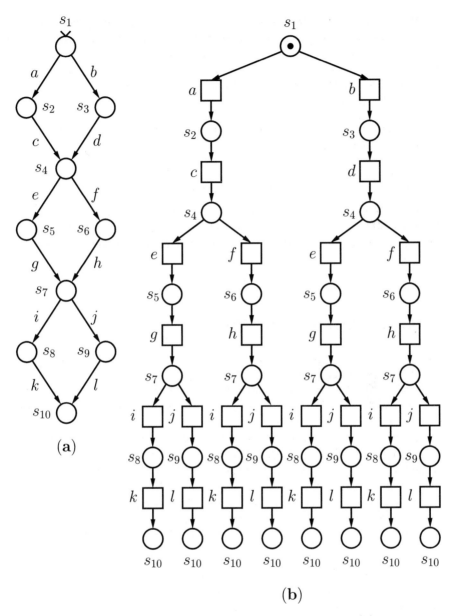

Fig. 4.4. A transition system (**a**) and its unfolding (**b**)

Which of them is "the" history of event 10? In the case of transition systems, the history of an event contains the events that *must necessarily* occur for the event to occur. If we adopt this point for products as well, we conclude that the first and fourth histories are not histories of 10: they contain the events 7 and 12, which are not necessary for 10 to occur.

However, there is no reason why we should choose the second or third history as "the" history of event 10. We conclude that an event of a product does not have a unique history, but a set of histories.

This example suggests that a strategy should no longer be an order on transition words, but on *sets of words*, i.e., an order on the powerset of $\mathbf{T}^*$. However, for many sets of words we can easily tell that they are not the sets of histories of an event. For instance, since the histories of an event always have the same length, all sets containing words of different length can be excluded. So maybe it is better to define strategies over the sets of words whose elements have the same length? Which is the right universe for strategies? While a good part of the theory that follows could be developed using the powerset of $\mathbf{T}^*$ as universe, the theory takes a much nicer shape if we restrict our attention to sets of histories being *Mazurkiewicz traces*, a well-known notion of concurrency theory introduced by Antoni Mazurkiewicz in the 1970s. In the next section we introduce some basic definitions and results about Mazurkiewicz traces.

4.3.1 Mazurkiewicz Traces

The definition of Mazurkiewicz traces is based on the notion of independence of transitions. Recall that a component $\mathcal{A}_i$ of $\mathbf{A}$ participates in the execution of a global transition $\mathbf{t} = \langle t_1, \ldots, t_n \rangle$ when $t_i \neq \epsilon$. We define:

Definition 4.15. *Two global transitions are* independent *if no component $\mathcal{A}_i$ of $\mathbf{A}$ participates in both of them.*

Example 4.16. The transitions $\langle t_1, \epsilon \rangle$ and $\langle \epsilon, u_1 \rangle$ of the product of Fig. 2.2 on p. 7 are independent, but the transitions $\langle t_1, \epsilon \rangle$ and $\langle t_4, u_2 \rangle$ are not, because $\mathcal{A}_1$ participates in both of them.

It follows easily from this definition that a pair $\mathbf{t}$ and $\mathbf{u}$ of independent transitions satisfies the following two properties for every $\mathbf{w}, \mathbf{w}' \in \mathbf{T}^*$:

(1) if $\mathbf{w\,t\,u\,w}'$ is a history of $\mathbf{A}$, then so is $\mathbf{w\,u\,t\,w}'$; and
(2) if $\mathbf{w\,t}$ and $\mathbf{w\,u}$ are histories of $\mathbf{A}$, then so are $\mathbf{w\,t\,u}$ and $\mathbf{w\,u\,t}$.

Example 4.17. The sequence $\langle t_1, \epsilon \rangle \langle \epsilon, u_1 \rangle \langle t_3, u_2 \rangle$ is a history of the product of Fig. 2.2 on p. 7, and so is $\langle \epsilon, u_1 \rangle \langle t_1, \epsilon \rangle \langle t_3, u_2 \rangle$, as demanded by (1). (In this case $\mathbf{w}$ is the empty sequence and $\mathbf{w}' = \langle t_3, u_2 \rangle$.) The sequences of length 1, $\langle t_1, \epsilon \rangle$ and $\langle \epsilon, u_1 \rangle$, are histories of the same product, and so are $\langle t_1, \epsilon \rangle \langle \epsilon, u_1 \rangle$ and $\langle \epsilon, u_1 \rangle \langle t_1, \epsilon \rangle$, as demanded by (2). (In this case $\mathbf{w}$ is the empty sequence.)

The independence relation induces an equivalence relation on the set $\mathbf{T}^*$ of transition words. Loosely speaking, two words are equivalent if one can be obtained from the other by swapping consecutive independent transitions.

Definition 4.18. *Two transition words* $\mathbf{w}, \mathbf{w}' \in \mathbf{T}^*$ *are* 1-equivalent, *denoted by* $\mathbf{w} \equiv_1 \mathbf{w}'$, *if* $\mathbf{w} = \mathbf{w}'$ *or if there are two independent transitions* $\mathbf{t}$ *and* $\mathbf{u}$ *and two words* $\mathbf{w}_1, \mathbf{w}_2 \in \mathbf{T}^*$ *such that* $\mathbf{w} = \mathbf{w}_1 \mathbf{t} \mathbf{u} \mathbf{w}_2$ *and* $\mathbf{w}' = \mathbf{w}_1 \mathbf{u} \mathbf{t} \mathbf{w}_2$. *Two words* $\mathbf{w}, \mathbf{w}' \in \mathbf{T}^*$ *are* equivalent *if* $\mathbf{w} \equiv \mathbf{w}'$, *where* $\equiv$ *denotes the transitive closure of* $\equiv_1$.

Since $\equiv_1$ is reflexive and symmetric, $\equiv$ is an equivalence relation. It follows easily from this definition and property (1) above that if $\mathbf{h}$ is a history of $\mathbf{A}$, then every word $\mathbf{w} \equiv \mathbf{h}$ is also a history of $\mathbf{A}$.

Definition 4.19. *A* Mazurkiewicz trace *(or just a* trace*) of a product* $\mathbf{A}$ *is an equivalence class of the relation* $\equiv$. *The trace of a word* $\mathbf{w}$ *is denoted by* $[\mathbf{w}]$, *and the set of all traces of* $\mathbf{A}$ *by* $[\mathbf{T}^*]$.
  A trace of $\mathbf{A}$ *is a* history trace *if all its elements are histories.*

Example 4.20. The sequence $\mathbf{w} = \langle t_1, \epsilon \rangle \langle \epsilon, u_1 \rangle \langle t_3, u_2 \rangle \langle t_5, \epsilon \rangle \langle \epsilon, u_3 \rangle$ is a history of the product of Fig. 2.2 on p. 7. Its corresponding history trace is:

$$
\begin{aligned}
[\mathbf{w}] = \{ \ & \langle t_1, \epsilon \rangle \langle \epsilon, u_1 \rangle \langle t_3, u_2 \rangle \langle t_5, \epsilon \rangle \langle \epsilon, u_3 \rangle , \\
& \langle t_1, \epsilon \rangle \langle \epsilon, u_1 \rangle \langle t_3, u_2 \rangle \langle \epsilon, u_3 \rangle \langle t_5, \epsilon \rangle , \\
& \langle \epsilon, u_1 \rangle \langle t_1, \epsilon \rangle \langle t_3, u_2 \rangle \langle t_5, \epsilon \rangle \langle \epsilon, u_3 \rangle , \\
& \langle \epsilon, u_1 \rangle \langle t_1, \epsilon \rangle \langle t_3, u_2 \rangle \langle \epsilon, u_3 \rangle \langle t_5, \epsilon \rangle \ \}.
\end{aligned}
$$

The sequence $\mathbf{w}' = \langle t_1, \epsilon \rangle \langle \epsilon, u_3 \rangle \langle t_1, \epsilon \rangle$ is not a history. Its corresponding trace is:

$$
\begin{aligned}
[\mathbf{w}'] = \{ \ & \langle t_1, \epsilon \rangle \langle \epsilon, u_3 \rangle \langle t_1, \epsilon \rangle , \\
& \langle \epsilon, u_3 \rangle \langle t_1, \epsilon \rangle \langle t_1, \epsilon \rangle , \\
& \langle t_1, \epsilon \rangle \langle t_1, \epsilon \rangle \langle \epsilon, u_3 \rangle \ \}.
\end{aligned}
$$

We conclude this section with a fundamental result. Loosely speaking, it states that a trace of a product is characterized by the projections of *any* of its elements onto the product's components.

Theorem 4.21. *For every* $i \in \{1, \ldots, n\}$, *let* $\mathbf{T}_i \subseteq \mathbf{T}$ *be the set of global transitions of* $\mathbf{A}$ *in which* $\mathcal{A}_i$ *participates. Two words* $\mathbf{w}, \mathbf{w}' \in \mathbf{T}^*$ *satisfy* $\mathbf{w} \equiv \mathbf{w}'$ *if and only if for every* $i \in \{1, \ldots, n\}$ *their projections onto* $\mathbf{T}_i$ *coincide.*

Proof. ($\Rightarrow$): Assume $\mathbf{w}' \equiv \mathbf{w}$, and let $i \in \{1, \ldots, n\}$ be an arbitrary index. We show that $\mathbf{w}$ and $\mathbf{w}'$ have the same projection onto $\mathbf{T}_i$. It suffices to prove the result for the case $\mathbf{w}' \equiv_1 \mathbf{w}$. By the definition of $\equiv_1$, there are two independent transitions $\mathbf{t}, \mathbf{u}$ such that $\mathbf{w} = \mathbf{w}_1 \mathbf{t} \mathbf{u} \mathbf{w}_2$ and $\mathbf{w}' = \mathbf{w}_1 \mathbf{u} \mathbf{t} \mathbf{w}_2$. By the definition of independence, at most one of $\mathbf{t}$ and $\mathbf{u}$ belongs to $\mathbf{T}_i$. So $\mathbf{t} \mathbf{u}$ and $\mathbf{u} \mathbf{t}$ have the same projection onto $\mathbf{T}_i$, and we are done.

($\Leftarrow$): Assume $\mathbf{w}$ and $\mathbf{w}'$ have the same projection onto $\mathbf{T}_i$ for every $i \in \{1, \ldots, n\}$. We first claim that the length of a word $\mathbf{v} \in \mathbf{T}^*$ is completely determined by the length of its projections onto the $\mathbf{T}_i$'s, so that $\mathbf{w}$ and $\mathbf{w}'$ have the same length. For this, observe that if exactly k components participate in a transition $\mathbf{t}$, then each occurrence of $\mathbf{t}$ in $\mathbf{v}$ appears in exactly k of the projections of $\mathbf{v}$ onto $\mathbf{T}_1, \ldots, \mathbf{T}_n$. So, if we attach weight $1/k$ to transitions with k participating components, then the length of $\mathbf{v}$ is equal to the total weight of all the projections of $\mathbf{v}$ on $\mathbf{T}_1, \ldots, \mathbf{T}_n$. This proves the claim.

We now prove $\mathbf{w} \equiv \mathbf{w}'$ by induction on the common length k of $\mathbf{w}$ and $\mathbf{w}'$. If $k = 0$ then both $\mathbf{w}$ and $\mathbf{w}'$ are the empty sequence, and we are done. If $k > 0$, then there are transitions $\mathbf{t}$ and $\mathbf{t}'$ and words $\mathbf{w}_1, \mathbf{w}'_1$ such that $\mathbf{w} = \mathbf{t}\,\mathbf{w}_1$ and $\mathbf{w}' = \mathbf{t}'\,\mathbf{w}'_1$. We consider two cases:

Case 1: $\mathbf{t} = \mathbf{t}'$. Then $\mathbf{w}_1$ and $\mathbf{w}'_1$ have the same projection onto $\mathbf{T}_i$ for every $i \in \{1, \ldots, n\}$. So, by induction hypothesis, we have $\mathbf{w}_1 \equiv \mathbf{w}'_1$, and so $\mathbf{w} = \mathbf{t}\,\mathbf{w}_1 \equiv \mathbf{t}\,\mathbf{w}'_1 = \mathbf{w}'$.

Case 2: $\mathbf{t} \neq \mathbf{t}'$. We first claim that $\mathbf{t}$ and $\mathbf{t}'$ are independent. Assume the contrary. Then some component $\mathcal{A}_i$ participates in both $\mathbf{t}$ and $\mathbf{t}'$. But then the projection of $\mathbf{w}$ on $\mathbf{T}_i$ starts with $\mathbf{t}$, and the projection of $\mathbf{w}'$ on $\mathbf{T}_i$ starts with $\mathbf{t}'$, a contradiction, and the claim is proved.

Let $\mathcal{A}_j$ be any of the components that participates in $\mathbf{t}'$. Since $\mathbf{w}$ and $\mathbf{w}'$ have the same projection onto $\mathbf{T}_j$, and $\mathbf{w}'$ contains at least one occurrence of $\mathbf{t}'$, the word $\mathbf{w}_1$ also contains at least one occurrence of $\mathbf{t}'$. So there exist words $\mathbf{w}_2$ and $\mathbf{w}_3$ such that $\mathbf{w} = \mathbf{t}\,\mathbf{w}_2\,\mathbf{t}'\,\mathbf{w}_3$, and w.l.o.g. we can further assume that $\mathbf{w}_2$ contains no occurrence of $\mathbf{t}'$ (notice that $\mathbf{w}_2$ may be empty).

We claim $\mathbf{w} \equiv \mathbf{t}'\,\mathbf{t}\,\mathbf{w}_2\,\mathbf{w}_3$. Since $\mathbf{t}$ and $\mathbf{t}'$ are independent, it suffices to prove that $\mathbf{t}'$ is independent of every transition occurring in $\mathbf{w}_2$. Assume this is not the case, i.e., assume that $\mathbf{w}_2$ contains some transition $\mathbf{u}$ such that $\mathbf{t}'$ and $\mathbf{u}$ are dependent. We have $\mathbf{u} \neq \mathbf{t}$, because $\mathbf{t}$ and $\mathbf{t}'$ are independent, and $\mathbf{u} \neq \mathbf{t}'$, because $\mathbf{t}'$ does not occur in $\mathbf{w}_2$. Since $\mathbf{t}'$ and $\mathbf{u}$ are dependent, some component $\mathcal{A}_k$ participates in both $\mathbf{t}'$ and $\mathbf{u}$. We examine the projections of $\mathbf{w}$ and $\mathbf{w}'$ onto $\mathbf{T}_k$. In the former, transition $\mathbf{u}$ appears before transition $\mathbf{t}'$ (recall that $\mathbf{t}'$ does not appear in $\mathbf{w}_2$). In the latter, transition $\mathbf{t}'$ appears before transition $\mathbf{u}$. But this contradicts our assumption that $\mathbf{w}$ and $\mathbf{w}'$ have the same projection onto $\mathbf{T}_k$, and proves the claim.

Since $\mathbf{w} \equiv \mathbf{t}'\,\mathbf{t}\,\mathbf{w}_2\,\mathbf{w}_3$, we can apply the first part of this theorem and conclude that the projections of $\mathbf{w}$ and $\mathbf{t}'\,\mathbf{t}\,\mathbf{w}_2\,\mathbf{w}_3$ onto $\mathbf{T}_1, \ldots, \mathbf{T}_n$ coincide. So the same holds for $\mathbf{w}'$ and $\mathbf{t}'\,\mathbf{t}\,\mathbf{w}_2\,\mathbf{w}_3$. Since $\mathbf{w}'$ also starts with $\mathbf{t}'$, we can continue as in Case 1, and prove $\mathbf{w}' \equiv \mathbf{t}'\,\mathbf{t}\,\mathbf{w}_2\,\mathbf{w}_3$. So, since both $\mathbf{w}$ and $\mathbf{w}'$ are equivalent to the same word, we have $\mathbf{w} \equiv \mathbf{w}'$. $\square$

Example 4.22. Consider the trace $[\mathbf{w}]$ of Ex. 4.20. In this case we have

$$\mathbf{T}_1 = \{\langle t_1, \epsilon \rangle, \langle t_2, \epsilon \rangle, \langle t_3, u_2 \rangle, \langle t_4, u_2 \rangle, \langle t_5, \epsilon \rangle\}, \text{ and}$$
$$\mathbf{T}_2 = \{\langle t_3, u_2 \rangle, \langle t_4, u_2 \rangle, \langle \epsilon, u_1 \rangle, \langle \epsilon, u_3 \rangle\}.$$

As guaranteed by Thm. 4.21, the projections of all the elements of $[\mathbf{w}]$ onto $\mathbf{T}_1$ coincide, and the same holds also for $\mathbf{T}_2$. The projections are

$$\langle t_1, \epsilon \rangle \ \langle t_3, u_2 \rangle \ \langle t_5, \epsilon \rangle \quad \text{and} \quad \langle \epsilon, u_1 \rangle \ \langle t_3, u_2 \rangle \ \langle \epsilon, u_3 \rangle .$$

At this point the reader might like to ask the following question: Does Thm. 4.21 still hold if we replace the projections of $\mathbf{w}$ and $\mathbf{w}'$ onto $\mathbf{T}_1, \ldots, \mathbf{T}_n$ by their projections onto $T_1, \ldots, T_n$, the sets of *local* transitions of $\mathcal{A}_1, \ldots, \mathcal{A}_n$? This would look more natural, since then the projections of a global history would be local histories of its components. However, the theorem then fails, as shown by the following example.

Example 4.23. Consider the product shown in Fig. 4.5(a), and the global histories $\mathbf{w}_1 = \langle t_1, u_1, \epsilon \rangle \ \langle \epsilon, u_2, v_1 \rangle$ and $\mathbf{w}_2 = \langle \epsilon, u_1, v_1 \rangle \ \langle t_1, u_2, \epsilon \rangle$. We have $[\mathbf{w}_1] = \{\mathbf{w}_1\} \neq \{\mathbf{w}_2\} = [\mathbf{w}_2]$. However, the projections of $\mathbf{w}_1$ and $\mathbf{w}_2$ onto the sets T_1, T_2, and T_3 of local transitions coincide; they are in both cases t_1, $u_1 u_2$, and v_1. So a trace is not characterized by the projections of its elements onto the sets of local transitions.

The Fig. 4.5(b) shows the unfolding of the product. The sequences $\mathbf{w}_1$ and $\mathbf{w}_2$ are the unique histories of events 3 and 4, respectively.

4.3.2 Search Strategies as Orders on Mazurkiewicz Traces

We define search strategies following the same steps of the transition system case (see Sect. 4.1). First, we formally define the set of histories of an event (Def. 4.26). Then we show that this set is always a Mazurkiewicz trace (Prop. 4.28). So an order on Mazurkiewicz traces induces an order on events, and so it makes sense to define strategies as orders on Mazurkiewicz traces (Def. 4.32).

We start by introducing the notion of the past of an event. Intuitively, this is the set of events that must occur for the event to occur.

Definition 4.24. *The* past *of an event e, denoted by $past(e)$, is the set of events e' such that $e' \leq e$ (recall that $e' < e$ if there is a path leading from e' to e).*[2]

It is easy to see that $past(e)$ is always a configuration.

Example 4.25. The past of event 10 in Fig. 3.3 on p. 17 is $past(10) = \{1, 3, 4, 6, 10\}$. While the past of an event is a configuration, not every configuration is the past of an event. For instance the configuration $\{2, 3\}$ is not the past of an event. However, it is easy to see that every configuration is the union of the pasts of some events. For instance, for $\{2, 3\}$ we have $past(2) = \{2\}$ and $past(3) = \{3\}$.

---

[2] In other papers the past of an event is called a *local configuration*. We avoid here this terminology, because it does not correspond to the way in which the word *local* is used in this book.

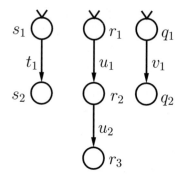

$$\mathbf{T} = \{\langle t_1, u_1, \epsilon\rangle, \langle \epsilon, u_1, v_1\rangle, \langle t_1, u_2, \epsilon\rangle, \langle \epsilon, u_2, v_1\rangle\}$$

(a)

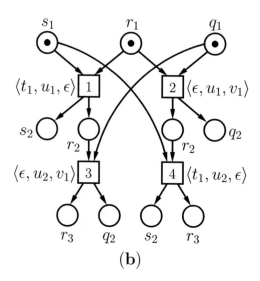

(b)

Fig. 4.5. A product of transition systems (a) and its unfolding (b)

Now we define the set of histories of an event as the set of realizations of its past.

Definition 4.26. *A transition word* $t_1 t_2 \ldots t_n$ *is a* history *of a configuration* C *if there is a realization* $e_1 e_2 \ldots e_n$ *of* C *such that* e_i *is labeled by* t_i *for every* $i \in \{1, \ldots, n\}$. *The set of histories of* C *is denoted by* $\mathbf{H}(C)$. *If* $C = past(e)$ *for some event* e, *then we also call the elements of* $\mathbf{H}(past(e))$ *histories of* e. *To simplify notation, we write* $\mathbf{H}(e)$ *instead of* $\mathbf{H}(past(e))$.

Example 4.27. The configuration $past(10) = \{1, 3, 4, 6, 10\}$ has two realizations, namely the occurrence sequences $1\,3\,4\,6\,10$ and $3\,1\,4\,6\,10$. So event 10 in Fig. 3.3 on p. 17 has two histories, which are the second and third histories in the list of four shown in Ex. 4.14 on p. 48.

The next proposition shows that a configuration is characterized by its set of histories, and that this set is always a Mazurkiewicz trace.

Proposition 4.28. *(a) Let C_1, C_2 be two configurations. Then $C_1 = C_2$ if and only if $\mathbf{H}(C_1) = \mathbf{H}(C_2)$.*
(b) Let C be a configuration. Then $\mathbf{H}(C)$ is a Mazurkiewicz trace.

Proof. (a) If $C_1 = C_2$, then $\mathbf{H}(C_1) = \mathbf{H}(C_2)$. Assume that $\mathbf{H}(C_1) = \mathbf{H}(C_2)$, and let $\mathbf{h} \in \mathbf{H}(C_1)$. We proceed by induction on the length k of $\mathbf{h}$. If $k = 0$, then $C_1 = \emptyset = C_2$ and we are done. If $k > 0$, then $\mathbf{h} = \mathbf{h}'\,\mathbf{t}$ for some history $\mathbf{h}'$ and some transition $\mathbf{t}$, and there are configurations C_1', C_2' and events e_1, e_2 labeled by $\mathbf{t}$ such that $C_1 = C_1' \cup \{e_1\}$, $C_2 = C_2' \cup \{e_2\}$, and $\mathbf{h}' \in \mathbf{H}(C_1'), \mathbf{H}(C_2')$. By induction hypothesis we have $C_1' = C_2'$. So it remains to prove $e_1 = e_2$. For this, let M be the marking reached after executing any of C_1' or C_2' (recall $C_1' = C_2'$). Since both e_1 and e_2 are labeled with $\mathbf{t}$, the set ${}^{\bullet}e_1$ contains some i-place if and only if ${}^{\bullet}e_2$ does. Since M contains exactly one i-place for each component $\mathcal{A}_i$, we have ${}^{\bullet}e_1 = {}^{\bullet}e_2$. By the definition of branching processes, if two events have the same set of input places and are labeled by the same global transition, then they have the same canonical names, which implies that they are equal. So $e_1 = e_2$.

(b) Let $\mathbf{h}$ be an arbitrary history of $\mathbf{H}(C)$. We prove $[\mathbf{h}] = \mathbf{H}(C)$.

$\mathbf{H}(C) \supseteq [\mathbf{h}]$ follows easily from property (1) of independent transitions. For $\mathbf{H}(C) \subseteq [\mathbf{h}]$, let $\mathbf{w}$ be an arbitrary realization of $\mathbf{H}(C)$. We have to show $\mathbf{w} \in [\mathbf{h}]$. We apply Thm. 4.21. For every $i \in \{1, \ldots n\}$, let $\mathbf{T}_i$ denote the set of global transitions in which component $\mathcal{A}_i$ participates. We claim that the projections of $\mathbf{w}$ and $\mathbf{h}$ on $\mathbf{T}_i$ coincide. By Thm. 4.21, this implies $[\mathbf{w}] = [\mathbf{h}]$, and so, in particular, $\mathbf{w} \in [\mathbf{h}]$.

To prove the claim, recall that the set of i-nodes of a branching process forms a tree that branches only at places (Prop. 3.11 (3)). It follows that for every two distinct i-events e and e', either $e < e'$, or $e' < e$, or there is a place x such that $x < e$ and $x < e'$. However, this last case is impossible, because then e and e' would be in conflict, contradicting the fact that C is a configuration and so conflict-free. So any two distinct i-events of C are causally related. Since in every realization of C causally related events appear in the same order, the projections of all realizations onto the set of i-events coincide. It follows that the projections of all histories of C onto $\mathbf{T}_i$ also coincide. Since both $\mathbf{w}$ and $\mathbf{h}$ are realizations of C, we are done. $\qquad\square$

Example 4.29. Consider again the configuration $past(10) = \{1, 3, 4, 6, 10\}$. Its two realizations correspond to the histories:

$$\langle t_1, \epsilon \rangle \ \langle \epsilon, u_1 \rangle \ \langle t_3, u_2 \rangle \ \langle t_5, \epsilon \rangle \ \langle t_1, \epsilon \rangle \text{, and}$$
$$\langle \epsilon, u_1 \rangle \ \langle t_1, \epsilon \rangle \ \langle t_3, u_2 \rangle \ \langle t_5, \epsilon \rangle \ \langle t_1, \epsilon \rangle \text{,}$$

which constitute a Mazurkiewicz trace.

Proposition 4.28 shows that we can define strategies for products as orders on the Mazurkiewicz traces of $\mathbf{A}$. Recall however that in the transition system case a strategy was defined as an order that refines the prefix order, the idea being that a history must be generated before any of its extensions are generated. We need the same condition in the general case.

Definition 4.30. *The* concatenation *of two traces* $[\mathbf{w}]$ *and* $[\mathbf{w}']$ *is denoted by* $[\mathbf{w}] [\mathbf{w}']$ *and defined as the trace* $[\mathbf{w} \, \mathbf{w}']$. *We say that* $[\mathbf{w}]$ *is a* prefix *of* $[\mathbf{w}']$ *if there is a trace* $[\mathbf{w}'']$ *such that* $[\mathbf{w}'] = [\mathbf{w}] [\mathbf{w}'']$.

We list some useful properties of trace concatenation and prefixes.

Proposition 4.31.

(a) The prefix relation on traces is an order.
(b) $[\mathbf{w_1}] [\mathbf{w_2}] \supseteq \{\mathbf{v_1} \, \mathbf{v_2} \mid \mathbf{v_1} \in [\mathbf{w_1}], \mathbf{v_2} \in [\mathbf{w_2}]\}$.
(c) If $[\mathbf{w_1}] = [\mathbf{w_2}]$ then $[\mathbf{w}] [\mathbf{w_1}] [\mathbf{w}'] = [\mathbf{w}] [\mathbf{w_2}] [\mathbf{w}']$ for all words $\mathbf{w}$ and $\mathbf{w}'$.
(d) If $[\mathbf{w}] [\mathbf{w_1}] [\mathbf{w}'] = [\mathbf{w}] [\mathbf{w_2}] [\mathbf{w}']$ for some words $\mathbf{w}$ and $\mathbf{w}'$, then $[\mathbf{w_1}] = [\mathbf{w_2}]$.

Proof. Parts (a), (b), and (c) follow easily from the definitions. We prove (d). Given a word $\mathbf{v}$ and $i \in \{1, \ldots, n\}$, let $\mathbf{v}|_i$ denote the projection of $\mathbf{v}$ onto $\mathbf{T}_i$, the set of transitions the ith component participates in. Choose an arbitrary $i \in \{1, \ldots, n\}$. By definition, $[\mathbf{w}] [\mathbf{w_1}] [\mathbf{w}'] = [\mathbf{w} \, \mathbf{w_1} \, \mathbf{w}']$ and $[\mathbf{w}] [\mathbf{w_2}] [\mathbf{w}'] = [\mathbf{w} \, \mathbf{w_2} \, \mathbf{w}']$. By Thm. 4.21, $(\mathbf{w} \, \mathbf{w_1} \, \mathbf{w}')|_i = (\mathbf{w} \, \mathbf{w_2} \, \mathbf{w}')|_i$. Since $(\mathbf{w} \, \mathbf{w_1} \, \mathbf{w}')|_i = \mathbf{w}|_i \, \mathbf{w_1}|_i \, \mathbf{w}'|_i$ and $(\mathbf{w} \, \mathbf{w_2} \, \mathbf{w}')|_i = \mathbf{w}'|_i \, \mathbf{w_1}|_i \, \mathbf{w}'|_i$ we have $\mathbf{w_1}|_i = \mathbf{w_2}|_i$. By Thm. 4.21, we get $[\mathbf{w_1}] = [\mathbf{w_2}]$. $\square$

We can now formulate the generalization of search strategies.

Definition 4.32. *A* search strategy *for* $\mathbf{A}$ *is an order on* $[\mathbf{T}^*]$ *that refines the prefix order on traces.*

4.4 Search Scheme for Products

We generalize the search scheme of Def. 4.6 to products. For this, we replace $H(e)$ by $\mathbf{H}(e)$, which by Prop. 4.28 is a Mazurkiewicz trace. It remains to replace $St(e)$ by a suitable generalization. For this, recall that $St(e)$ is the state reached after the execution of $H(e)$. So we would have to replace it by the set of global states reached after the execution of the different histories in $\mathbf{H}(e)$. However, since all these histories are realizations of $past(e)$, by Prop. 3.18 on p. 25 all of them lead to the same global state.

Definition 4.33. *Let C be a configuration of the unfolding of* **A***. The global state reached by C, denoted by* $\mathbf{St}(C)$*, is the global state reached by the execution of any of the histories of* $\mathbf{H}(C)$*.*

To lighten the notation we define $\mathbf{St}(e)$ as a shorthand for $\mathbf{St}(past(e))$.

Example 4.34. In Fig. 3.3 on p. 17 we have $past(10) = \{1, 3, 4, 6, 10\}$. The marking reached by all the realizations of $past(10)$ puts a token on the unique output place of event 10 and on the output place of event 4 labeled by r_3. We have $\mathbf{St}(10) = \langle s_2, r_3 \rangle$.

Here is the generalized search scheme:

Definition 4.35. *Let $\prec$ be a search strategy on* $[\mathbf{T}^*]$*. An event e of the unfolding of* **A** *is* feasible *if no event $e' < e$ is a terminal. A feasible event e is a* terminal *if either*

(a) e is labeled with a transition of **G***, or*
(b) there is a feasible event $e' \prec e$, called the companion *of e, such that* $\mathbf{St}(e') = \mathbf{St}(e)$*.*

A terminal is successful *if it is of type (a). The $\prec$-final prefix is the prefix of the unfolding of* **A** *containing the feasible events.*

It is easy to show that the scheme is well-defined and sound for every strategy (compare with Lemma 4.8, Prop. 4.9 and Prop. 4.10).

Lemma 4.36. *Let $\prec$ be an arbitrary search strategy, and let (F, T) be a pair of sets of events satisfying the conditions of Def. 4.35 for the sets of feasible and terminal events, respectively. For every event $e \in F$, every history of $\mathbf{H}(e)$ has length at most $nK + 1$, where n is the number of components of* **A** *and K is the number of reachable global states of* **A***.*

Proof. Assume that some history of $\mathbf{H}(e)$ has length greater than $nK + 1$. Then, by the pigeonhole principle there is a component $\mathcal{A}_i$ of **A** and two i-events $e_1 < e_2 < e$ such that $\mathbf{St}_i(e_1) = \mathbf{St}_i(e_2)$. Since $e_1 < e_2$ and the search strategy $\prec$ refines the prefix order, we have $e_1 \prec e_2$. By condition (b) we have $e_2 \in T$. Since $e_2 < e$, e cannot be feasible, i.e., $e \notin F$, and we are done. $\square$

A direct corollary of the proof above is that for all non-terminal feasible events e the maximal length of the histories in $\mathbf{H}(e)$ is at most nK.

Proposition 4.37. *The search scheme of Def. 4.35 is well-defined for every search strategy $\prec$, i.e., there is a unique set of feasible events and a unique set of terminal events satisfying the conditions of the definition. Moreover, the $\prec$-final prefix is finite.*

Proof. Analogous to the proof of Prop. 4.9. $\square$

Proposition 4.38. *The search scheme of Def. 4.35 is sound for every strategy.*

Proof. If the final prefix is successful then it contains a terminal e labeled by a goal transition $\mathbf{g}$. So every history of $\mathbf{H}(e)$ contains $\mathbf{g}$ and therefore $\mathbf{g}$ is executable. □

In the worst case, the size of the final prefix can be exponential in the number K of reachable global states of $\mathbf{A}$. This is not surprising, since this is already the case for transition systems, which are products with only one component. As in the case of transition systems, we can do better by using *total* strategies.

Theorem 4.39. *If $\prec$ is a total search strategy on $[\mathbf{T}^*]$, then the $\prec$-final prefix generated by the search scheme of Def. 4.35 with $\prec$ as search strategy has at most K non-terminal events.*

Proof. Analogous to the proof of Thm. 4.13. □

4.4.1 Counterexample to Completeness

Unfortunately, a direct generalization of Thm. 4.11 *does not hold*: the search scheme of Def. 4.35 is not complete for every strategy, as shown by the next example.

Example 4.40. Figure 4.6 shows a product of transition systems with four components. The corresponding Petri net is shown in Fig. 4.7, while the unfolding is shown in Fig. 4.8. In this case the unfolding is finite, and can be represented in full.

We wish to solve the executability problem for the global transition $\mathbf{i} = \langle i_1, i_2, i_3, i_4 \rangle$. Let $\prec$ be a search strategy that orders the events of the unfolding according to the numbering shown in Fig. 4.8 (a lower number corresponds to higher priority). We use the generalization of the search scheme of Def. 4.6, with $H(e)$ replaced by $\mathbf{H}(e)$ and $St(e)$ by $\mathbf{St}(e)$. The $\prec$-final prefix is the branching process containing events 1 to 9. To see this, observe that events 8 and 10 are terminals, with events 7 and 9 as companions, respectively, because

$$\mathbf{St}(8) = \{s_5, t_4, u_5, v_4\} = \mathbf{St}(7) \quad \text{and} \quad \mathbf{St}(10) = \{s_4, t_5, u_4, v_5\} = \mathbf{St}(9) \, .$$

The prefix with events 1 to 9 cannot be extended, because the only two possible extensions, namely events 11 and 12, have terminals among their predecessors. So this prefix is the final prefix. Since events 8 and 10 are unsuccessful terminals, the final prefix is unsuccessful. Since the global transition $\mathbf{i}$ is executable, the search scheme is not complete for this search strategy.

We can ask at which point the completeness proof of Thm. 4.11 breaks down in the case of products. In the *Contradiction* part of the completeness

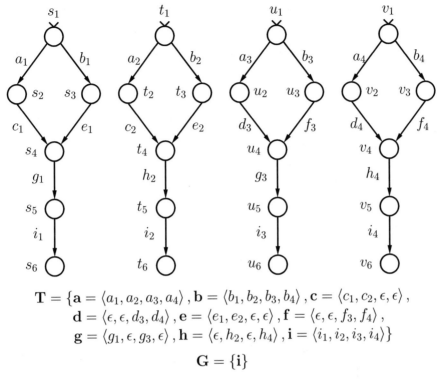

$$\mathbf{T} = \{\mathbf{a} = \langle a_1, a_2, a_3, a_4 \rangle, \mathbf{b} = \langle b_1, b_2, b_3, b_4 \rangle, \mathbf{c} = \langle c_1, c_2, \epsilon, \epsilon \rangle,$$
$$\mathbf{d} = \langle \epsilon, \epsilon, d_3, d_4 \rangle, \mathbf{e} = \langle e_1, e_2, \epsilon, \epsilon \rangle, \mathbf{f} = \langle \epsilon, \epsilon, f_3, f_4 \rangle,$$
$$\mathbf{g} = \langle g_1, \epsilon, g_3, \epsilon \rangle, \mathbf{h} = \langle \epsilon, h_2, \epsilon, h_4 \rangle, \mathbf{i} = \langle i_1, i_2, i_3, i_4 \rangle\}$$

$$\mathbf{G} = \{\mathbf{i}\}$$

Fig. 4.6. An instance of the executability problem

proof we consider two events e' and e'_s, both satisfying $e' < e'_m$ and $e'_s < e'_m$ for a certain event e'_m. We then argue that there are three possible cases: $e' < e'_s$, $e' = e'_s$, and $e'_s < e'$. However, in the case of products we also have a *fourth* case: the events e' and e'_s can also be concurrent. This fourth case occurs in Fig. 4.8. For the reader that has read the proof of Thm. 4.11 in detail: Event 12 (playing the role of e_m) does not belong to the final prefix, and event 8 (playing the role of e_s) is its spoiler. The companion e' of e_s is event 7, and e'_m is event 11. The spoiler e'_s of event e'_m 11 is event 10. But the events 7 and 10 are concurrent.

4.5 Adequate Search Strategies

Intuitively, the problem in the counterexample of Fig. 4.8 is that the events are added "in the wrong order". For instance, if the events 7, 8, 9, 10 were added in the order 7, 10, 8, 9, then events 8 and 9 would be marked as unsuccessful terminals, but we would still be able to add event 11, which would then be a successful terminal.

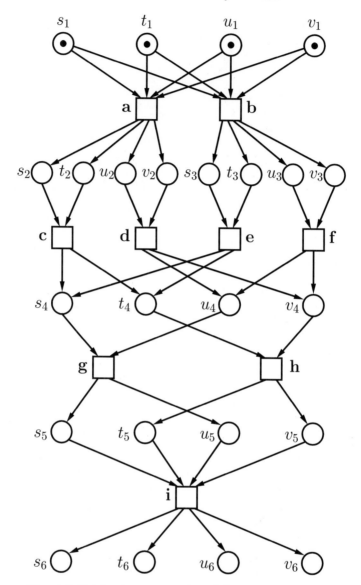

Fig. 4.7. Petri net representation of the product of Fig. 4.6

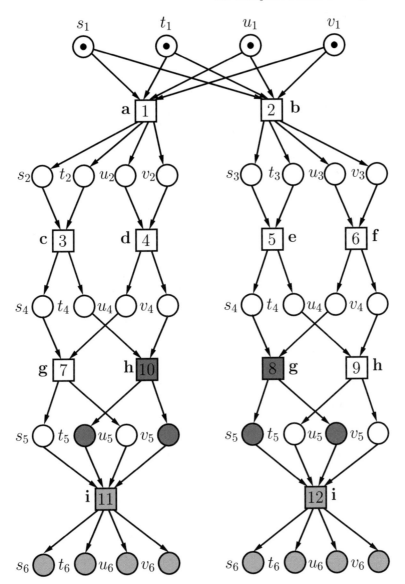

Fig. 4.8. Unfolding of the product of Fig. 4.6

The question is, which are the search strategies that in combination with the search scheme lead to complete search procedures? The next definition introduces such a class of strategies.

Definition 4.41. *A strategy* $\prec$ *on* $[\mathbf{T}^*]$ *is* adequate *if*

- *it is* well-founded, *and*
- *it is* preserved by extensions: *For all traces* $[\mathbf{w}], [\mathbf{w}'], [\mathbf{w}''] \in [\mathbf{T}^*]$, *if* $[\mathbf{w}] \prec [\mathbf{w}']$, *then* $[\mathbf{w}] [\mathbf{w}''] \prec [\mathbf{w}'] [\mathbf{w}'']$.

The following surprising result is due to Chatain and Khomenko. The proof requires some notions of the theory of well-quasi-orders, and can be found in Sect. 5.4 of the next chapter.

Proposition 4.42. *Every strategy on* $[\mathbf{T}^*]$ *preserved by extensions is well-founded.*

It follows that a strategy is adequate if and only if it is preserved by extensions. However, since the term "adequate" has already found its place in the literature, we keep it.

We prove that the search scheme of Def. 4.35 together with an adequate search strategy always yields a complete search procedure.

Theorem 4.43. *The search scheme of Def. 4.35 is complete for all adequate strategies.*

Proof. Let $\prec$ be an adequate search strategy. Assume that some goal transition $\mathbf{g} \in \mathbf{G}$ is executable, but no terminal of the final prefix is successful. We derive a contradiction.

We follow the scheme of the completeness proof of Thm. 4.11, just changing the definition of minimal witness, and using the definition of an adequate strategy to derive the contradiction.

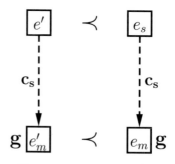

Fig. 4.9. Illustration of the proof of Thm. 4.43

Witnesses. Let an event of the unfolding of **A** be a *witness* if it is labeled with **g**. Using the same argument as in the proof of Thm. 4.11, we conclude that for every witness e there is an unsuccessful terminal $e_s < e$ that we call the *spoiler* of e.

Minimal witnesses. Since $\prec$ is well-founded by definition, the set of witnesses has at least one minimal element e_m w.r.t. $\prec$. Let e_s be the spoiler of e_m (see Fig. 4.9), and let $[\mathbf{c_s}]$ be a trace satisfying $\mathbf{H}(e_m) = \mathbf{H}(e_s)\,[\mathbf{c_s}]$. Since e_s is an unsuccessful terminal, it has a companion $e' \prec e_s$ such that $\mathbf{St}(e') = \mathbf{St}(e_s)$, and so $\mathbf{H}(e')\,[\mathbf{c_s}]$ is also a history of **A**. Let e'_m be the event satisfying $\mathbf{H}(e'_m) = \mathbf{H}(e')[\mathbf{c_s}]$. Then e'_m is labeled with **g**, and so it is a witness.

Contradiction. Since $\prec$ is preserved by extensions and $\mathbf{H}(e') \prec \mathbf{H}(e_s)$ holds, we have $\mathbf{H}(e'_m) = \mathbf{H}(e')[\mathbf{c_s}] \prec \mathbf{H}(e_s)[\mathbf{c_s}] = \mathbf{H}(e_m)$, and so $\mathbf{H}(e'_m) \prec \mathbf{H}(e_m)$. But this implies $e'_m \prec e_m$, which contradicts the minimality of e_m. $\qquad\Box$

Let us summarize the results of this section and Sect. 4.4. The search scheme of Def. 4.35 is well-defined and sound for all search strategies. Moreover,

- the final prefix has at most K non-terminal events (where K is the number of reachable global states) for total strategies, and
- the scheme is complete for adequate strategies.

The obvious question is whether total *and* adequate strategies exist. In the rest of the section we show that this is indeed the case.

4.5.1 The Size and Parikh Strategies

In order to avoid confusions, we use the following notational convention:

Notation 2. *We denote strategies by adding a mnemonic subscript to the symbol $\prec$, as in $\prec_x$. Given a strategy $\prec_x$, we write $[\mathbf{w}] =_x [\mathbf{w}']$ to denote that neither $[\mathbf{w}] \prec_x [\mathbf{w}']$ nor $[\mathbf{w}'] \prec_x [\mathbf{w}]$ holds.*

A simple example of an adequate strategy is the size strategy.

Definition 4.44. *The size strategy $\prec_s$ on $[\mathbf{T}^*]$ is defined as:* $[\mathbf{w}] \prec_s [\mathbf{w}']$ *if* $|\mathbf{w}| < |\mathbf{w}'|$, *i.e., if* $\mathbf{w}$ *is shorter than* $\mathbf{w}'$.

Notice that the size strategy is well-defined because all words that belong to a trace have the same length. Observe also that, as required of a strategy, it refines the prefix order. Finally, the size strategy is clearly adequate, because $[\mathbf{w}] \prec_s [\mathbf{w}']$ implies $|\mathbf{w}| < |\mathbf{w}'|$ implies $|\mathbf{w}\mathbf{w}''| < |\mathbf{w}'\mathbf{w}''|$ implies $[\mathbf{w}][\mathbf{w}''] \prec_s [\mathbf{w}'][\mathbf{w}'']$ for every trace $[\mathbf{w}], [\mathbf{w}'], [\mathbf{w}'']$.

Unfortunately, as we saw in Ex. 4.12 on p. 47, the size strategy may lead to very large final prefixes, even for transition systems. In the worst case, the prefix can be exponentially larger than the transition system itself, and so potentially much too large for verification purposes.

The Parikh strategy is a refinement of the size strategy that compares not only the total number of occurrences of transitions, but also the number of occurrences of each individual transition. In order to define it, we introduce the *Parikh image* of a trace.

Definition 4.45. *Let* $[\mathbf{w}]$ *be a trace. The* Parikh mapping *of* $[\mathbf{w}]$, *denoted by* $\mathcal{P}([\mathbf{w}])$, *is the mapping that assigns to each global transition* $\mathbf{t}$ *the number of times that* $\mathbf{t}$ *occurs in* $\mathbf{w}$.

Notice that the Parikh mapping is well-defined because all the words of a trace have the same Parikh mapping. The Parikh strategy is defined in two stages: first, the sizes of the traces are compared, and then, if necessary, their Parikh mappings.

Definition 4.46. *Let* $<_a$ *be a total order on* $\mathbf{T}$, *called the* alphabetical order. *The* Parikh strategy $\prec_P$ *on* $[\mathbf{T}^*]$ *is defined as follows:* $[\mathbf{w}] \prec_P [\mathbf{w}']$ *if either* $[\mathbf{w}] \prec_s [\mathbf{w}']$, *or* $[\mathbf{w}] =_s [\mathbf{w}']$ *and there is a global transition* $\mathbf{t}$ *such that*

- $\mathcal{P}([\mathbf{w}])(\mathbf{t}) < \mathcal{P}([\mathbf{w}'])(\mathbf{t})$, *and*
- $\mathcal{P}([\mathbf{w}])(\mathbf{t}') = \mathcal{P}([\mathbf{w}'])(\mathbf{t}')$ *for every* $\mathbf{t}' <_a \mathbf{t}$.

The Parikh strategy refines the prefix order because the size strategy does. It is easily seen to be adequate: Since $\mathcal{P}([\mathbf{w}][\mathbf{w}']) = \mathcal{P}([\mathbf{w}]) + \mathcal{P}([\mathbf{w}'])$, we have that $[\mathbf{w}] \prec_P [\mathbf{w}']$ implies $[\mathbf{w}][\mathbf{w}''] \prec_P [\mathbf{w}'][\mathbf{w}'']$ for every trace $[\mathbf{w}], [\mathbf{w}'], [\mathbf{w}'']$.

The Parikh strategy leads to smaller final prefixes than the size strategy, and it is in fact a useful strategy in practical applications. However, it is easy to show that it is not a total strategy, not even for products with only one component. So Thm. 4.39 cannot be applied to it.

4.5.2 Distributed Strategies

In this section we show that the problem of finding a total adequate strategy on the set $[\mathbf{T}^*]$ of traces can be reduced to the much simpler problem of finding a total adequate strategy for the set $\mathbf{T}^*$ of words.

Recall Thm. 4.21: Given a trace, the projections of its elements onto $\mathbf{T}_1, \ldots, \mathbf{T}_n$ coincide, where $\mathbf{T}_i$ is the set of global transitions in which the ith component participates. Moreover, these projections characterize the trace, i.e., different traces have different projections. It follows that searching for total adequate orders on Mazurkiewicz traces reduces to searching for total adequate orders on their tuples of projections onto $\mathbf{T}_1, \ldots, \mathbf{T}_n$. Since these are just tuples of words, we can try the following approach: find a total adequate order on $\mathbf{T}^*$, and then use some generic procedure to "lift" it to a total adequate order on tuples of words.

In the following we develop this approach. We start with a useful notational convention:

Notation 3. *We write* $[\mathbf{w}] = [\mathbf{w}_1, \ldots, \mathbf{w}_n]$ *to denote that* $\mathbf{w}_1, \ldots, \mathbf{w}_n$ *are the projections of* $\mathbf{w}$ *onto* $\mathbf{T}_1, \ldots, \mathbf{T}_n$ *and that* $[\mathbf{w}]$ *is the unique trace with this property.*

Example 4.47. For instance, we have

$$[\langle t_1, \epsilon \rangle \, \langle \epsilon, u_1 \rangle \, \langle t_3, u_2 \rangle \, \langle t_5, \epsilon \rangle \, \langle \epsilon, u_3 \rangle] = [\, \langle t_1, \epsilon \rangle \, \langle t_3, u_2 \rangle \, \langle t_5, \epsilon \rangle \, , \\ \langle \epsilon, u_1 \rangle \, \langle t_3, u_2 \rangle \, \langle \epsilon, u_3 \rangle \,] \,.$$

The following little proposition shows that the prefix order on words and the prefix order on traces fit nicely with each other.

Proposition 4.48. *If* $[\mathbf{w}] = [\mathbf{w}_1, \ldots, \mathbf{w}_n]$ *and* $[\mathbf{w}'] = [\mathbf{w}'_1, \ldots, \mathbf{w}'_n]$ *then* $[\mathbf{w}]\,[\mathbf{w}'] = [\mathbf{w}_1\,\mathbf{w}'_1, \ldots, \mathbf{w}_n\,\mathbf{w}'_n]$.

Proof. By definition we have $[\mathbf{w}]\,[\mathbf{w}'] = [\mathbf{w}\,\mathbf{w}']$. Since for every $i \in \{1, \ldots, n\}$ the projection of $\mathbf{w}\,\mathbf{w}'$ onto $\mathbf{T}_i$ is $\mathbf{w}_i\,\mathbf{w}'_i$, we are done. □

We are now ready to define the "lifting" procedure and prove its correctness.

Definition 4.49. *Let* $\prec$ *be a total search strategy on* $\mathbf{T}^*$. *The distributed strategy* $\prec^d$ *is the total search strategy on* $[\mathbf{T}^*]$ *defined as follows. Given* $[\mathbf{w}] = [\mathbf{w}_1, \ldots, \mathbf{w}_n]$ *and* $[\mathbf{w}'] = [\mathbf{w}'_1, \ldots, \mathbf{w}'_n]$, *we have* $[\mathbf{w}] \prec^d [\mathbf{w}']$ *if there is an index* $i \in \{1, \ldots, n\}$ *such that* $\mathbf{w}_i \prec \mathbf{w}'_i$, *and* $\mathbf{w}_j = \mathbf{w}'_j$ *for every* $1 \leq j < i$.

By Prop. 4.48, and since $\prec$ refines the prefix order on words, $\prec^d$ refines the prefix order on traces. Moreover, if $\prec$ is adequate and total then so is $\prec^d$:

Theorem 4.50. *If* $\prec$ *is a total adequate strategy on* $\mathbf{T}^*$, *then* $\prec^d$ *is a total adequate strategy on* $[\mathbf{T}^*]$.

Proof. By the definition of an adequate strategy and Prop. 4.42, it suffices to prove that $\prec^d$ is preserved by extensions. Let $[\mathbf{w}] = [\mathbf{w}_1, \ldots, \mathbf{w}_n]$ and $[\mathbf{w}'] = [\mathbf{w}'_1, \ldots, \mathbf{w}'_n]$ be traces such that $[\mathbf{w}] \prec^d [\mathbf{w}']$, and let $[\mathbf{w}''] = [\mathbf{w}''_1, \ldots, \mathbf{w}''_n]$ be an arbitrary trace. By definition, there is an index i such that $\mathbf{w}_i \prec \mathbf{w}'_i$ and $\mathbf{w}_j = \mathbf{w}'_j$ for every $j < i$. Then we have $\mathbf{w}_j\,\mathbf{w}''_j = \mathbf{w}'_j\,\mathbf{w}''_j$ for every $j < i$ and, since $\prec$ is preserved by extensions, $\mathbf{w}_i\,\mathbf{w}''_i \prec \mathbf{w}'_i\,\mathbf{w}''_i$. So $\mathbf{w}\,\mathbf{w}'' \prec \mathbf{w}'\,\mathbf{w}''$. □

So to finish our quest for a total adequate strategy on $[\mathbf{T}^*]$ we just have to find a total adequate strategy on $\mathbf{T}^*$. But this is easy:

Definition 4.51. *Let* $<_a$ *be the alphabetical order on* $\mathbf{T}$. *The* lexicographic *strategy on* $\mathbf{T}^*$, *denoted by* $\prec_l$, *is defined as follows:* $\mathbf{w} \prec_l \mathbf{w}'$ *if either* $\mathbf{w}$ *is a proper prefix of* $\mathbf{w}'$ *or there are words* $\overline{\mathbf{w}}, \mathbf{v}, \mathbf{v}'$ *and transitions* $\mathbf{a}$ *and* $\mathbf{b}$ *such that* $\mathbf{a} <_a \mathbf{b}$, $\mathbf{w} = \overline{\mathbf{w}}\,\mathbf{a}\,\mathbf{v}$, *and* $\mathbf{w}' = \overline{\mathbf{w}}\,\mathbf{b}\,\mathbf{v}'$. *The* size-lexicographic *strategy on* $\mathbf{T}^*$, *denoted by* $\prec_{sl}$, *is defined as follows:* $\mathbf{w} \prec_{sl} \mathbf{w}'$ *if either* $\mathbf{w} \prec_s \mathbf{w}'$ *or* $\mathbf{w} =_s \mathbf{w}'$ *and* $\mathbf{w} \prec_l \mathbf{w}'$.

Theorem 4.52. $\prec_{sl}$ *is a total adequate strategy on* $\mathbf{T}^*$, *and so* $\prec_{sl}^d$ *is a total adequate strategy on* $[\mathbf{T}^*]$.

Proof. By Thm. 4.50 it suffices to prove the first part. Clearly, $\prec_{sl}$ is a well-founded total order on $\mathbf{T}^*$. We show that it is preserved by extensions. Let $\mathbf{w}, \mathbf{w}', \mathbf{w}''$ be words such that $\mathbf{w} \prec_{sl} \mathbf{w}'$. There are two possible cases:

- $\mathbf{w} \prec_s \mathbf{w}'$. Then $\mathbf{w}\,\mathbf{w}'' \prec_s \mathbf{w}\,\mathbf{w}''$ and so $\mathbf{w}\,\mathbf{w}'' \prec_{sl} \mathbf{w}\,\mathbf{w}''$.
- $\mathbf{w} =_s \mathbf{w}'$ and $\mathbf{w} \prec_l \mathbf{w}'$. Then there are words $\overline{\mathbf{w}}, \mathbf{v}, \mathbf{v}'$ and transitions $\mathbf{a}$ and $\mathbf{b}$ such that $\mathbf{a} <_a \mathbf{b}$, $\mathbf{w} = \overline{\mathbf{w}}\,\mathbf{a}\,\mathbf{v}$ and $\mathbf{w}' = \overline{\mathbf{w}}\,\mathbf{b}\,\mathbf{v}'$. But then we have $\mathbf{w}\,\mathbf{w}'' = \overline{\mathbf{w}}\,\mathbf{a}\,\mathbf{v}\,\mathbf{w}'' \prec_l \overline{\mathbf{w}}\,\mathbf{b}\,\mathbf{v}'\,\mathbf{w}'' = \mathbf{w}'\,\mathbf{w}''$, and so $\mathbf{w}\,\mathbf{w}'' \prec_{sl} \mathbf{w}'\,\mathbf{w}''$.

$\square$

Since $\prec_{sl}^d$ is a total adequate order on $[\mathbf{T}^*]$, it is also complete, and so the search procedure based on it will return the correct answer when applied to the product of Fig. 4.6 on p. 59.

Example 4.53. Consider again the executability problem for $\mathbf{G} = \{\mathbf{i}\}$ in the product of Fig. 4.6 on p. 59. The unfolding is shown in Fig. 4.8 on p. 61. Table 4.1 shows for every event e the projections of $\mathbf{H}(e)$ onto $\mathbf{T}_1, \ldots, \mathbf{T}_4$ (columns $\mathbf{T}_1$ to $\mathbf{T}_4$). On the left table the events are ordered according to their number, while on the right table they are ordered according to $\prec_{sl}^d$.

Table 4.1. Histories of the events in Fig. 4.8 sorted according to event numbers (left) and according to $\prec_{sl}^d$ (right)

Event	$\mathbf{T}_1$	$\mathbf{T}_2$	$\mathbf{T}_3$	$\mathbf{T}_4$
1	a	a	a	a
2	b	b	b	b
3	ac	ac	a	a
4	a	a	ad	ad
5	be	be	b	b
6	b	b	bf	bf
7	acg	ac	adg	ad
8	beg	be	bfg	bf
9	be	beh	bf	bfh
10	ac	ach	ad	adh
11	acgi	achi	adgi	adhi
12	begi	behi	bfgi	bfhi

Event	$\mathbf{T}_1$	$\mathbf{T}_2$	$\mathbf{T}_3$	$\mathbf{T}_4$
1	a	a	a	a
4	a	a	ad	ad
2	b	b	b	b
6	b	b	bf	bf
3	ac	ac	a	a
10	ac	ach	ad	adh
5	be	be	b	b
9	be	beh	bf	bfh
7	acg	ac	adg	ad
8	beg	be	bfg	bf
11	acgi	achi	adgi	adhi
12	begi	behi	bfgi	bfhi

So a search procedure based on $\prec_{sl}^d$ generates the events in order 1, 4, 2, 6, 3, 10, 5, 9, 7, 8, 11, and marks events 9 and 8 as terminals with corresponding events 10 and 7, respectively. Even though event 12 is not generated, the final prefix is still successful because it contains event 11, which is a successful terminal. Intuitively, in this example the adequate order guarantees that the events of the "left side" of Fig. 4.8 on p. 61 are always added to the unfolding a bit earlier than their counterparts on the "right side" of the unfolding.

Notice, however, that adequacy is *only a sufficient condition* for the completeness of the associated search procedure. This is illustrated by the prefix order on traces. While it is obviously a search strategy, it is not adequate: for instance, if $\mathbf{a}, \mathbf{b}, \mathbf{c}$ are pairwise-dependent transitions, then [$\mathbf{a}$] is a prefix of [$\mathbf{a}\,\mathbf{b}$], but [$\mathbf{a}$] [$\mathbf{c}$] is not a prefix of [$\mathbf{a}\,\mathbf{b}$] [$\mathbf{c}$], and therefore the prefix order on traces is not preserved by extensions. However, the search procedure based on the prefix strategy is still complete. This fact is a consequence of the following generalization of Thm. 4.43:

Theorem 4.54. *Let $\prec_1$ and $\prec_2$ be two strategies on $[\mathbf{T}^*]$. If $\prec_1$ is adequate and refines $\prec_2$, then the search procedure with $\prec_2$ as strategy is complete.*

Proof. Recall the definition of $\prec_1$ refines $\prec_2$: for every two events e, e' of the unfolding, $e \prec_2 e'$ implies $e \prec_1 e'$.

It suffices to show that if an unfolding contains events labeled by goal transitions, then the $\prec_2$-final prefix contains at least one successful terminal.

Let e_m be a $\prec_1$-minimal event labeled by a goal transition. This event exists, because $\prec_1$ is adequate and therefore well-founded. We prove by contradiction that e_m is $\prec_2$-feasible, and so a $\prec_2$-successful terminal.

Assume e_m is not $\prec_2$-feasible. Then some event $e_s < e_m$ (the spoiler of e_m) is a $\prec_2$-terminal. Since $\prec_1$ is a strategy, we have $e_s \prec_1 e_m$, and so, by the minimality of e_m, the event e_s cannot be labeled by a goal transition. So e_s is not a successful $\prec_2$-terminal. It follows that e_s is unsuccessful. Let $e' \prec_2 e_s$ be the companion of e_s. Since $\prec_1$ refines $\prec_2$, we also have $e' \prec_1 e_s$. Let [$\mathbf{c}$] be the trace satisfying $\mathbf{H}(e_s)\,[\mathbf{c}] = \mathbf{H}(e_m)$. Since $\mathbf{St}(e') = \mathbf{St}(e_s)$, there is an event e'_m satisfying $\mathbf{H}(e')\,[\mathbf{c}] = \mathbf{H}(e'_m)$. This event is labeled by the same goal transition as e_m and, since $\prec_1$ is preserved by extensions, we have $e'_m \prec_1 e_m$. But this contradicts the minimality of e_m. □

Corollary 4.55. *The search scheme of Def. 4.35 is complete for the distributed prefix strategy.*

Proof. It is easy to see that $\prec^d_{sl}$ refines the prefix strategy on traces. Since $\prec^d_{sl}$ is adequate, we can apply Thm. 4.54. □

4.6 Complete Search Scheme for Arbitrary Strategies

We have seen that the search scheme of Def. 4.35, called S in this section for brevity, is not complete for every search strategy.

This result should not be interpreted as *forbidding* the use of some strategies. It only states that they cannot be used *in combination with S*. In this section we show that S can be modified in a rather straightforward way to yield a new search scheme complete for *every* strategy. The price to pay is that the new search scheme may lead to larger final prefixes in the worst case. In particular, Thm. 4.39, stating that the combination of S with a total adequate strategy does not generate more non-terminals than the number of reachable states of the product, does not hold for the new scheme. This approach is originally due to Bonet, Haslum, Hickmott and Thiébaux.

Recall that S defines a terminal as a feasible event satisfying one of these properties:

(a) e is labeled with a transition of $\mathbf{G}$, or
(b) there is a feasible event $e' \prec e$ such that $\mathbf{St}(e') = \mathbf{St}(e)$.

We replace (b) by a *stronger* condition (b′):

(b′) there is a feasible event $e' \prec e$ such that $\mathbf{St}(e') = \mathbf{St}(e)$ and $P(e', e)$,

where $P(e', e)$ is a to-be-determined predicate on pairs of events. The question is: how to choose $P(e', e)$ so that the resulting scheme is complete for all strategies, without losing soundness or finiteness.

The perhaps surprising, but in fact very simple observation is that we can take $P(e', e) \Leftrightarrow e' \ll e$, where $\ll$ is any strategy for which S is complete. As we shall see, the new scheme, whatever the strategy, always generates at least (and possibly more than) the events generated by S with strategy $\ll$. So, if the set $\mathbf{G}$ of goal transitions is executable, then S with strategy $\ll$ generates an event labeled by some transition of $\mathbf{G}$, and since this event is also generated by the new scheme, the new scheme is also complete.

Before giving a formal definition of the new scheme, let us consider once more the example of Fig. 4.6, whose full unfolding is shown again in Fig. 4.10. The numbers inside the boxes correspond to the total strategy $\prec$ for which S is not complete (events 8 and 10 are terminals, and so the search procedure never adds events 11 or 12). For $\ll$ we take the size strategy $\prec_s$, which is adequate and so complete in combination with S.

The new search procedure adds events in the order given by $\prec$; however, when it adds event 8, it observes that $7 \not\prec_s 8$ holds, and so that condition (b′) fails. So the procedure does not mark event 8 as a terminal. In the same way, event 10 is not marked either. So events 11 and 12 are feasible in the new scheme, and become part of the final prefix.

This same example allows us to illustrate the practical interest in the new search scheme. In Sect. 5.3 we shall consider depth-first strategies (see the section for a formal definition), and will show that, unfortunately, they are not complete for S. However, they can be safely used in combination with the new scheme. This is useful, because in favorable cases depth-first strategies may quickly lead to a successful terminal, which allows us to stop the search. For instance, consider Fig. 4.11, which shows the unfolding of Fig. 4.8, but orders the events according to a depth-first strategy. In combination with this strategy, the new scheme stops after the addition of event 6, which is

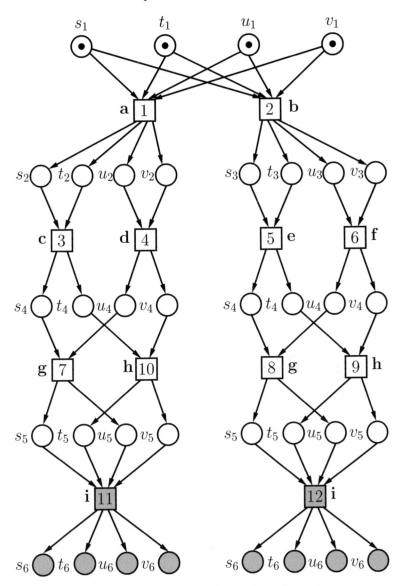

Fig. 4.10. Unfolding of the product of Fig. 4.6

a successful terminal. This is a better result than the one obtained with scheme
S and the distributed version of the size-lexicographic strategy, which requires
us to generate 11 events.

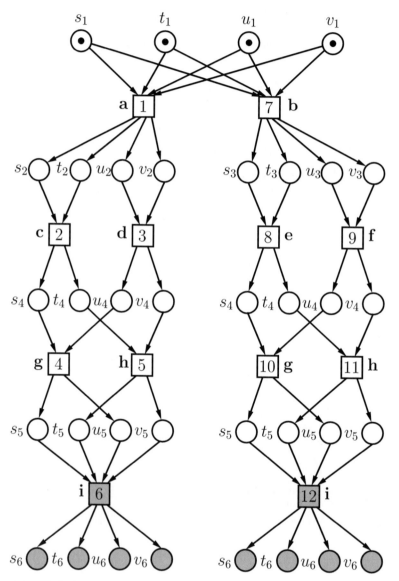

Fig. 4.11. Unfolding of the product of Fig. 4.6 with depth-first strategy; only events
1 to 6 are part of the final prefix

Summarizing: when the answer to the executability problem is positive, the new scheme can reach a successful terminal faster by making use of its freedom for choosing strategies. On the other hand, when the answer to the problem is negative, the new scheme can never outperform S, because it generates at least as many events, and in unfavorable cases it may generate many more events.

We conclude the section with the formal definition of the new search scheme.

Definition 4.56. *Let $\prec$ be a strategy on $[\mathbf{T}^*]$, and let $\ll$ be any strategy on $[\mathbf{T}^*]$ that together with the search scheme of Def. 4.35 yields a complete search procedure.*
An event e of the unfolding of $\mathbf{A}$ is feasible *if no event $e' < e$ is a terminal. A feasible event e is a* terminal *if either*

(a) e is labeled with a transition of $\mathbf{G}$, or
(b') there is a feasible event $e' \prec e$, called the companion *of e, such that $\mathbf{St}(e') = \mathbf{St}(e)$ and $e' \ll e$.*

A terminal is successful *if it is of type (a). The $\prec$-final prefix is the prefix of the unfolding of $\mathbf{A}$ containing the feasible events.*

Well-definedness (including finiteness) and soundness for arbitrary strategies are proved exactly as for the scheme of Def. 4.35; see proofs of Props. 4.37 and 4.38. Completeness is also easy:

Theorem 4.57. *The search scheme of Def. 4.56 is complete for every strategy.*

Proof. Let S and S' be the search schemes of Defs. 4.35 and 4.56, respectively. Since the combination of S and $\ll$ is complete, the $\ll$-final prefix contains a successful terminal e_t. So e_t is feasible and labeled by some goal transition. We show that e_t is a feasible event of S' for any strategy. Since e_t is labeled by a goal transition, this implies that e_t is a successful terminal of S', and so that S' is complete for every strategy.

Fix any strategy $\prec$, and assume that e_t is not feasible in S'. Then, some event $e < e_t$ is an unsuccessful terminal of S'. Let e' be the companion of e. By condition (b'), we have $e' \ll e$. But then e is a terminal of S, and since $e < e_t$ the event e_t is not feasible, contradicting the assumption. □

Bibliographical Notes

The search schemes of Defs. 4.6 and 4.35 for the executability problem owe very much to the work of Khomenko, Koutny, and Vogler on canonical prefixes of Petri net unfoldings [73]. They observed that this kind of seemingly circular definition is actually correct. The immediate consequence is that for any arbitrary search strategy $\prec$ there is a unique $\prec$-final prefix (Khomenko, Koutny, and Vogler would call it the canonical prefix).

Mazurkiewicz traces were introduced by Mazurkiewicz in the early 1970s and have been very extensively studied. The standard reference is [31]. The counterexample of Sect. 4.4.1 is taken from [40, 41].

Adequate search strategies were introduced in [40, 41] under the name of adequate orders. The size strategy was introduced by McMillan in [84]. The section on distributed strategies is taken from [39].

The complete search scheme for arbitrary strategies presented in Sect. 4.6 is due to Bonet, Haslum, Hickmott, and Thiébaux, and as far as we know still unpublished in this form at the time this book goes to print. An earlier version of the approach was presented in [15].

5

More on the Executability Problem

In this chapter we present some additional results on the executability problem, and in particular on adequate strategies, that are not used in the rest of the book. The reader interested in the essentials of the model checking procedure for LTL can safely skip them and move to Chap. 6.

In Sect. 5.1 we introduce *complete prefixes*. These are prefixes of the unfolding which, loosely speaking, contain all reachable states. Once a complete prefix is computed, it can be used to solve many different verification problems.

The other sections of the chapter present further results on adequate strategies. Section 5.2 introduces a second total adequate strategy, different from the distributed version of the size-lexicographic strategy that was defined in the previous chapter. Section 5.3 generalizes the concept of breadth-first and depth-first search to products. Finally, Sect. 5.4 proves Prop. 4.42, stating that every strategy on Mazurkiewicz traces preserved by extensions is well-founded.

5.1 Complete Prefixes

Consider the special case of the executability problem in which the set $\mathbf{G}$ of goal transitions is empty. Obviously, the answer to the question of whether $\mathbf{G}$ contains an executable transition is "no", and we do not need to construct any branching process to answer it. However, the case $\mathbf{G} = \emptyset$ is interesting for another reason. We show in this section that, given an arbitrary adequate strategy $\prec$, every reachable state of the product is represented by at least one reachable state of the $\prec$-final prefix. So, in particular, the $\prec$-final prefix can be seen as a (potentially very compact) representation of the complete set of reachable global states. For this reason, this prefix is known in the literature as the $\prec$-*complete prefix* (or just the complete prefix if the strategy $\prec$ is clear from the context). In this section we prove this fact, show that the global reachability problem for complete finite prefixes (formally defined below) is NP-complete, and briefly discuss the applications of this result.

Recall that in the search scheme of Def. 4.35 on p. 57 an event is a terminal if (a) it is labeled by a transition of $\mathbf{G}$ or (b) there is a feasible event $e' \prec e$ such that $\mathbf{St}(e') = \mathbf{St}(e)$. If $\mathbf{G} = \emptyset$ then case (a) cannot occur. This leads to the following definition of the complete prefix:

Definition 5.1. *Let* $\prec$ *be an adequate search strategy on* $[\mathbf{T}^*]$. *An event* e *of the unfolding of* $\mathbf{A}$ *is* feasible *if no event* $e' < e$ *is a terminal. A feasible event* e *is a* terminal *if there is a feasible event* $e' \prec e$, *called the* companion *of* e, *such that* $\mathbf{St}(e') = \mathbf{St}(e)$. *The* $\prec$-complete prefix *is the prefix of the unfolding of* $\mathbf{A}$ *containing the feasible events.*

The fact that this definition is not circular follows immediately from the fact that it is a special case of Def. 4.35 with $\mathbf{G} = \emptyset$.

Example 5.2. Consider the product of Fig. 2.2 on p. 7, whose unfolding can be found in Fig. 3.3 on p. 17. Consider the distributed size lexicographic strategy $\prec_{sl}^d$, where the alphabetical order $<_a$ on global transitions is given by:

$$\langle t_1, \epsilon \rangle <_a \langle t_2, \epsilon \rangle <_a \langle t_3, u_2 \rangle <_a \langle t_4, u_2 \rangle <_a \langle t_5, \epsilon \rangle <_a \langle \epsilon, u_1 \rangle <_a \langle \epsilon, u_3 \rangle .$$

Recall that $\prec_{sl}^d$ is a total adequate strategy on traces. Fig. 5.1 shows the complete finite prefix for this strategy. The events 7, 11, and 12, shown in dark grey, are terminals. All of them have event 4 as companion. Table 5.1 shows for every event e the projections of the history $\mathbf{H}(e)$ onto $\mathbf{T}_1$ and $\mathbf{T}_2$. The events are numbered in the order in which they are added to the complete prefix, and the column $\mathbf{St}(e)$ shows the state reached by $past(e)$.

Table 5.1. Projections of histories for the events in Fig. 5.1

Event	Projection on $\mathbf{T}_1$	Projection on $\mathbf{T}_2$	$\mathbf{St}(e)$
1		$\langle \epsilon, u_1 \rangle$	$\langle s_1, r_2 \rangle$
2	$\langle t_1, \epsilon \rangle$		$\langle s_2, r_1 \rangle$
3	$\langle t_2, \epsilon \rangle$		$\langle s_3, r_1 \rangle$
4	$\langle t_1, \epsilon \rangle\ \langle t_3, u_2 \rangle$	$\langle \epsilon, u_1 \rangle\ \langle t_3, u_2 \rangle$	$\langle s_4, r_3 \rangle$
5	$\langle t_1, \epsilon \rangle\ \langle t_3, u_2 \rangle$	$\langle \epsilon, u_1 \rangle\ \langle t_3, u_2 \rangle\ \langle \epsilon, u_3 \rangle$	$\langle s_4, r_1 \rangle$
6	$\langle t_1, \epsilon \rangle\ \langle t_3, u_2 \rangle$	$\langle \epsilon, u_1 \rangle\ \langle t_3, u_2 \rangle\ \langle \epsilon, u_3 \rangle\ \langle \epsilon, u_1 \rangle$	$\langle s_4, r_2 \rangle$
7	$\langle t_2, \epsilon \rangle\ \langle t_4, u_2 \rangle$	$\langle \epsilon, u_1 \rangle\ \langle t_4, u_2 \rangle$	$\langle s_4, r_3 \rangle$
8	$\langle t_1, \epsilon \rangle\ \langle t_3, u_2 \rangle\ \langle t_5, \epsilon \rangle$	$\langle \epsilon, u_1 \rangle\ \langle t_3, u_2 \rangle$	$\langle s_1, r_3 \rangle$
9	$\langle t_1, \epsilon \rangle\ \langle t_3, u_2 \rangle\ \langle t_5, \epsilon \rangle\ \langle t_1, \epsilon \rangle$	$\langle \epsilon, u_1 \rangle\ \langle t_3, u_2 \rangle$	$\langle s_2, r_3 \rangle$
10	$\langle t_1, \epsilon \rangle\ \langle t_3, u_2 \rangle\ \langle t_5, \epsilon \rangle\ \langle t_2, \epsilon \rangle$	$\langle \epsilon, u_1 \rangle\ \langle t_3, u_2 \rangle$	$\langle s_3, r_3 \rangle$
11	$\langle t_1, \epsilon \rangle\ \langle t_3, u_2 \rangle\ \langle t_5, \epsilon \rangle\ \langle t_1, \epsilon \rangle$ $\langle t_3, u_2 \rangle$	$\langle \epsilon, u_1 \rangle\ \langle t_3, u_2 \rangle\ \langle \epsilon, u_3 \rangle\ \langle \epsilon, u_1 \rangle$ $\langle t_3, u_2 \rangle$	$\langle s_4, r_3 \rangle$
12	$\langle t_1, \epsilon \rangle\ \langle t_3, u_2 \rangle\ \langle t_5, \epsilon \rangle\ \langle t_2, \epsilon \rangle$ $\langle t_4, u_2 \rangle$	$\langle \epsilon, u_1 \rangle\ \langle t_3, u_2 \rangle\ \langle \epsilon, u_3 \rangle\ \langle \epsilon, u_1 \rangle$ $\langle t_4, u_2 \rangle$	$\langle s_4, r_3 \rangle$

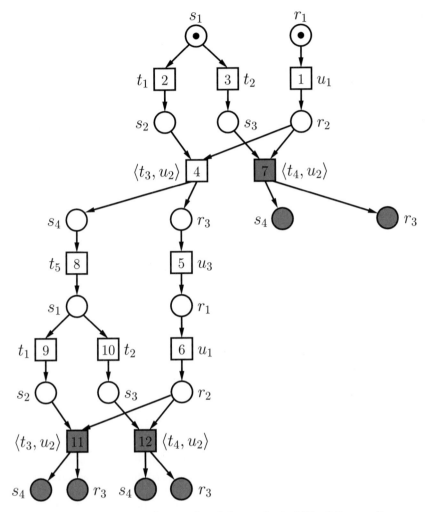

Fig. 5.1. The complete prefix of the product of Fig. 2.2 on p. 7

We show that every reachable global state of a product **A** "corresponds" to some configuration of the complete prefix.

Theorem 5.3. *Let* $\prec$ *be an adequate search strategy on* $[\mathbf{T}^*]$. *A global state* **s** *of* **A** *is reachable if and only if some configuration* C *of the* $\prec$-*complete prefix of* **A** *containing no terminals satisfies* $\mathbf{St}(C) = \mathbf{s}$.

Proof. We start with the first statement.

($\Leftarrow$:) Obvious, because every realization of C corresponds to a history of **A** whose execution leads to **s**.

($\Rightarrow$:) Since **s** is reachable, at least one history of **A** leads to it. Let **h** be a history of **A** leading to **s** such that the trace [**h**] is minimal w.r.t. $\prec$.

(Notice that $[\mathbf{h}]$ exists because $\prec$ is well-founded.) By Prop. 3.7 on p. 19, some occurrence sequence of the unfolding of $\mathbf{A}$ is labeled by $\mathbf{h}$. The set of events occurring in this sequence is realizable, and so, by definition, it constitutes a configuration C. This configuration satisfies $\mathbf{H}(C) = [\mathbf{h}]$ and $\mathbf{St}(C) = \mathbf{s}$.

We prove that C contains no terminals and is therefore contained in the complete prefix. Assume that C contains a terminal e with companion e'. Let $\mathbf{c}$ be any computation such that $\mathbf{H}(C) = \mathbf{H}(e)\,[\mathbf{c}]$. Since $\mathbf{St}(e') = \mathbf{St}(e)$, we have that $\mathbf{H}(e')\,[\mathbf{c}]$ is also a history trace of $\mathbf{A}$. Let C' be the configuration satisfying $\mathbf{H}(C') = \mathbf{H}(e')\,[\mathbf{c}]$. We have $\mathbf{St}(C') = \mathbf{s}$ and, since $\prec$ is preserved by extensions, $\mathbf{H}(C') \prec \mathbf{H}(C)$ holds, contradicting the minimality of $[\mathbf{h}]$. This proves that C contains no terminals. Moreover, it implies that all events of C are feasible, and so that C is a configuration of the complete prefix.   □

5.1.1 Some Complexity Results

It follows from Thm. 5.3 that a global transition $\mathbf{t}$ of a product is executable if and only if the complete prefix contains an event labeled by it. Indeed, if $\mathbf{t}$ is executable, then it is enabled by some reachable marking. By Thm. 5.3, the complete prefix contains a configuration containing no terminal leading to this marking, which can be extended with an event labeled by $\mathbf{t}$, and also belonging to the prefix. Note that the event labeled with $\mathbf{t}$ may itself be a terminal. So we have the following result:

Proposition 5.4. *The following problem can be solved in linear time:*
Given: A complete prefix of a product $\mathbf{A}$, a set $\mathbf{G} \subseteq \mathbf{T}$ of global transitions.
Decide: Can some transition of $\mathbf{G}$ ever be executed?

This must be compared with Thm. 3.24 on p. 36, which states that the executability problem is PSPACE-complete for products. In the executability problem we ask the same question, but the input is the product $\mathbf{A}$ itself, not a complete prefix. There is no contradiction between the two results, because in the worst case the complete prefix of $\mathbf{A}$ is exponentially larger than $\mathbf{A}$, and so "linear time in the size of the complete prefix" may mean "exponential time in the size of $\mathbf{A}$".

The same results (PSPACE-completeness with $\mathbf{A}$ as input, linear time with the complete prefix as input) hold for the *local state reachability* problem: Given a product $\mathbf{A}$ and a local state s of the ith component, decide if there is a reachable global state $\mathbf{s} = \langle s_1, \dots, s_n \rangle$ such that $s_i = s$. The proof is a simple reduction from and to the executability problem.

Let us now examine the problem of deciding if a *global* state is reachable. If the input is the product $\mathbf{A}$, then the problem is again PSPACE-complete, as can be easily shown by mutual reduction to the executability problem or by a slight modification of the proof of Thm. 3.24 on p. 36. But if the input is the complete prefix we have:

Proposition 5.5. *The following problem is NP-complete:*
Given: A complete prefix of a product **A**, *a global state* **s**.
Decide: Is **s** *reachable?*

Proof. To prove membership in NP, we start by observing that in an occurrence sequence of the complete prefix no event can occur twice. This can be easily proved by structural induction on the causal order: minimal events w.r.t. the order can obviously occur at most once, and if the immediate causal predecessors of an event can occur at most once, then so can the event itself. Now, if **s** is reachable, we can guess a sequence of events of the complete prefix, check that it is an occurrence sequence and that it leads to a reachable marking labeled by **s**, and do all this checking in polynomial time.

NP-hardness can be proved by means of a reduction from the propositional logic satisfiability problem (SAT). The proof is very similar to that of Prop. 3.21 on p. 31. □

Finally, we can consider a third version of the global reachability problem in which the input is the transition system $\mathcal{T}_\mathbf{A}$. Since the states of $\mathcal{T}_\mathbf{A}$ are the global states of **A**, in this case the problem can be solved in linear time.

An interesting way of interpreting these results is to consider the product **A**, its complete prefix, and the transition system $\mathcal{T}_\mathbf{A}$ as three representations of the set of reachable global states. The product **A** is a very succinct representation, while $\mathcal{T}_\mathbf{A}$ is very "verbose". The complete prefix lies in between. The price to pay for a succinct representation is a higher cost in retrieving information. In the case of **A**, almost any interesting information has "PSPACE-complete cost" (it is well known that most problems of interest are PSPACE-complete for products). In the case of $\mathcal{T}_\mathbf{A}$, almost any kind of information (for instance, deciding any property expressible in CTL and LTL, two popular temporal logics) has polynomial cost in the size of $\mathcal{T}_\mathbf{A}$. Again, the complete prefix lies in between. If we are interested in *local* properties, i.e., in properties concerning a *bounded* number of components, then retrieving the information has polynomial cost. For instance, deciding the executability of one transition has linear cost, and deciding the mutual exclusion of two local states has quadratic cost. However, global information, like the reachability of a global state, has "NP-complete cost".

It is important to notice the difference between "complete prefix" (as defined in this work) and "prefix in which every reachable state is represented". Let us call the latter a *full* prefix. While every complete prefix is full, not every full prefix is complete. Intuitively, when constructing a complete prefix the only information we have about which global states are reachable comes from the states $\mathbf{St}(e)$ associated with the events. These are the only global states that are explicitly constructed and stored by a search procedure. In particular, when adding a new event e, the search procedure cannot check whether $\mathbf{St}(e)$ is already represented in the prefix constructed so far; it can only check whether $\mathbf{St}(e)$ is also the state associated with some other event. "Minimal" full prefixes can be constructed by performing this check (reachability of a global state can be done using Prop. 5.5), and can therefore be much more compact representations of the set of reachable states than complete prefixes. However, retrieving information from them is more costly: the second author has shown that certain nested local state reachability problems with full prefixes as input are PSPACE-complete. The exact lower bound of these nested local state reachability problems for the much less succinct complete prefixes is an open question.

By Prop. 5.5 we should not expect to find polynomial algorithms for the global reachability problem with a complete prefix as input. Let us however give a rough estimate of the complexity of a naive exponential algorithm. Assume that the product $\mathbf{A}$ has k components, and that its complete prefix has size n. Assume further that $\mathbf{s} = \langle s_1, \ldots, s_k \rangle$. By Thm. 5.3 and Prop. 3.14 on p. 23, $\mathbf{s}$ is reachable if and only if the complete prefix contains a set $\{p_1, \ldots, p_k\}$ of places such that

(1) p_i and p_j are concurrent for every $1 \le i < j \le k$, and
(2) p_i is labeled by s_i for every $i \in \{1, \ldots, k\}$.

To check if such a set exists, we proceed in two steps. First, in a preprocessing step we compute all concurrent pairs of places. It is easy to see that this can be done in $O(n^2)$ time (and space). Then, for each subset $\{p_1, \ldots, p_k\}$ we check (1) and (2) in time $O(k^2)$ by going through the places pairwise. Since there are $O((n/k)^k)$ possible subsets, the existence of a set satisfying (1) and (2) can be decided in $O(n^k/k^{k-2})$ time with a $O(n^2)$ preprocessing step. See also Sect. 3.4, especially Prop. 3.20 on p. 29.

The important observation here is that the algorithm is only exponential in the number k of components, which is usually much smaller than n.

5.1.2 Reducing Verification Problems to SAT

In the rest of the section we show that the reachability problem with a complete prefix as input can be reduced in an elegant way to SAT. In fact, similar reductions can be given for many other problems. These reductions are important, because they allow us to apply SAT solvers to reachability problems.

In a first preprocessing step we remove all terminals and their output places from the complete prefix. The reason is Thm. 5.3: since all global states are reachable by configurations containing no terminals, they can be safely removed.

The heart of the result is the construction of a formula $\phi_{\mathbf{A}}$ over a set of Boolean variables containing a variable $\mathbf{e}$ for every event e, and a variable $\mathbf{p}$ for every place p of the preprocessed complete prefix. In the following we present this construction, but without paying much attention to efficiency questions; many encoding tricks can be used to reduce the size of $\phi_{\mathbf{A}}$.

An assignment to the variables of $\phi_{\mathbf{A}}$ determines and is completely determined by the pair (E, P), where E and P are the sets of events e and places

p such that the variables $\mathbf{e}$ and $\mathbf{p}$ are set to true by the assignment, respectively. So we identify an assignment and its associated pair, and speak of "the assignment (E, P)". The formula $\phi_{\mathbf{A}}$ has the following fundamental property:

> An assignment (E, P) satisfies $\phi_{\mathbf{A}}$ if and only if E is a configuration, and P is the marking reached by any realization of E.

So in $\phi_{\mathbf{A}}$ we can interpret the variable $\mathbf{e}$ as "the event e has occurred", and the variable $\mathbf{p}$ as "the place p is marked".

The formula $\phi_{\mathbf{A}}$ is a conjunction of formulas ϕ_p, one for each place p of the preprocessed complete prefix. Assume that p has an input event e and output events $e_1, e_2, \ldots, e_n$. We set

$$\phi_p = \left(\left(\bigvee_{i=1}^{n} \mathbf{e}_i \right) \rightarrow \mathbf{e} \right) \wedge \left(\bigwedge_{1 \leq i < j \leq n} \neg(\mathbf{e}_i \wedge \mathbf{e}_j) \right) \wedge \left(\mathbf{p} \leftrightarrow (\mathbf{e} \wedge \bigwedge_{i=1}^{n} \neg \mathbf{e}_i) \right)$$

The first conjunct expresses that if any of $e_1, \ldots, e_n$ have occurred, then e must also have occurred. The second conjunct expresses that at most one of $e_1, \ldots, e_n$ have occurred. Finally, the third conjunct expresses that p is marked if and only if e has occurred and none of $e_1, \ldots, e_n$ has occurred. So, if an assignment (E, P) satisfies the first two conjuncts for every place p, then E is causally closed and conflict-free, and therefore a configuration (Prop. 3.18). Moreover, P is the marking reached by any realization of C.

The preprocessed complete prefix may contain places having no input event, no output events, or (in pathological cases) having neither input nor output events. If a place has no input event, then its associated formula is obtained by replacing all occurrences of the input event variable $\mathbf{e}$ in the formula above by *true*. If it has no output events, then all occurrences of output event variables $\mathbf{e}_i$ are replaced by *false*. In particular, if the place has neither input nor output events we get $\phi_p = \mathbf{p}$, expressing the fact that the place p is marked in all configurations.

We illustrate the construction by means of an example.

Example 5.6. Consider the Petri net of Fig. 5.2. It is easy to see that it is the Petri net representation of a product with two components, one with states labeled s_i, and one with states labelled r_i. Figure 5.3 shows the complete prefix for the $\prec_{sl}^d$ strategy. The name of a node (place or event) is written inside the node, whereas its label is written next to it. As usual, the names of the events correspond to the order in which they are added to the unfolding. For the names of the places we have chosen Greek letters. Events 5 and 7 (that are ignored by the encoding together with their output places) are terminals with event 1 as their companion. Table 5.2 shows the conjuncts ϕ_p of $\phi_{\mathbf{A}}$ for every $p \in \{\alpha, \ldots, \zeta, \kappa, \lambda, \mu, \nu\}$. (The places θ, ι, and ξ are removed by the preprocessing step.)

With the help of the formula $\phi_{\mathbf{A}}$ we can reduce many safety problems to the satisfiability problem of a SAT formula. We give some examples:

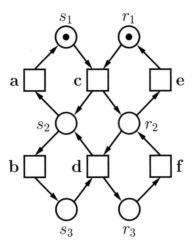

Fig. 5.2. A Petri net model

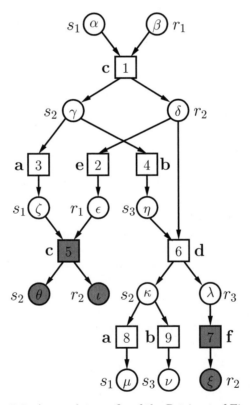

Fig. 5.3. A complete prefix of the Petri net of Fig. 5.2

Table 5.2. The conjuncts of $\phi_\mathbf{A}$ for the complete prefix of Fig. 5.3

p	ϕ_p
α	$\alpha \leftrightarrow \neg 1$
β	$\beta \leftrightarrow \neg 1$
γ	$((3 \vee 4) \rightarrow 1) \wedge \neg(3 \wedge 4) \wedge (\gamma \leftrightarrow (1 \wedge \neg 3 \wedge \neg 4))$
δ	$((2 \vee 6) \rightarrow 1) \wedge \neg(2 \wedge 6) \wedge (\delta \leftrightarrow (1 \wedge \neg 2 \wedge \neg 6))$
ϵ	$\epsilon \leftrightarrow 2$
ζ	$\zeta \leftrightarrow 3$
η	$(6 \rightarrow 4) \wedge (\eta \leftrightarrow (4 \wedge \neg 6))$
κ	$((8 \vee 9) \rightarrow 6) \wedge \neg(8 \wedge 9) \wedge (\kappa \leftrightarrow (6 \wedge \neg 8 \wedge \neg 9))$
λ	$\lambda \leftrightarrow 6$
μ	$\mu \leftrightarrow 8$
ν	$\nu \leftrightarrow 9$

- Is $\langle s_2, r_3 \rangle$ a reachable state of $\mathbf{A}$?
  This is the case if and only if some reachable marking of the complete prefix marks a place labeled by s_2 and a place labeled by r_3. This is the case if and only if the formula

$$\phi_\mathbf{A} \wedge (\gamma \vee \kappa) \wedge \lambda$$

  is satisfiable.
- Does every reachable marking mark either s_1 or r_2?
  This is the case if and only if the formula

$$\phi_\mathbf{A} \rightarrow ((\alpha \vee \zeta \vee \mu) \vee \delta)$$

  is valid, i.e., if and only if its negation is unsatisfiable.
- Can the Petri net deadlock?
  This is an interesting property. By definition, the Petri net of Fig. 5.2 can deadlock if and only if some reachable marking does not enable any transition. Assume that for every transition $\mathbf{t} \in \{\mathbf{a}, \ldots, \mathbf{f}\}$ we have constructed a formula $enables(\mathbf{t})$ which holds for an assignment (P, E) if and only if P enables some event labeled by $\mathbf{t}$. Then, the net is deadlock-free if and only if the formula

$$\phi_\mathbf{A} \rightarrow (enables(\mathbf{a}) \vee enables(\mathbf{b}) \vee \ldots \vee enables(\mathbf{f}))$$

  is valid.
  We explain how to construct the formula $enables(\mathbf{t})$ by means of an example. The formula $enables(\mathbf{c})$ should be true for the assignments that mark a place labeled by r_1 and a place labeled by r_1. So we have:

$$enables(\mathbf{c}) = (\alpha \vee \zeta \vee \mu) \wedge (\beta \vee \epsilon) .$$

The formula $\phi_{\mathbf{A}}$ can be seen as a database that can be queried in order to solve different problems. This approach has been studied from an experimental point of view in different papers (see the Bibliographical Notes at the end of the chapter). The main conclusion is that the bottleneck of the approach lies in the construction of the complete prefix. In practice, the time required for the construction of the complete prefix is usually far larger than the time required by a state-of-the-art SAT solver to solve the SAT instances corresponding to typical queries.

5.2 Least Representatives

In this section we present another total adequate strategy due to Niebert and Qu. It can be seen as a way of refining the Parikh strategy so that it becomes a total order. Historically, this strategy is older than the previous one we presented in Sect. 4.5.2 (see Bibliographical Notes). Its main feature is that it does not use the product structure, i.e., it is not a distributed strategy.

Recall that a trace is an equivalence class of words. The classical way to deal with equivalence classes is to assign them representatives. A function *rep* that assigns to each trace $[\mathbf{w}]$ a representative $rep([\mathbf{w}]) \in [\mathbf{w}]$ can be used to lift an order $\prec$ on $\mathbf{T}^*$ to an order $\prec^r$ on traces as follows: $[\mathbf{w}] \prec^r [\mathbf{w}']$ if $rep([\mathbf{w}]) \prec rep([\mathbf{w}'])$. In this section we follow this path and choose as representative of a trace its smallest word according to the lexicographic order.

Definition 5.7. *Let* $[\mathbf{w}]$ *be a trace. The* least lexicographic representative *of* $[\mathbf{w}]$, *denoted by* $[\mathbf{w}]_l$, *is defined as follows:* $[\mathbf{w}]_l \in [\mathbf{w}]$, *and* $[\mathbf{w}]_l \prec_l \mathbf{w}'$ *for every* $\mathbf{w}' \in [\mathbf{w}] \setminus \{[\mathbf{w}]_l\}$, *where* $\prec_l$ *denotes the lexicographic order on sequences of global transitions. The order* $\prec^r_l$ *on traces is defined by* $[\mathbf{w}] \prec^r_l [\mathbf{w}']$ *if* $[\mathbf{w}]_l \prec_l [\mathbf{w}']_l$.

Notice that $\prec^r_l$ is *not* a strategy, because it does not refine the prefix order, as shown by the following example.

Example 5.8. If the transitions $\mathbf{a}$ and $\mathbf{b}$ are independent, then we have $\mathbf{a}\,\mathbf{b} \prec_l \mathbf{b}$ and so $[\mathbf{b}\,\mathbf{a}] \prec^r_l [\mathbf{b}]$, even though $[\mathbf{b}]$ is a prefix of $[\mathbf{b}]\,[\mathbf{a}] = [\mathbf{b}\,\mathbf{a}]$.

However, we can use it to refine the Parikh strategy.

Definition 5.9. *The* Parikh-lexicographic strategy $\prec_{PL}$ *on* $[\mathbf{T}^*]$ *is defined as follows:* $[\mathbf{w}] \prec_{PL} [\mathbf{w}']$ *if* $[\mathbf{w}] \prec_P [\mathbf{w}']$ *or* $[\mathbf{w}] =_P [\mathbf{w}']$ *and* $[\mathbf{w}] \prec^r_l [\mathbf{w}']$.

Since the lexicographic order on words is total, so is the Parikh-lexicographic strategy. We prove that it is not only total, but also adequate. We start with a basic property of the lexicographic representatives.

Lemma 5.10. *If* $[\mathbf{w}\,\mathbf{w}']_l = \mathbf{w}\,\mathbf{w}'$ *then* $[\mathbf{w}]_l = \mathbf{w}$.

Proof. We prove the contrapositive. Assume $[\mathbf{w}]_l = \mathbf{v}$ and $\mathbf{v} \neq \mathbf{w}$. Then $\mathbf{v} \equiv \mathbf{w}$, which implies that $\mathbf{w}$ and $\mathbf{v}$ have the same length, and $\mathbf{v} \prec_l \mathbf{w}$. It follows $\mathbf{v}\,\mathbf{w}' \equiv \mathbf{w}\,\mathbf{w}'$ and $\mathbf{v}\,\mathbf{w}' \prec_l \mathbf{w}\,\mathbf{w}'$, and so $[\mathbf{w}\,\mathbf{w}']_l \neq \mathbf{w}\,\mathbf{w}'$. □

The second lemma shows the relation between $[\mathbf{w}\,\mathbf{t}]_l$ and $[\mathbf{w}]_l$, where $\mathbf{t}$ is a global transition. Notice that $[\mathbf{w}]_l = \mathbf{w}'$ does not necessarily imply $[\mathbf{w}\,\mathbf{t}]_l = \mathbf{w}'\,\mathbf{t}$. For instance, if $\mathbf{a}$ and $\mathbf{b}$ are independent then we have $[\mathbf{b}]_l = \mathbf{b}$ and $[\mathbf{b}\mathbf{a}]_l = \mathbf{a}\mathbf{b} \neq [\mathbf{b}]_l\mathbf{a}$.

Lemma 5.11. *Let* $[\mathbf{w}]$ *be a trace and let* $\mathbf{t}$ *be a transition. Then there exist words* $\mathbf{w}_1, \mathbf{w}_2 \in \mathbf{T}^*$ *such that* $[\mathbf{w}]_l = \mathbf{w}_1\,\mathbf{w}_2$, $[\mathbf{w}\,\mathbf{t}]_l = \mathbf{w}_1\mathbf{t}\mathbf{w}_2$ *and* $\mathbf{t}$ *is independent of every transition occurring in* $\mathbf{w}_2$.

Proof. Let $\mathbf{w}_1, \mathbf{w}_2 \in \mathbf{T}^*$ be the unique words such that $[\mathbf{w}\,\mathbf{t}]_l = \mathbf{w}_1\,\mathbf{t}\,\mathbf{w}_2$ and $\mathbf{w}_2$ contains no occurrence of $\mathbf{t}$. Since $\mathbf{w}\,\mathbf{t} \equiv \mathbf{w}_1\,\mathbf{t}\,\mathbf{w}_2$, the transition $\mathbf{t}$ is independent of every transition of $\mathbf{w}_2$. So in order to prove the result it only remains to show $[\mathbf{w}]_l = \mathbf{w}_1\,\mathbf{w}_2$. For this, let $\mathbf{w}_1'\,\mathbf{w}_2'$ be the words satisfying $[\mathbf{w}]_l = \mathbf{w}_1'\,\mathbf{w}_2'$, $|\mathbf{w}_1'| = |\mathbf{w}_1|$ and $|\mathbf{w}_2'| = |\mathbf{w}_2|$. In the rest of the proof we show that $\mathbf{w}_1' = \mathbf{w}_1$ and $\mathbf{w}_2' = \mathbf{w}_2$. We start by showing $\mathbf{w}_1' = \mathbf{w}_1$.

Claim 1: $\mathbf{w}_1' \preceq_l \mathbf{w}_1$. We first prove $\mathbf{w}_1'\,\mathbf{w}_2'\,\mathbf{t} \equiv \mathbf{w}_1\,\mathbf{w}_2\,\mathbf{t}$:

$$
\begin{aligned}
\mathbf{w}_1'\,\mathbf{w}_2'\,\mathbf{t} &= [\mathbf{w}]_l\,\mathbf{t} && (\mathbf{w}_1'\,\mathbf{w}_2' = [\mathbf{w}]_l) \\
&\equiv \mathbf{w}\,\mathbf{t} && (\mathbf{w} \equiv [\mathbf{w}]_l) \\
&\equiv [\mathbf{w}\,\mathbf{t}]_l && (\mathbf{w}\,\mathbf{t} \text{ and } [\mathbf{w}\,\mathbf{t}]_l \text{ are elements of } [\mathbf{w}\,\mathbf{t}]) \\
&= \mathbf{w}_1\,\mathbf{t}\,\mathbf{w}_2 && (\text{def. of } \mathbf{w}_1, \mathbf{w}_2) \\
&\equiv \mathbf{w}_1\,\mathbf{w}_2\,\mathbf{t} && (\mathbf{t} \text{ is independent of every transition of } \mathbf{w}_2)
\end{aligned}
$$

Now we have:

$$
\begin{aligned}
& \mathbf{w}_1'\,\mathbf{w}_2'\,\mathbf{t} \equiv \mathbf{w}_1\,\mathbf{w}_2\,\mathbf{t} \\
\Rightarrow\ & \mathbf{w}_1'\,\mathbf{w}_2' \equiv \mathbf{w}_1\,\mathbf{w}_2 \\
\Rightarrow\ & [\mathbf{w}]_l \equiv \mathbf{w}_1\,\mathbf{w}_2 && (\mathbf{w}_1'\,\mathbf{w}_2' = [\mathbf{w}]_l) \\
\Rightarrow\ & [\mathbf{w}]_l \preceq_l \mathbf{w}_1\,\mathbf{w}_2 && (\text{def. of least representative}) \\
\Rightarrow\ & \mathbf{w}_1'\,\mathbf{w}_2' \preceq_l \mathbf{w}_1\,\mathbf{w}_2 && (\mathbf{w}_1'\,\mathbf{w}_2' = [\mathbf{w}]_l) \\
\Rightarrow\ & \mathbf{w}_1' \preceq_l \mathbf{w}_1 && (\mathbf{w}_1 \text{ and } \mathbf{w}_1' \text{ have the same length})
\end{aligned}
$$

Claim 2: $\mathbf{w}_1 \preceq_l \mathbf{w}_1'$. Since $\mathbf{w}_1$ and $\mathbf{w}_1'$ have the same length, it suffices to prove $\mathbf{w}_1\,\mathbf{v} \preceq_l \mathbf{w}_1'\,\mathbf{v}'$ for some words $\mathbf{v}$ and $\mathbf{v}'$. We prove $\mathbf{w}_1\,\mathbf{t}\,\mathbf{w}_2 \preceq_l \mathbf{w_1}'\,\mathbf{w_2}'\,\mathbf{t}$.

$$
\begin{aligned}
& \mathbf{w} \equiv [\mathbf{w}]_l && (\mathbf{w} \text{ and } [\mathbf{w}]_l \text{ are elements of } [\mathbf{w}]) \\
\Rightarrow\ & \mathbf{w}\,\mathbf{t} \equiv [\mathbf{w}]_l\,\mathbf{t} && \\
\Rightarrow\ & [\mathbf{w}\,\mathbf{t}]_l \preceq_l [\mathbf{w}]_l\,\mathbf{t} && (\text{def. of least representative}) \\
\Rightarrow\ & \mathbf{w}_1\,\mathbf{t}\,\mathbf{w}_2 \preceq_l \mathbf{w_1}'\,\mathbf{w_2}'\,\mathbf{t} && (\mathbf{w}_1\,\mathbf{t}\,\mathbf{w}_2 = [\mathbf{w}\,\mathbf{t}]_l,\ \mathbf{w}_1'\,\mathbf{w}_2' = [\mathbf{w}]_l)
\end{aligned}
$$

By Claims 1 and 2, and since the lexicographic order is total, we get $\mathbf{w}_1 \preceq_l \mathbf{w}_1'$. Now we prove $\mathbf{w}_2 = \mathbf{w}_2'$.

Claim 3: $\mathbf{w}_2' \preceq_l \mathbf{w}_2$. In Claim 1 we proved $\mathbf{w}_1' \mathbf{w}_2' \preceq_l \mathbf{w}_1 \mathbf{w}_2$. Since $\mathbf{w_1} = \mathbf{w}_1'$, we get $\mathbf{w}_1' \mathbf{w}_2' \preceq_l \mathbf{w}_1' \mathbf{w}_2$, and the claim follows.

Claim 4: $\mathbf{w}_2 \preceq_l \mathbf{w}_2'$. In Claim 1 we proved $\mathbf{w}_1 \mathbf{w}_2 \mathbf{t} \equiv \mathbf{w}_1' \mathbf{w}_2' \mathbf{t}$. Now we have:

$$
\begin{array}{rl}
& \mathbf{w}_1 \mathbf{w}_2 \mathbf{t} \equiv \mathbf{w}_1' \mathbf{w}_2' \mathbf{t} \\
\Rightarrow & \mathbf{w}_1 \mathbf{w}_2 \mathbf{t} \equiv \mathbf{w}_1 \mathbf{w}_2' \mathbf{t} \quad (\mathbf{w}_1' = \mathbf{w}_1) \\
\Rightarrow & \mathbf{w}_2 \equiv \mathbf{w}_2' \\
\Rightarrow & \mathbf{w}_1 \mathbf{t} \mathbf{w}_2 \equiv \mathbf{w}_1 \mathbf{t} \mathbf{w}_2' \\
\Rightarrow & \mathbf{w}_1 \mathbf{t} \mathbf{w}_2 \preceq_l \mathbf{w}_1 \mathbf{t} \mathbf{w}_2' \quad ([\mathbf{w}\,\mathbf{t}]_l = \mathbf{w}_1 \mathbf{t} \mathbf{w}_2,\ \text{def. of least representative}) \\
\Rightarrow & \mathbf{w}_2 \preceq_l \mathbf{w}_2'
\end{array}
$$

By Claims 1 and 2, and since the lexicographic order is total, we get $\mathbf{w}_2 \prec_l \mathbf{w}_2'$. $\qquad\square$

We can now proceed to prove the result.

Theorem 5.12. *The Parikh-lexicographic strategy on traces is adequate and total.*

Proof. Totality follows immediately from the definition. We show that the strategy is preserved by extensions, which by Prop. 4.42 implies that it is adequate. Assume $[\mathbf{w}] \prec_{PL} [\mathbf{w}']$. We show that $[\mathbf{w}] [\mathbf{w}''] \prec_{PL} [\mathbf{w}'] [\mathbf{w}'']$ holds for every trace $[\mathbf{w}'']$. It suffices to consider the case in which $\mathbf{w}''$ has length 1, since the result can then be easily proved by induction on the length of $\mathbf{w}''$. So we assume that $\mathbf{w}'' = \mathbf{t}$ for some transition $\mathbf{t}$ and prove $[\mathbf{w}\,\mathbf{t}] \prec_{PL} [\mathbf{w}'\,\mathbf{t}]$.

If $[\mathbf{w}] \prec_P [\mathbf{w}']$, then we have $[\mathbf{w}\,\mathbf{t}] \prec_P [\mathbf{w}'\,\mathbf{t}]$ (recall that the Parikh strategy is adequate), and we are done. So we consider the case in which $[\mathbf{w}] =_P [\mathbf{w}']$ and $[\mathbf{w}] \prec_l [\mathbf{w}']$, i.e., $[\mathbf{w}]_l \prec_l [\mathbf{w}']_l$. Without loss of generality we can assume $[\mathbf{w}]_l = \mathbf{w}$ and $[\mathbf{w}']_l = \mathbf{w}'$. Moreover, $[\mathbf{w}] =_P [\mathbf{w}']$ implies $[\mathbf{w}\,\mathbf{t}] =_P [\mathbf{w}'\,\mathbf{t}]$, and so in order to prove $[\mathbf{w}\,\mathbf{t}] \prec_{PL} [\mathbf{w}'\,\mathbf{t}]$ it suffices to show $[\mathbf{w}\,\mathbf{t}] \prec_l [\mathbf{w}'\,\mathbf{t}]$, i.e., $[\mathbf{w}\,\mathbf{t}]_l \prec_l [\mathbf{w}'\,\mathbf{t}]_l$. So, summarizing, we can assume $\mathbf{w} \prec_l \mathbf{w}'$ and it suffices to prove $[\mathbf{w}\,\mathbf{t}]_l \prec_l [\mathbf{w}'\,\mathbf{t}]_l$.

Since $[\mathbf{w}] =_P [\mathbf{w}']$, the words $\mathbf{w}$ and $\mathbf{w}'$ have the same length. So, since $\mathbf{w} \prec_l \mathbf{w}'$, there are words $\overline{\mathbf{w}}, \mathbf{v}, \mathbf{v}' \in \mathbf{T}^*$ and transitions $\mathbf{a} \prec_l \mathbf{b}$ such that

$$\mathbf{w} = \overline{\mathbf{w}}\,\mathbf{a}\,\mathbf{v} \quad \text{and} \quad \mathbf{w}' = \overline{\mathbf{w}}\,\mathbf{b}\,\mathbf{v}' \tag{5.1}$$

Moreover, by Lemma 5.11 there are words $\mathbf{w}_1, \mathbf{w}_2, \mathbf{w}_1', \mathbf{w}_2' \in \mathbf{T}^*$ such that:

$$[\mathbf{w}\,\mathbf{t}]_l = \mathbf{w}_1 \mathbf{t} \mathbf{w}_2 \quad \text{and} \quad [\mathbf{w}'\,\mathbf{t}]_l = \mathbf{w}_1' \mathbf{t} \mathbf{w}_2' \tag{5.2}$$

$$\mathbf{w} = \mathbf{w}_1 \mathbf{w}_2 \quad \text{and} \quad \mathbf{w}' = \mathbf{w}_1' \mathbf{w}_2' \tag{5.3}$$

$$\mathbf{w}_2 \mathbf{t} \equiv \mathbf{t} \mathbf{w}_2 \quad \text{and} \quad \mathbf{w}_2' \mathbf{t} \equiv \mathbf{t} \mathbf{w}_2' \tag{5.4}$$

Observe that (5.1) and (5.3) give two different decompositions of $\mathbf{w}$ and $\mathbf{w}'$. To prove $[\mathbf{w}\,\mathbf{t}]_l \prec_l [\mathbf{w}'\,\mathbf{t}]_l$ we consider two cases:

- $|\overline{\mathbf{w}}| < |\mathbf{w}_1|$. By (5.1) and (5.3) there are (possibly empty) words $\mathbf{v}_1, \mathbf{v}_1' \in \mathbf{T}^*$ such that

$$\overline{\mathbf{w}}\,\mathbf{a}\,\mathbf{v}_1 = \mathbf{w}_1 \quad \text{and} \quad \overline{\mathbf{w}}\,\mathbf{b}\,\mathbf{v}_1' = \mathbf{w}_1' \tag{5.5}$$

Since $\mathbf{a} \prec_l \mathbf{b}$ we have

$$[\mathbf{w}\,\mathbf{t}]_l \overset{(5.2)}{=} \mathbf{w}_1\,\mathbf{t}\,\mathbf{w}_2 \overset{(5.5)}{=} \overline{\mathbf{w}}\,\mathbf{a}\,\mathbf{v}_1\,\mathbf{t}\,\mathbf{w}_2 \prec_l \overline{\mathbf{w}}\,\mathbf{b}\,\mathbf{v}_1'\,\mathbf{t}\,\mathbf{w}_2' \overset{(5.5)}{=} \mathbf{w}_1'\,\mathbf{t}\,\mathbf{w}_2' \overset{(5.2)}{=} [\mathbf{w}'\,\mathbf{t}]_l$$

- $|\overline{\mathbf{w}}| \geq |\mathbf{w}_1|$. By (5.1) and (5.3) there are (possibly empty) words $\mathbf{v}_2, \mathbf{v}_2' \in \mathbf{T}^*$ such that

$$\mathbf{w}_2 = \mathbf{v}_2\,\mathbf{a}\,\mathbf{v} \quad \text{and} \quad \mathbf{w}_2' = \mathbf{v}_2'\,\mathbf{b}\,\mathbf{v}' \tag{5.6}$$

Moreover, again by (5.1) and (5.3), these words satisfy

$$\mathbf{w}_1\,\mathbf{v}_2 = \mathbf{w}_1'\,\mathbf{v}_2' \tag{5.7}$$

Claim: $\mathbf{w}_1\,\mathbf{t}\,\mathbf{v}_2\,\mathbf{a}\,\mathbf{v} \preceq_l \mathbf{w}_1'\,\mathbf{t}\,\mathbf{v}_2'\,\mathbf{a}\,\mathbf{v}$.
It suffices to prove $\mathbf{w}_1\,\mathbf{t}\,\mathbf{v}_2\,\mathbf{a}\,\mathbf{v} \equiv \mathbf{w}_1'\,\mathbf{t}\,\mathbf{v}_2'\,\mathbf{a}\,\mathbf{v}$ and $[\mathbf{w}_1\,\mathbf{t}\,\mathbf{v}_2\,\mathbf{a}\,\mathbf{v}]_l = \mathbf{w}_1\,\mathbf{t}\,\mathbf{v}_2\,\mathbf{a}\,\mathbf{v}$. For the first part:

$$
\begin{array}{lll}
& \mathbf{t}\,\mathbf{w}_2 \equiv \mathbf{w}_2\,\mathbf{t} & (5.4) \\
\Rightarrow & \mathbf{t}\,\mathbf{v}_2 \equiv \mathbf{v}_2\,\mathbf{t} & \text{(by (5.6) and (5.4) } \mathbf{t} \text{ is independent} \\
& & \text{of every transition in } \mathbf{v}_2) \\
\Rightarrow & \mathbf{w}_1\,\mathbf{t}\,\mathbf{v}_2 \equiv \mathbf{w}_1\,\mathbf{v}_2\,\mathbf{t} & \\
\Rightarrow & \mathbf{w}_1\,\mathbf{t}\,\mathbf{v}_2 \equiv \mathbf{w}_1'\,\mathbf{v}_2'\,\mathbf{t} & \text{(by 5.7)} \\
\Rightarrow & \mathbf{w}_1\,\mathbf{t}\,\mathbf{v}_2 \equiv \mathbf{w}_1'\,\mathbf{t}\,\mathbf{v}_2' & \text{(by (5.6) and (5.4) } \mathbf{t} \text{ is independent} \\
& & \text{of every transition in } \mathbf{v}_2') \\
\Rightarrow & \mathbf{w}_1\,\mathbf{t}\,\mathbf{v}_2\,\mathbf{a}\,\mathbf{v} \equiv \mathbf{w}_1'\,\mathbf{t}\,\mathbf{v}_2'\,\mathbf{a}\,\mathbf{v} &
\end{array}
$$

For the second part:

$$[\mathbf{w}_1\,\mathbf{t}\,\mathbf{v}_2\,\mathbf{a}\,\mathbf{v}]_l \overset{(5.6)}{=} [\mathbf{w}_1\,\mathbf{t}\,\mathbf{w}_2]_l \overset{(5.2)}{=} \mathbf{w}_1\,\mathbf{t}\,\mathbf{w}_2 \overset{(5.6)}{=} \mathbf{w}_1\,\mathbf{t}\,\mathbf{v}_2\,\mathbf{a}\,\mathbf{v}$$

Now we have:

$$
\begin{array}{rl}
[\mathbf{w}\,\mathbf{t}]_l \overset{(5.2)}{=} \mathbf{w}_1\,\mathbf{t}\,\mathbf{w}_2 & \overset{(5.6)}{=} \mathbf{w}_1\,\mathbf{t}\,\mathbf{v}_2\,\mathbf{a}\,\mathbf{v} \\
& \overset{(\text{Claim})}{\preceq_l} \mathbf{w}_1'\,\mathbf{t}\,\mathbf{v}_2'\,\mathbf{a}\,\mathbf{v} \\
& \prec_l \mathbf{w}_1'\,\mathbf{t}\,\mathbf{v}_2'\,\mathbf{b}\,\mathbf{v}' \overset{(5.6)}{=} \mathbf{w}_1'\,\mathbf{t}\,\mathbf{w}_2' \overset{(5.2)}{=} [\mathbf{w}'\,\mathbf{t}]_l
\end{array}
$$

$\square$

5.3 Breadth-First and Depth-First Strategies

The two most popular classes of strategies for transition systems are the breadth-first and depth-first strategies. Loosely speaking, a breadth-first strategy gives priority to short histories over long ones, while a depth-first strategy gives priority to extending a branch of the final prefix over generating other branches. Breadth-first strategies are good for finding the shortest history satisfying some property, while depth-first strategies are the key to many efficient algorithms.

We have introduced two total strategies that are complete for the scheme of Def. 4.35 on p. 57: the distributed version of the size-lexicographic strategy (Def. 4.51 on p. 65) and the Parikh-lexicographic strategy (Def. 5.9). In this section we study the question of whether total strategies exist that are not only complete, but also breadth-first or depth-first. We shall see that the answers are positive and negative, respectively.

5.3.1 Total Breadth-First Strategies

Let $\mathcal{A}$ be a transition system with T as set of transitions and let $\prec$ be a total strategy on T^*. Recall that $\prec$ induces an order on the events of the unfolding of $\mathcal{A}$. We say that $\prec$ is *breadth-first* if $|H(e)| < |H(e')|$ implies $e \prec e'$ for any two events e, e'. The generalization to products is immediate. Let $\mathbf{A}$ be a product with $\mathbf{T}$ as set of global transitions, and let $\prec$ be a total strategy on $[\mathbf{T}^*]$. We say that $\prec$ is *breadth-first* if $|\mathbf{H}(e)| < |\mathbf{H}(e')|$ implies $e \prec e'$ for any two events e, e'.

Recall that the size strategy $\prec_s$ (Def. 4.44 on p. 63) induces the order on events given by: $e \prec_s e'$ if and only if $|H(e)| < |H(e')|$. So a total strategy is breadth-first if it refines the size strategy. Since the Parikh-lexicographic strategy refines the Parikh strategy (Def. 4.45 on p. 64), which in turn refines the size strategy, the Parikh-lexicographic strategy is breadth-first.

Distributed strategies (Def. 4.49 on p. 65) are not breadth-first, because, loosely speaking, they compare the projections of two traces without first comparing their sizes. But this can be easily changed. Consider the strategy that gives priority to the shortest of two given traces, and, if the traces have the same length, gives priority to the smallest of the two w.r.t. the size-lexicographic strategy. This strategy is still total and breadth-first.

5.3.2 Total Depth-First Strategies

We first formalize the notion of depth-first strategy for transition systems.

Definition 5.13. *Let $\mathcal{A}$ be a transition system with T as set of transitions and let $\prec$ be a total strategy on T^*. We say that $\prec$ is depth-first if it satisfies the following property for any three events e, e', e'' of the unfolding: if $e \# e'$ and $e \prec e'$, then $e < e''$ implies $e'' \prec e'$.*

So, intuitively, a depth-first strategy extends existing branches of the current prefix before generating new ones. In the case of products, branches correspond to configurations, and extending a branch corresponds to extending a configuration with a new event. In the transition system case, a configuration C can be extended by an event e only if $e' < e$ for every $e' \in C$. In the product case this is no longer true: C can be extended by e only if either $e' < e$ or e' co e hold for every $e' \in C$. This suggests that, after adding one event e, a depth-first strategy should give priority to the events that are causally related or concurrent to e over the events that are in conflict with e. More formally, one is tempted to define depth-first strategies for products as follows:

A total strategy $\prec$ on $[\mathbf{T}^*]$ is depth-first if it satisfies the following property for every three events e, e', e'': if $e \# e'$ and $e \prec e'$, then $e < e''$ implies $e'' \prec e'$ and e co e'' implies $e'' \prec e'$.

Unfortunately, this definition is inconsistent, in the sense that many products have no depth-first strategies at all. The following example shows one of them.

Example 5.14. Consider a product with two components. The first component can choose between transitions a and b, and the second one between transitions c and d. There are no synchronization constraints, and so these choices are independent of each other. It is easy to see that the full unfolding contains

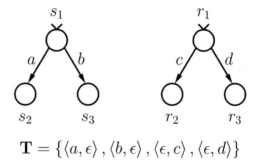

$$\mathbf{T} = \{\langle a, \epsilon \rangle, \langle b, \epsilon \rangle, \langle \epsilon, c \rangle, \langle \epsilon, d \rangle\}$$

Fig. 5.4. A product without depth-first strategies according to the first definition

four events, one for each global transition. Call these events e_a, e_b, e_c, and e_d, respectively. We have $e_a \# e_b$ and $e_c \# e_d$, while all other pairs of events are concurrent.

Assume there exists a depth-first strategy $\prec$. We can assume w.l.o.g. that $e_a \prec e_b$ and $e_c \prec e_d$. Then, since e_a co e_d and e_c co e_b hold, we have $e_d \prec e_b$ and $e_b \prec e_d$, contradicting that $\prec$ is an order.

The lesson learned from this example is that, after exploring an event e, we cannot always give priority to events concurrent with e over events in conflict with e. Loosely speaking, strategies cannot satisfy "co before #". On the other hand, depth-first strategies must definitely give priority to the causal descendants of an event over the events in conflict with it, i.e., they must satisfy "$<$ before $\#$". It follows that strategies cannot satisfy "co before $<$" either, because "co before $<$" and "$<$ before $\#$" imply together "co before $\#$".

We now investigate the possibility of defining "$<$ before co". That is, causal successors are given priority over both concurrent events and events in conflict.

Definition 5.15. *A total strategy $\prec$ on* $[\mathbf{T}^*]$ *is* depth-first *if it satisfies the following properties for every three events e, e', e'':*

(1) if $e \# e'$, $e \prec e'$, and $e < e''$, then $e'' \prec e'$; and
(2) if e co e', $e \prec e'$, and $e < e''$, then $e'' \prec e'$.

Let us compute the order in which these depth-first strategies would explore events when applied to the example of Fig. 4.6 on p. 59.

Example 5.16. Consider again the executability problem for $\mathbf{G} = \{\mathbf{i}\}$ in the product of Fig. 4.6 on p. 59. The unfolding is shown in Fig. 4.8 on p. 61. We consider a search procedure based on a depth-first strategy as defined in Def. 5.15. Assume that the strategy gives priority to event 1 over event 2 (the other possibility is analogous). The next event cannot be 2, because it is in conflict with 1. So the next event must be 3 or 4. Both cases are similar, because after adding 3 the next event must be 4, and vice versa. The search procedure continues with 7 and 10 (or vice versa), and then with 11. At this point the procedure can stop, since it has found a successful terminal.

The depth-first strategy performs in this example better than the size-lexicographic or Parikh-lexicographic strategies: it generates only six events instead of 11.

Definition 5.15 looks attractive, and for some years the problem of whether these strategies were complete for the search scheme of Def. 4.35 on p. 57 remained open. Unfortunately, the answer to this question is negative. We prove this by showing that *any* search procedure based on the search scheme of Def. 4.35 and a depth-first strategy of Def. 5.15 returns the wrong answer to the following instance of the executability problem: Can transition $\mathbf{i}$ of the product of Fig. 5.5 be executed? The answer is "yes" because, for instance, the sequence $\mathbf{b\,d\,i}$ is a global history of the product. However, every search procedure of this class returns "no".

We claim that every search procedure of the class produces either the final prefix shown in Fig. 5.7 or a symmetric one. Since $\mathbf{b}$ and $\mathbf{d}$ are the only two global transitions enabled at the initial global state, the procedure must start by exploring either event 1 or event 12. Due to the symmetry of the product, both cases are similar, and so w.l.o.g. we can assume that event 1 is chosen. After that, the order in which events can be explored is almost completely determined by the depth-first condition. The procedure must continue with

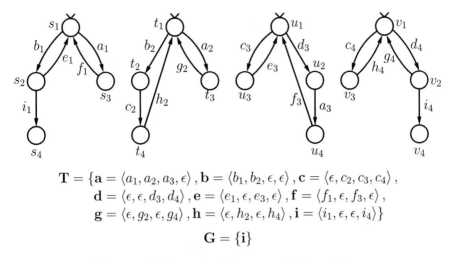

$$\mathbf{T} = \{\mathbf{a} = \langle a_1, a_2, a_3, \epsilon \rangle, \mathbf{b} = \langle b_1, b_2, \epsilon, \epsilon \rangle, \mathbf{c} = \langle \epsilon, c_2, c_3, c_4 \rangle,$$
$$\mathbf{d} = \langle \epsilon, \epsilon, d_3, d_4 \rangle, \mathbf{e} = \langle e_1, \epsilon, e_3, \epsilon \rangle, \mathbf{f} = \langle f_1, \epsilon, f_3, \epsilon \rangle,$$
$$\mathbf{g} = \langle \epsilon, g_2, \epsilon, g_4 \rangle, \mathbf{h} = \langle \epsilon, h_2, \epsilon, h_4 \rangle, \mathbf{i} = \langle i_1, \epsilon, \epsilon, i_4 \rangle\}$$

$$\mathbf{G} = \{\mathbf{i}\}$$

Fig. 5.5. An instance of the executability problem

event 2, because 2 is a causal descendant of 1, and 12 is not. Event 2 is followed by event 3 and then 4 (both have priority over event 12 because they are causally related to event 2, which is in conflict with event 12). Event 5 may or may not be explored next, but in fact the moment at which it is added is irrelevant, since whenever it is added it is marked as a terminal event:

$$\mathbf{St}(5) = \langle s_1, t_1, u_2, v_2 \rangle = \mathbf{St}(1)$$

The search procedure continues with events 6, 7, and then with events 8 and 9 (or 9 and 8). Finally, it explores events 10, 11, and 12, not necessarily in this order, but marking all of them as terminals, because:

$$\mathbf{St}(10) = \langle s_1, t_1, u_2, v_2 \rangle = \mathbf{St}(1)$$
$$\mathbf{St}(11) = \mathbf{St}(12) = \langle s_2, t_2, u_1, v_1 \rangle = \mathbf{St}(6)$$

No further events can be added, and so, since no event labeled by $\mathbf{i}$ is ever explored, the search procedure wrongly claims that $\mathbf{i}$ is not executable.

Our examples indicate that there does not seem to be a simple way of generalizing depth-first strategies to the case of products while preserving completeness. Any other candidate one might come up with should be tested on the example of Fig. 5.5. Consider for instance the following approach. Since in products with only one component the sets T and $\mathbf{T}$ of local and global transitions coincide, we can define depth-first strategies on $\mathbf{T}^*$ as in Def. 5.13. Now, we can call a strategy $\prec$ on $[\mathbf{T}^*]$ depth-first if $\prec = \prec_{df}^d$ for some depth-first strategy $\prec_{df}$ on $\mathbf{T}^*$. In other words, we define depth-first strategies for products as the distributed strategies obtained from depth-first strategies for transition systems. While we do not know if *all* these strategies also fail on the example of Fig. 5.5, we can show that *some* of them do. Consider the

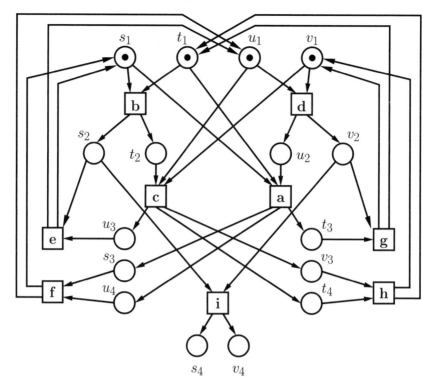

Fig. 5.6. Petri net representation of the product of Fig. 5.5

lexicographic strategy $\prec_l$ on $\mathbf{T}^*$. Clearly, $\prec_l$ is a depth-first search strategy on $\mathbf{T}^*$. Table 5.3 shows the projections onto the four components of the product of the event histories, sorted according to the strategy $\prec_l^d$. The final prefix is the one of Fig. 5.7.

Notice that $\prec_l^d$ is based on two arbitrary orders: the order of the components of the product and the order of the global transitions. It is not difficult to see that, as long as the order on global transitions is the alphabetical order, the final prefix remains unsuccessful for any order of the components.[1] If we change the order on global transitions, then we can have a final prefix that contains **i**. For instance, if we modify the alphabetical order by declaring that **b** is smaller than **a**, and keep the order on the components, then the first two events generated by the search procedure are labeled by **d** and **b** enabling an event labelled with **i**, which is then bound to be added some events later. However, finding the right order on transitions seems to require deep insight into the semantics of the product.

---

[1] For another order of the components the final prefix may differ from the one shown in Fig. 5.7, but it does not contain any event labeled by **i**.

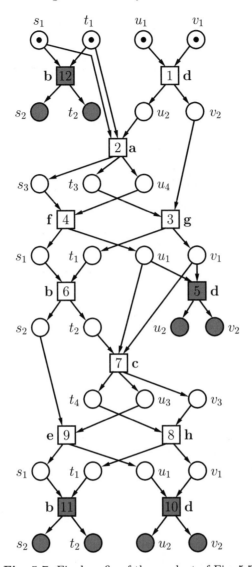

Fig. 5.7. Final prefix of the product of Fig. 5.5

5.4 Strategies Preserved by Extensions Are Well-Founded

We have defined an adequate strategy on $[\mathbf{T}^*]$ as a well-founded strategy that is preserved by extensions (see Def. 4.41 on p. 62). In this section we show a result due to Chatain and Khomenko, stating that every order preserved by extensions is necessarily well-founded. So in fact the well-foundedness condition of Def. 4.41 on p. 62 is redundant.

Table 5.3. Projections of event histories sorted according to $\prec_l^d$

Event	$\mathbf{T}_1$	$\mathbf{T}_2$	$\mathbf{T}_3$	$\mathbf{T}_4$
1			d	d
2	a	a	da	d
3	a	ag	da	dg
4	af	a	daf	d
5	af	ag	dafd	dgd
6	afb	agb	daf	dg
7	afb	agbc	dafc	dgc
8	afb	agbch	dafc	dgch
9	afbe	agbc	dafce	dgc
10	afbe	agbc	dafced	dgchd
11	afbeb	agbchb	dafce	bf
12	b	b		

The proof makes use of the theory of well-quasi-orders.

Definition 5.17. *An order $\prec$ on a set X is a* well-quasi-order *if every infinite subset $Y \subseteq X$ contains an infinite $\prec$-chain, i.e., an infinite set $\{y_1, y_2, \ldots\} \subseteq Y$ such that $y_1 \prec y_2 \prec y_3 \prec \ldots$.*

The following lemma presents two basic properties of well-quasi-orders.

Lemma 5.18. *(1) Well-quasi-orders are well-founded.*
(2) If $\prec$ is a well-quasi-order and $\prec'$ refines $\prec$, then $\prec'$ is also a well-quasi-order.

Proof. (1) We prove the contrapositive. Let $\prec$ be a non-well-founded order on a set X. Then there is an infinite *descending* chain $x_1 \succ x_2 \succ x_3 \succ \ldots$. But this implies that the set $Y = \{x_1, x_2, x_3, \ldots\}$ contains no infinite $\prec$-chain, and so $\prec$ is not a well-quasi-order.
    (2) If $\prec'$ refines $\prec$ then every $\prec$-chain is also a $\prec'$-chain. □

Lemma 5.18 suggests a way to prove that a given order is well-founded: show that it refines some well-quasi-order. This is the way we proceed, choosing the subword order (defined below) as well-quasi-order. (The fact that the subword order is a well-quasi-order is known as Higman's lemma.)
    In the rest of the section we

- introduce the subword order on $\mathbf{T}^*$ (Def. 5.19),
- lift it to a subtrace order on $[\mathbf{T}^*]$, the set of traces (Def. 5.20),
- show that the subtrace order is a well-quasi-order (Lemma 5.21), and
- prove that every strategy preserved by extensions refines the subtrace order (Lemma 5.22).

Definition 5.19. *Given* $\mathbf{w}, \mathbf{w}' \in \mathbf{T}^*$ *such that* $\mathbf{w} \neq \mathbf{w}'$, *we say that* $\mathbf{w}$ *is a subword of* $\mathbf{w}'$, *denoted by* $\mathbf{w} \prec_{sw} \mathbf{w}'$ *if* $\mathbf{w} \neq \mathbf{w}'$ *and there exist words* $\mathbf{u}_1, \ldots, \mathbf{u}_k, \mathbf{v}_0, \ldots, \mathbf{v}_k \in \mathbf{T}^*$ *such that* $\mathbf{w} = \mathbf{u}_1 \mathbf{u}_2 \ldots \mathbf{u}_k$ *and* $\mathbf{w}' = \mathbf{v}_0 \mathbf{u}_1 \mathbf{v}_1 \mathbf{u}_2 \ldots \mathbf{v}_{k-1} \mathbf{u}_k \mathbf{v}_k$.

Loosely speaking, $\mathbf{w}$ is a subword of $\mathbf{w}'$ if it can be obtained from $\mathbf{w}'$ through deletion of letters. It is easy to see that $\prec_{sw}$ is an order on words.

Higman's lemma [63] states that the subword order is a well-quasi-order. Both the subword order and Higman's lemma can be lifted to traces.

Definition 5.20. *Given* $[\mathbf{w}], [\mathbf{w}'] \in [\mathbf{T}^*]$, *we say that* $[\mathbf{w}]$ *is a subtrace of* $[\mathbf{w}']$, *denoted by* $[\mathbf{w}] \prec_{st} [\mathbf{w}']$ *if* $\mathbf{v} \prec_{sw} \mathbf{v}'$ *for some* $\mathbf{v} \in [\mathbf{w}]$ *and* $\mathbf{v}' \in [\mathbf{w}']$.

Lemma 5.21. *The subtrace relation is a well-quasi-order.*

Proof. We first show that the subtrace relation is an order, i.e., irreflexive and transitive (Def. 4.1 on p. 41). Transitivity follows immediately from the transitivity of $\prec_{sw}$. Irreflexivity follows from the fact that all the words of a trace have the same length, while all subwords of a word $\mathbf{w}$ are shorter than $\mathbf{w}$. To show that $\prec_{st}$ is a well-quasi-order, take an arbitrary infinite subset $X \subseteq [\mathbf{T}^*]$. Then, the set X' of words contained in the elements of X is also infinite. Since the subword order is a well-quasi-order, X' contains an infinite chain $\mathbf{w}_1 \prec_{sw} \mathbf{w}_2 \prec_{sw} \mathbf{w}_3 \ldots$. But then $[\mathbf{w}_1] \prec_{st} [\mathbf{w}_2] \prec_{st} [\mathbf{w}_3] \ldots$. $\quad\square$

We can now prove the key lemma:

Lemma 5.22. *Every strategy on* $[\mathbf{T}^*]$ *preserved by extensions refines the subtrace order.*

Proof. Let $\prec$ be a strategy on $[\mathbf{T}^*]$ preserved by extensions. Let $[\mathbf{w}], [\mathbf{w}'] \in [\mathbf{T}^*]$ such that $[\mathbf{w}] \prec_{st} [\mathbf{w}']$. We show $[\mathbf{w}] \prec [\mathbf{w}']$.

Assume w.l.o.g. $\mathbf{w} \prec_{sw} \mathbf{w}'$. By the definition of the subword order, there exist $\mathbf{u}_1, \ldots, \mathbf{u}_k$ and $\mathbf{v}_0, \ldots, \mathbf{v}_k$ such that $\mathbf{w} = \mathbf{u}_1 \mathbf{u}_2 \ldots \mathbf{u}_k$ and $\mathbf{w}' = \mathbf{v}_0 \mathbf{u}_1 \mathbf{v}_1 \mathbf{u}_2 \ldots \mathbf{v}_{k-1} \mathbf{u}_k \mathbf{v}_k$. We proceed by induction on k, with the convention that if $k = 0$ then $\mathbf{w}$ is the empty word and $\mathbf{w}' = \mathbf{v}_0$. If $k = 0$, then $\mathbf{w}$ is a prefix of $\mathbf{w}'$, and so $[\mathbf{w}] \prec [\mathbf{w}']$ because, by definition, strategies refine the prefix order. If $k > 0$, then let $\widetilde{\mathbf{w}} = \mathbf{u}_1 \mathbf{u}_2 \ldots \mathbf{u}_{k-1}$ and $\widetilde{\mathbf{w}}' = \mathbf{v}_0 \mathbf{u}_1 \mathbf{v}_1 \mathbf{u}_2 \ldots \mathbf{u}_{k-1} \mathbf{v}_{k-1}$. By induction hypothesis, $[\widetilde{\mathbf{w}}] \prec [\widetilde{\mathbf{w}}']$. Since $\prec$ is preserved by extensions, we have $[\widetilde{\mathbf{w}} \, \mathbf{u_k}] = [\widetilde{\mathbf{w}}] [\mathbf{u_k}] \prec [\widetilde{\mathbf{w}}'] [\mathbf{u_k}] = [\widetilde{\mathbf{w}}' \, \mathbf{u_k}]$. Since $\prec$ refines the prefix order, we have $[\widetilde{\mathbf{w}}' \, \mathbf{u_k}] \preceq [\widetilde{\mathbf{w}}' \, \mathbf{u_k}] [\mathbf{v_k}]$ (notice that $\mathbf{v}_k$ may be empty). So, finally,

$$[\mathbf{w}] = [\widetilde{\mathbf{w}} \, \mathbf{u_k}] \prec [\widetilde{\mathbf{w}}' \, \mathbf{u_k}] \preceq [\widetilde{\mathbf{w}}' \, \mathbf{u_k}] [\mathbf{v_k}] = [\mathbf{w}']$$

and we are done. $\quad\square$

The main result of the section follows easily:

Theorem 5.23. *Every strategy on* $[\mathbf{T}^*]$ *that is preserved by extensions is also well-founded.*

Proof. Let $\prec$ be a strategy on $[\mathbf{T}^*]$ preserved by extensions. By Lemma 5.22, $\prec$ refines the subtrace order. By Lemma 5.21, $\prec$ refines a well-quasi-order. By Lemma 5.18(2), $\prec$ is itself a well-quasi-order. By Lemma 5.18(1), $\prec$ is well-founded.   □

Corollary 5.24. *A search strategy on* $[\mathbf{T}^*]$ *is adequate if and only if it is preserved by extensions.*

Bibliographical Notes

Complete prefixes were introduced by McMillan in [84], although not under this name. There is rather substantial experimental evidence showing that they are reasonably small for many concurrent systems. For instance, experiments of this kind have been conducted in [84, 87, 40, 41, 39, 107]. Many other papers have experimentally studied the complexity of different verification problems with a complete prefix as input. The deadlock problem was studied by McMillan in [84, 85], Melzer and Römer in [88], Heljanko in [58], and Khomenko and Koutny in [70]. Esparza and Schröter studied the global reachability problem in [42] (see also [109]). Both problems were studied by Heljanko in [56, 58, 60] and by Khomenko in [69]. Heljanko also studies nested local state reachability problems in compact "full prefixes" in [59].

These papers rely on different algorithmic techniques. In [84], McMillan used a branch-and-bound technique. In [88], Melzer and Römer observed that the deadlock problem (and in fact also the reachability problem) could be solved using Integer Linear Programming, and obtained experimental results using a commercial Integer Programming tool. Khomenko and Koutny developed in [70] a specialized algorithm for solving Integer Linear programming problems, and showed that it was faster than the commercial package. In [56, 58], Heljanko used a reduction to logic programs with stable model semantics, another NP-complete problem. The search for stable models is implemented by using the **smodels** system [96]. However, a SAT mapping similar to the one shown in this section is immediate from these results as remarked on p. 25 of Chap. 4.2 in [60]. In [42], Esparza and Schröter compare the performance of different algorithms.

The Parikh-lexicographic strategy was defined by Niebert and Qu in [92]. It is very similar to a total adequate strategy of [40] that also compares two traces in three steps, but differs from the Parikh-lexicographic strategy only in the last one. There, instead of comparing the lexicographically smallest representatives of the two traces, it compares their Foata normal forms.

The counterexample showing that depth-first strategies are not complete is due to Esparza, Kanade, and Schwoon [38]. Theorem 5.23 (every strategy preserved by extensions is well-founded) is due to Chatain and Khomenko [23].

6

Search Procedures for the Repeated Executability Problem

The repeated executability problem consists of deciding if some infinite history of the system executes a goal transition infinitely often. We provide search procedures for this problem. We start with the transition system case and then continue with the generalization to products. As in the last section, we give a search scheme for transition systems that is sound and complete for every search strategy. Then, we generalize the search scheme to a scheme for products, and show that the scheme yields a complete search procedure for every *adequate* search strategy.

6.1 Search Scheme for Transition Systems

We fix a transition system $\mathcal{A} = \langle S, T, \alpha, \beta, is \rangle$ and a set of transitions $R \subseteq T$. We wish to solve the problem of whether some infinite history of $\mathcal{A}$ executes some transition of R infinitely often. We define the following search scheme.

Definition 6.1. *Let $\prec$ be a search strategy on T^*. An event e is* feasible *if no event $e' < e$ is a terminal. A feasible event e is a* terminal *if there exists a feasible event $e' \prec e$, called the* companion *of e, such that $St(e') = St(e)$ and at least one of (a) $e' < e$ or (b) $\#_R(e') \geq \#_R(e)$ holds, where $\#_R(e)$ denotes the number of occurrences of transitions of R in the history $H(e)$.*

A terminal is successful *if it satisfies (a) and $\#_R(e') < \#_R(e)$ holds. The $\prec$-final prefix is the prefix of the unfolding of $\mathcal{A}$ containing the feasible events.*

The intuition behind terminals of type (a) is easy. Let c be the computation satisfying $H(e')\,c = H(e)$. Since $St(e) = St(e')$, we can repeat c infinitely often. If $\#_R(e') < \#_R(e)$, then some transition of R occurs in c, and the search is successful. If not, we can still label e as terminal because, loosely speaking, for any infinite computation extending $H(e)$ and containing a transition of R infinitely often there is a corresponding computation extending $H(e')$.

Terminals of type (b) are a bit more delicate. The example below shows a case in which they are required.

Example 6.2. Consider the instance of the repeated executability problem shown in Fig. 6.1(**a**). The transition system has the infinite computation $a\,(r\,c)^\omega$, which executes an infinite number of transitions of R.

The final prefix for a breadth-first strategy $\prec$ (i.e., $e \prec e'$ if and only if $|H(e)| < |H(e')|$) is shown in Fig. 6.1(**b**). The events are numbered in the order in which they are added by the search procedure. Event 3 is *not* a terminal of type (b), because even though $2 \prec 3$ holds, we have $\#_R(2) = 0 < 1 = \#_R(3)$. Event 4 is a terminal of type (b) with event 1 as the companion. Event 5 is a terminal of type (a) with event 1 as companion. We have $H(1)\,r\,c = H(5)$, and so event 5 is a successful terminal because the computation $r\,c$ contains a transition of R.

We can now show that the search scheme obtained by dropping the condition $\#_R(e') \geq \#_R(e)$ in the terminals of type (b) is no longer complete. The new final prefix is shown in Fig. 6.1(**c**). This time event 3 is a terminal of type (b) with event 2 as the companion. Event 4 is a terminal of type (b) with 1 as companion. Both terminals are unsuccessful, and thus the search procedure system is incomplete, i.e., even though the infinite computation $a\,(r\,c)^\omega$ exists the final prefix is not successful.

It is easy to see that the search scheme of Def. 6.1 is well-defined, finite, and sound for every search strategy.

Proposition 6.3. *The search scheme of Def. 6.1 is well-defined for every strategy $\prec$. Moreover, the $\prec$-final prefix is finite.*

Proof. Well-definedness is proved as in Prop. 4.9 on p. 45. In particular, Lemma 4.8 on p. 45 (feasible events have histories of length at most $|S| + 1$) still holds: As usual, if $|H(e)| > |S| + 1$ then there are events e', e'' such that $e'' < e' < e$ and $St(e'') = St(e')$, and so e' is a terminal of type (a). For soundness, assume that a terminal e with companion e' is successful. Since $e' < e$, some computation c satisfies $H(e')\,c = H(e)$. Since $\#_R(e') < \#_R(e)$, this c contains some transition $r \in R$. Since $St(e') = St(e)$, the sequence $H(e')\,c^\omega$ is an infinite history containing infinitely many occurrences of r. $\square$

Completeness is, as usual, a bit more delicate.

Theorem 6.4. *The search scheme of Def. 6.1 is complete for every strategy.*

Proof. Assume that $\mathcal{A}$ has an infinite history containing infinitely many occurrences of R-transitions, but the final prefix contains no successful terminals. We derive a contradiction following the general scheme of the proof of Thm. 4.11 on p. 46.

Witnesses. We call an event e of the unfolding of $\mathcal{A}$ a *witness* if $\#_R(e) > |S| + 1$. We make the following two observations:

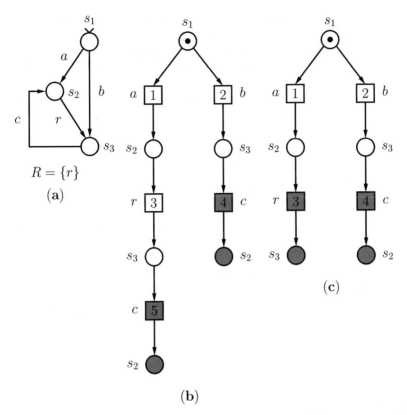

Fig. 6.1. An instance of the repeated executability problem (**a**), its corresponding final prefix (**b**), and final prefix with the condition $\#_R(e') \geq \#_R(e)$ dropped (**c**)

- $\mathcal{A}$ has a history containing infinitely many occurrences of transitions of R if and only if the unfolding of $\mathcal{A}$ contains witnesses.

  The only-if direction is obvious. For the if direction, we use the same argument as for soundness. Let e be a witness. Since $\#_R(e) > |S| + 1$, the history $H(e)$ contains more than $|S| + 1$ occurrences of R-transitions. By the pigeonhole principle, e has two distinct predecessors, say e' and e'', both labeled with transitions of R, such that $St(e') = St(e'')$. Assume w.l.o.g. that $e'' < e'$, and that c is the computation satisfying $H(e') = H(e'') c$. Then $H(e'') c^\omega$ is an infinite history containing infinitely many occurrences of R-transitions.

- If e is a witness, then some predecessor of e is a terminal.

  We have just seen that for every witness e there exist events $e'' < e' < e$ such that $St(e') = St(e'')$. If e' is feasible, then e' is a terminal of type (a). If e' is not feasible, then, by the definition of feasibility, some predecessor of e' is a terminal.

Since $\mathcal{A}$ has a history containing infinitely many occurrences of transitions of R, the unfolding of $\mathcal{A}$ contains witnesses. Since the final prefix is unsuccessful, each witness has an unsuccessful terminal in its past, which we call the *spoiler* of the witness.

Minimal witnesses. Let e_m be a minimal witness w.r.t. the order $\ll$ defined as in the proof of Thm. 4.11 on p. 46 ($e \ll e'$ if either $l(e) < l(e')$ or $l(e) = l(e')$ and $e_s \prec e'_s$) and let e_s be its spoiler. Since e_s is an unsuccessful terminal, it has a companion $e' \prec e_s$ such that $St(e') = St(e_s)$. Moreover, since e_s is unsuccessful, either it satisfies (a) and $\#_R(e') = \#_R(e_s)$, or it satisfies (b), and in both cases $\#_R(e') \geq \#_R(e_s)$ holds. Since $St(e') = St(e_s)$, the sequence $H(e')\,c_s$ is also a history of $\mathcal{A}$. Let e'_m be the event satisfying $H(e'_m) = H(e')\,c_s$. Since $\#_R(e') \geq \#_R(e_s)$, we have $\#_R(H(e'_m)) = \#_R(H(e')\,c_s) = \#_R(H(e')) + \#_R(c_s) \geq \#_R(H(e_s)) + \#_R(c_s) = \#_R(H(e_m))$ and so $\#_R(e'_m) \geq \#_R(e_m)$. But then, since e_m is a witness, so is e'_m. Let e'_s be the spoiler of e'_m.

Contradiction. This part is exactly as in the proof of Thm. 4.11 on p. 46. Since both $e' < e'_m$ and $e'_s < e'_m$ hold, there are three possible cases, namely $e'_s < e'$, $e'_s = e'$ and $e' < e'_s$, and all three lead to contradiction.   □

As for the executability problem, one way to reduce the size of the final prefix is to require the strategy $\prec$ to be a total order. However, in this case the number of non-terminals of the final prefix may grow quadratically in the number of states of $\mathcal{A}$.

Theorem 6.5. *If $\prec$ is a total order on T^*, then the $\prec$-final prefix of Def. 6.1 has at most $|S|^2$ non-terminal events.*

Proof. Given an event e, if $H(e)$ contains more than $|S|$ occurrences of transitions of R, then there are events $e_1 < e_2 \leq e$ labeled by transitions of R such that $St(e_1) = St(e_2)$, and so e_2 is a terminal. Therefore, for every non-terminal event e of the final prefix we have $\#_R(e) \leq |S|$.

We prove that for any state $s \in S$ there are at most $|S|$ non-terminal events such that $St(e) = s$. Assume the contrary, and let $e_1, \ldots, e_{|S|+1}$ be pairwise different non-terminal events such that $St(e_i) = s$ for all $1 \leq i \leq |S|+1$. Since $\#_R(e_i) \leq |S|$ for all $1 \leq i \leq |S|+1$, by the pigeonhole principle there are two non-terminal events $e_j \neq e_k$ such that $\#_R(e_j) = \#_R(e_k)$. Since $\prec$ is a total order we have that either $e_j \prec e_k$ or $e_k \prec e_j$. So either e_j or e_k is a terminal of type (b), a contradiction.

Since for each state $s \in S$ there are at most $|S|$ non-terminal events such that $St(e) = s$, the final prefix contains at most $|S|^2$ non-terminal events.   □

We can ask whether there exist search procedures such that the maximal number of non-terminal events is linear in $|S|$, instead of quadratic. The answer is affirmative. The *nested-depth-first-search* algorithm, due to Courcoubetis, Vardi, Wolper, and Yannakakis, is a linear-time algorithm for the repeated executability problem of transition systems. In a first phase, the algorithm uses depth-first search to sort the transitions of the set R. Recall that depth-first search traverses every transition twice: a first time when the search discovers the transition, and a second time when it backtracks along the transition. Transition t is defined to be smaller than t' if the depth-first search backtracks through t (visits t for the second time) before it backtracks through t'. In a second phase, the algorithm conducts a depth-first search for each transition $t \in R$ *in the order defined by the first search*. This search, however, stops if t is hit again, or if a state that has already been visited while searching from smaller transitions is discovered. This guarantees that in the second phase each transition is explored at most twice.[1]

It is a simple exercise to formulate the nested-depth-first search algorithm as a search procedure. The crucial point for us is that the search scheme underlying the nested-depth-first search algorithm is not correct for every strategy: its correctness relies on properties of depth-first search. Unfortunately, as mentioned in Sect. 5.3, depth-first search strategies do not lead to complete search procedures in the case of products. In other words, a direct generalization of the nested-depth-first-search algorithm to products does not yield a correct search procedure.

6.2 Search Scheme for Products

We fix a product $\mathbf{A} = \langle \mathcal{A}_1, \ldots, \mathcal{A}_n, \mathbf{T} \rangle$, where $\mathcal{A}_i = \langle S_i, T_i, \alpha_i, \beta_i, is_i \rangle$, and a set of global transitions $\mathbf{R} \subseteq \mathbf{T}$. The problem to solve is whether some infinite global history of $\mathbf{A}$ executes transitions of $\mathbf{R}$ infinitely often. We call the elements of $\mathbf{R}$ (global) $\mathbf{R}$-transitions, and call the events labeled by them $\mathbf{R}$-events.

We generalize the search scheme of Def. 6.1 to products. Following the ideas introduced in Sect. 4.4, we replace $St(e)$ by $\mathbf{St}(e)$, and $H(e)$ by $\mathbf{H}(e)$. The remaining question is how to generalize $\#_R(e)$. Recall that in the transition system case we defined $\#_R(e)$ as the number of occurrences of transitions of R in $H(e)$.

Definition 6.6. *Let e be an event, and let $\mathbf{h}$ be any history of the trace $\mathbf{H}(e)$. We denote by $\#_{\mathbf{R}}([\mathbf{h}])$ the number of occurrences of $\mathbf{R}$-transitions in $\mathbf{h}$, and define $\#_{\mathbf{R}}(e) = \#_{\mathbf{R}}([\mathbf{h}])$.*

Notice that $\#_{\mathbf{R}}(e)$ is well-defined because every transition occurs the same number of times in all histories of $\mathbf{H}(e)$.

Example 6.7. Consider again the product of Fig. 2.2 on p. 7 with the Petri net representation shown in Fig. 2.4 on p. 10, and choose $\mathbf{R} = \{\langle t_1, \epsilon \rangle\}$. Consider the history trace $[\mathbf{h}]$, where

---

[1] Actually, the nested-depth-first-search algorithm interleaves the two phases, but this is not relevant for our discussion.

$$\mathbf{h} = \langle t_1, \epsilon \rangle \, \langle \epsilon, u_1 \rangle \, \langle t_3, u_2 \rangle \, \langle t_5, \epsilon \rangle \, \langle \epsilon, u_3 \rangle .$$

The trace $[\mathbf{h}]$ contains four elements, namely

$$\langle t_1, \epsilon \rangle \, \langle \epsilon, u_1 \rangle \, \langle t_3, u_2 \rangle \, \langle t_5, \epsilon \rangle \, \langle \epsilon, u_3 \rangle ,$$
$$\langle t_1, \epsilon \rangle \, \langle \epsilon, u_1 \rangle \, \langle t_3, u_2 \rangle \, \langle \epsilon, u_3 \rangle \, \langle t_5, \epsilon \rangle ,$$
$$\langle \epsilon, u_1 \rangle \, \langle t_1, \epsilon \rangle \, \langle t_3, u_2 \rangle \, \langle t_5, \epsilon \rangle \, \langle \epsilon, u_3 \rangle , \text{ and}$$
$$\langle \epsilon, u_1 \rangle \, \langle t_1, \epsilon \rangle \, \langle t_3, u_2 \rangle \, \langle \epsilon, u_3 \rangle \, \langle t_5, \epsilon \rangle .$$

These four histories only differ in the order in which global transitions occur. They all contain one single occurrence of $\mathbf{R}$-transitions, and so $\#_{\mathbf{R}}([\mathbf{h}]) = 1$.

Furthermore, we have $[\mathbf{h}] = [\mathbf{h_1}, \mathbf{h_2}]$, where

$$\mathbf{h}_1 = \langle t_1, \epsilon \rangle \, \langle t_3, u_2 \rangle \, \langle t_5, \epsilon \rangle \quad \text{and} \quad \mathbf{h}_2 = \langle \epsilon, u_1 \rangle \, \langle t_3, u_2 \rangle \, \langle \epsilon, u_3 \rangle .$$

It is possible to compute $\#_{\mathbf{R}}([\mathbf{h}])$ directly from $\mathbf{h}_1$ and $\mathbf{h}_2$. If an $\mathbf{R}$-transition has k participants, then its occurrence is recorded in k components. If we give each of these records a weight of $1/k$, then we can compute $\#_{\mathbf{R}}([\mathbf{h}])$ as the weighted sum over all components of $[\mathbf{h}]$ of the number of occurrences of $\mathbf{R}$-transitions. In our example, the occurrence of $\langle t_1, \epsilon \rangle$ is recorded only by the first component, and so it has weight 1. If we had $\mathbf{R} = \{\langle t_3, u_2 \rangle\}$, then each of the occurrences of $\langle t_3, u_2 \rangle$ in $\mathbf{h}$ would have weight $1/2$.

We are now ready to define the search scheme for products.

Definition 6.8. *Let $\prec$ be a search strategy on $[\mathbf{T}^*]$. An event e is* feasible *if no event $e' < e$ is a terminal. A feasible event e is a* terminal *if there exists a feasible event $e' \prec e$, called the* companion *of e, such that $\mathbf{St}(e') = \mathbf{St}(e)$ and at least one of (a) $e' < e$ or (b) $\#_{\mathbf{R}}(e') \geq \#_{\mathbf{R}}(e)$ holds.*

A terminal is successful *if it satisfies (a) and $\#_{\mathbf{R}}(e') < \#_{\mathbf{R}}(e)$. The $\prec$-final prefix is the prefix of the unfolding of $\mathbf{A}$ containing the feasible events.*

As happened in the executability case, this search scheme is well-defined and sound for every strategy, but not complete for every search strategy. The proof of well-definedness and soundness is so close to that of the transition system case that we leave it as an easy exercise for the reader.

Example 6.9. Modify the product of Fig. 4.6 on p. 59 as follows: Turn each transition i_j into a self loop (i.e., set $\beta(i_1) = s_5, \ldots, \beta(i_4) = v_5$). Then, transition $\mathbf{i}$ can occur infinitely often; for instance, $\mathbf{a\,c\,d\,g\,h\,(i)}^\omega$ is an infinite global history of the new product. Set $\mathbf{R} = \{\mathbf{i}\}$, and run the search procedure consisting of the search scheme of Def. 6.8 with a strategy that assigns priorities to events according to the numbering shown in Fig. 4.8 on p. 61. This procedure marks events 10 and 8 as unsuccessful terminals. Event 8 has event 7 as companion, because $\#_{\mathbf{R}}(8) = 0 = \#_{\mathbf{R}}(7)$, and similarly event 10 has event 9 as companion. So neither event 11 nor event 12 is a feasible event, and the search procedure is unsuccessful.

As could be expected, the search scheme is however complete for adequate strategies. Before proving it, we show it at work on an example.

Example 6.10. Consider again the product of Fig. 2.2 on p. 7 having the Petri net representation shown in Fig. 2.4 on p. 10. We construct the final prefix for $\mathbf{R} = \{\langle t_1, \epsilon \rangle\}$ and the distributed size-lexicographic strategy, i.e., $\prec = \prec_{sl}^d$. We take the same order as in Ex. 5.2 on p. 74.

The final prefix is shown in Fig. 6.2. Notice that in this example it happens to be identical to the complete prefix of Ex. 5.2 on p. 74 shown in Fig. 5.1 on p. 75 but this is of course not true in general. Events are numbered according to the order in which they are added. Event 7 is a terminal because $\mathbf{St}(7) = \langle s_4, r_3 \rangle = \mathbf{St}(4)$, $4 \prec 7$, and $1 = \#_R(4) \geq \#_R(7) = 0$. To see that $4 \prec 7$ holds, consider the distributions of the history traces of both events:

$$\mathbf{H}(4) = [\,\langle t_1, \epsilon \rangle \langle t_3, u_2 \rangle \;, \; \langle \epsilon, u_1 \rangle \langle t_3, u_2 \rangle\,], \text{ and}$$
$$\mathbf{H}(7) = [\,\langle t_2, \epsilon \rangle \langle t_4, u_2 \rangle \;, \; \langle \epsilon, u_1 \rangle \langle t_4, u_2 \rangle\,].$$

We start by comparing the first components. Since $\langle t_1, \epsilon \rangle$ is smaller than $\langle t_2, \epsilon \rangle$, no further comparisons are necessary, and we conclude $\mathbf{H}(4) \prec \mathbf{H}(7)$. Since the events 4 and 7 are not causally related, event 7 is an unsuccessful terminal.

Events 11 and 12 are terminals of type (a), both having event 4 as companion. Event 11 is successful, because it is a causal successor of event 4, and $\#_R(4) = 1 < 2 = \#_R(11)$. Event 12 is an unsuccessful terminal.

Theorem 6.11. *The search scheme of Def. 6.8 is complete for every adequate strategy.*

Proof. Let $\prec$ be an arbitrary adequate strategy. Assume that $\mathbf{A}$ has an infinite global history containing infinitely many occurrences of $\mathbf{R}$-transitions, but the final prefix contains no successful terminals. We derive a contradiction, following the general scheme of the proof of Thm. 4.11 on p. 46.

Witnesses. Let K be the number of reachable global states of $\mathbf{A}$. We call an event e of the unfolding of $\mathbf{A}$ a *witness* if $\#_R(e) > nK + 1$. We make the following two observations:

- $\mathbf{A}$ has an infinite global history containing infinitely many occurrences of transitions of $\mathbf{R}$ if and only if the unfolding of $\mathbf{A}$ contains witnesses.
  The proof is very similar to that of the corresponding observation in Thm. 6.4. The only-if direction is obvious. For the if direction, let e be a witness. Since $\#_R(e) > nK + 1$, there is a component of $\mathbf{A}$, say $\mathcal{A}_i$, that participates in at least $K + 1$ events labeled with transitions from $\mathbf{R}$. Since the i-events of a history are causally ordered, these $K + 1$ events are pairwise causally ordered. By the pigeonhole principle, at least two of them, say e' and e'', satisfy $\mathbf{St}(e') = \mathbf{St}(e'')$. Assume w.l.o.g. that $e'' < e'$ holds, and that $\mathbf{c}$ is the computation trace satisfying $\mathbf{H}(e') = \mathbf{H}(e'')[\mathbf{c}]$. Then $\mathbf{H}(e'')([\mathbf{c}])^\omega$ is an infinite history trace of $\mathbf{A}$ containing infinitely many occurrences of R-transitions.

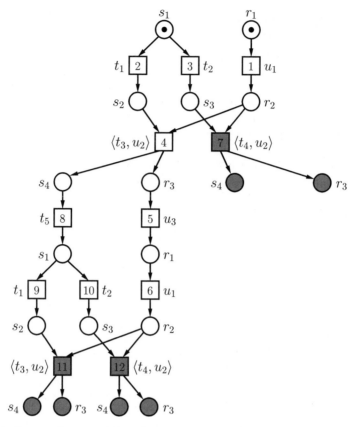

Fig. 6.2. Repeated executability final prefix of the product of Fig. 2.2 on p. 7 for $\mathbf{R} = \{\langle t_1, \epsilon \rangle\}$

- If e is a witness, then some predecessor of e is a terminal.
  Replace $St(e)$ by $\mathbf{St}(e)$ in the corresponding part of the proof of Thm. 4.11 on p. 46.

Since $\mathbf{A}$ has an infinite global history containing infinitely many occurrences of $\mathbf{R}$-transitions, the unfolding of $\mathbf{A}$ contains witnesses. Since the final prefix is unsuccessful, each witness has an unsuccessful terminal in its past, which we call the *spoiler* of the witness.

Minimal witnesses. As in the proof of Thm. 4.43 on p. 62, let e_m be a witness that is minimal w.r.t. $\prec$, let e_s be its spoiler, and let $[\mathbf{c_s}]$ be the computation trace satisfying $\mathbf{H}(e_m) = \mathbf{H}(e_s)[\mathbf{c_s}]$. Since e_s is an unsuccessful terminal, it has a companion $e' \prec e_s$ such that $\mathbf{St}(e') = \mathbf{St}(e_s)$. Moreover, since e_s is unsuccessful, either it satisfies (a) and $\#_\mathbf{R}(e') = \#_\mathbf{R}(e_s)$, or it satisfies (b), and in both cases $\#_\mathbf{R}(e') \geq \#_\mathbf{R}(e_s)$ holds. Since $\mathbf{St}(e') = \mathbf{St}(e_s)$, the trace $\mathbf{H}(e')[\mathbf{c_s}]$ is also a history trace of $\mathbf{A}$. Let e'_m be the event satisfying $\mathbf{H}(e'_m) =$

$\mathbf{H}(e')\,[\mathbf{c_s}]$. Since $\#_{\mathbf{R}}(e') \geq \#_{\mathbf{R}}(e_s)$, we have $\#_{\mathbf{R}}(\mathbf{H}(e')\,[\mathbf{c_s}]) \geq \#_{\mathbf{R}}(\mathbf{H}(e_s)\,[\mathbf{c_s}])$, and so $\#_{\mathbf{R}}(e'_m) \geq \#_{\mathbf{R}}(e_m)$. But then, since e_m is a witness, so is e'_m.

Contradiction. This part is exactly as in the proof of Thm. 4.43 on p. 62. $\square$

As in the transition system case, we can show that the number of non-terminal events of the final prefix is at most quadratic on the number of reachable global states of **A**. However, the bound on the size of the prefix also includes a factor bounded by the number of components of **A**.

Theorem 6.12. *Let C_R be any set of components such that for every transition $\mathbf{t} \in \mathbf{R}$ at least one component $\mathcal{A}_i \in C_R$ participates in $\mathbf{t}$. Let K be the number of reachable global states of **A**.*

If $\prec$ is a total adequate search strategy on $[\mathbf{T}^*]$, then the $\prec$-final prefix generated by the search scheme of Def. 6.8 with $\prec$ as search strategy has at most $|C_R|K^2$ feasible non-terminal events.

Proof. Given an event e, if $\mathbf{H}(e)$ contains more than $|C_R|K$ occurrences of transitions of $\mathbf{R}$, then by the pigeonhole principle there is a component $\mathcal{A}_j \in C_R$ such that more than K events of $past(e)$ are j-events. Since the j-events of a configuration are all causally related, two of them satisfy $e'' < e' < e$ and $\mathbf{St}(e'') = \mathbf{St}(e')$. So e' is a terminal. Therefore, for every feasible non-terminal event e of the final prefix we have $\#_R(e) \leq |C_R|K$.

Proceed now as in the proof of Thm. 6.5. $\square$

Notice that the set of all components is always a possible choice for C_R, which leads to $|C_R| = n$ and so to an nK^2 bound. In the particular case in which one fixed component participates in *all* transitions of **R** we have $|C_R| = 1$ and we obtain a K^2 bound. This special case will in fact happen when we consider the model checking problem in Chap. 8.

Bibliographical Notes

The repeated executability problem has been studied in great detail for transition systems. Courcoubetis, Vardi, Wolper, and Yannakakis proposed the nested-depth-first search algorithm in [26]. The algorithm was further improved by Holzmann, Peled, and Yannakakis in [66], and is implemented in the Spin model checker [65]. Couvreur presented an alternative algorithm inspired by Tarjan's procedure for the computation of strongly connected components in [27]. A similar algorithm was proposed by Geldenhuys and Valmari [45]. These algorithms are discussed and compared (and slightly improved) by Esparza and Schwoon in [112].

Depth-first search is difficult to implement in a parallel or distributed setting. For this reason, the research community working on parallel model checking algorithms has also studied solutions to the repeated executability problem not requiring depth-first search. In particular, Brim and Barnat have discovered breadth-first algorithms similar to our search procedures for transition systems [18].

Heljanko considers in [59] the complexity of model checking using prefixes of unfoldings. However, [59] does not use a specialized search scheme as presented in Def. 6.8, and so the results do not carry over to the search scheme presented here.

The repeated executability problem for products was studied by the authors in [35, 36], and the contents of this chapter are taken from there.

7

Search Procedures for the Livelock Problem

In this chapter we present search procedures for the livelock problem. They are a bit more technical than those for the executability and repeated executability problems. As in the former chapters, we first present a search scheme for transition systems which is complete for arbitrary search strategies. Then, we generalize it for products, showing along the way several pitfalls that must be avoided.

7.1 Search Scheme for Transition Systems

We fix a transition system $\mathcal{A} = \langle S, T, \alpha, \beta, is \rangle$, and partition the set T into a set V of *visible* and a set $I = T \setminus V$ of *invisible* transitions. We also fix a set $L \subseteq V$ of *livelock monitors*.

A *livelock* is an infinite history of the form $h\,t\,c$, where $h \in T^*$ is a finite history, $t \in L$ is a livelock monitor, and $c \in I^\omega$ is an infinite computation containing only invisible transitions. We call the occurrence of t after the history h the *livelock's root*. Intuitively, livelocks are undesirable behaviors in which right after the livelock's root the system enters an infinite loop of unobservable actions. We wish to solve the problem of whether $\mathcal{A}$ has some livelock.

Example 7.1. Figure 7.1 shows an instance of the livelock problem. It has several livelocks. For instance, the infinite histories $a\,c\,(f\,i)^\omega$ and $a\,b\,d\,g\,(i\,f)^\omega$ are livelocks with (the only occurrences of) transitions c and b as roots. However, the infinite history $a\,b\,(d\,g\,h)^\omega$ is not a livelock because h is a visible transition. Notice that whereas a livelock's root is always the occurrence of a livelock monitor, the converse does not hold in general. In particular, a livelock history may contain several instances of livelock monitor transitions.

Our solution to the livelock problem requires us to slightly modify the definition of unfolding. In order to present this modification it is useful to

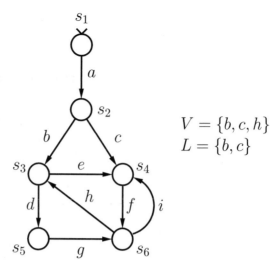

Fig. 7.1. An instance of the livelock problem for transition systems

imagine a nondeterministic program which on input $\mathcal{A}$ behaves as follows. The program has a variable v that ranges over the states of $\mathcal{A}$, intended to store the current state of the system. The initial value of v is the initial state *is*. Moreover, the program has a Boolean flag f, initially set to 0. The program repeatedly chooses a transition t enabled at the current state (stored in v), executes it, and updates v to the target state of t. If t happens to be a livelock monitor, then after updating v the program nondeterministically chooses between setting f to 0 or to 1. Clearly, $\mathcal{A}$ has a livelock if and only if in some execution the program sets f to 1 and then executes an infinite sequence of invisible transitions. We say that the program is in *main mode* or in *livelock mode* if the current value of f is 0 or 1, respectively.

We define a new unfolding that instead of the possible executions of $\mathcal{A}$ models the possible executions of the nondeterministic program as described above. Recall that if the current prefix generated so far contains a node labeled by a state s, and s enables a transition t, then we add a new event e to the prefix, labeled by t. In this chapter, if t belongs to the set L of livelock monitors (and only in this case), we add not only the event e, but also a second event e_d, labeled by t as well. We call e_d the *duplicate* of e. The addition of e and e_d reflects the nondeterministic choice between the main mode and the livelock mode. We call the new unfolding defined this way the *d-unfolding* of $\mathcal{A}$.

The search procedure defined below explores a finite prefix of the d-unfolding. It also has a main mode and a livelock mode. In the main mode, its goal is to compute all the livelock monitors that can be executed from the initial state. When it adds the event e_d, the search procedure enters the livelock mode, whose goal is to determine whether there is an infinite computation rooted at e_d and containing only invisible transitions.

Example 7.2. Figure 7.1 is an instance of the livelock problem. A prefix of the d-unfolding is shown in Fig. 7.2 (this prefix will actually be the final prefix of the search procedure). Events 10 and 17 are the duplicates of events 2 and 3.

In order to distinguish between the events belonging to the two search modes, we introduce the following definition.

Definition 7.3. *An event of the d-unfolding of $\mathcal{A}$ is* visible *if it is labeled by a visible transition, and* invisible *otherwise. An event e of the d-unfolding of $\mathcal{A}$ is of*

- *type 0 if no event $e' \leq e$ is a duplicate;*
- *type 1 if exactly one event $e' \leq e$ is a duplicate, and all events e'' satisfying $e' < e'' \leq e$ are invisible;*
- *type 2 if it is not of type 0 or type 1.*

If e is of type 1, then we denote by $d(e)$ the unique duplicate preceding e.

The events of type 0 and 1 correspond to the main and the livelock modes. The events of type 2 will not be explored by the search procedures, or, more precisely, events of type 2 explored by the search will be labeled as terminals.

Definition 7.4. *Let $\prec$ be an arbitrary strategy on T^*.*

An event e of the d-unfolding of $\mathcal{A}$ is feasible *if no event $e' < e$ is a terminal.*

A feasible event e of type 0 is a terminal if there is a feasible event $e' \prec e$ of type 0, called the companion of e, such that $St(e') = St(e)$.

A feasible event e of type 1 is a terminal if there is a feasible event $e' \prec e$ of type 1, called the companion of e, such that $St(e') = St(e)$ and

- *(1a) $d(e') \prec d(e)$; or*
- *(1b) $d(e') = d(e)$ and $e' < e$; or*
- *(1c) $d(e') = d(e)$ and $\#_I(e') \geq \#_I(e)$,*
  where $\#_I(e)$ denotes the number of events e'' satisfying $d(e) < e'' \leq e$.

A feasible event of type 2 is always a terminal.

A terminal is successful *if it is of type (1b). The $\prec$-final prefix is the prefix of the unfolding of $\mathcal{A}$ containing the feasible events.*

The intuition behind the terminals is rather simple. When adding events of type 0 (main search mode) we are looking for the transitions of L that are reachable from the initial state. Therefore, we can stop whenever we hit a state we have seen before, because the transitions we would explore from the event e will be explored from its companion e'. When adding events of type 1 (livelock mode) we are searching for infinite sequences of invisible transitions. For terminals of type (1a) the reasoning is that, loosely speaking, if some infinite sequence of invisible transitions starts at the event $d(e)$, then there is also such a corresponding sequence starting at $d(e')$, and it will be found from there. A terminal of type (1b) signals that such a sequence has been found: Since $e' < e$, there is a computation c such that $H(e) = H(e')c$, and since $St(e') = St(e)$, it corresponds to a loop of invisible transitions that can be executed infinitely often. Terminals of type (1c) are similar to the unsuccessful terminals for the repeated executability problem. Notice that in the livelock case the set R is replaced with the set I of invisible transitions.

Example 7.5. Figure 7.1 shows an instance of the livelock problem. Fig. 7.2 shows the final prefix generated by a search procedure consisting of the search scheme of Def. 7.4 and the following strategy. Events of type 0 have priority over events of type 1, which have priority over events of type 2. The numbering of events in the final prefix corresponds to the order in which they are added by the strategy.

Terminals of type 0 (events $5, 7, 8$, and 9) are shown in dark grey, terminals of type 1 (events $14, 16$, and 17) are line patterned, and terminals of type 2 (only event 18) are cross patterned. Type 0 events (if they are not terminals) are in white, and type 1 events (again, if they are not terminals) are light grey. The events are numbered according to the order in which they have been added to the prefix.

Events $5, 7, 8$, and 9 are terminals of type 0 with $3, 6, 2$, and 3 as companions, respectively. Events 10 and 17 are the duplicates of the events 2 and 3, respectively. Event 14 is a terminal of type (1c) with event 13 as companion: $d(13) = 10 = d(14)$ and $\#_I(13) = 2 = \#_I(14)$. Event 16 is a successful terminal of type (1b) with event 13 as companion and corresponds to the livelock: $a\, b\, d\, g\, (i\, f)^\omega$ with b as root. Event 17 is a terminal of type (1a) with event 12 as companion (we have $d(12) = 10 \prec 17 = d(17)$). Finally, event 18 is a terminal of type 2.

We prove well-definedness and soundness of the search scheme for every strategy.

Lemma 7.6. *Let $\prec$ be an arbitrary strategy, and let (F, T) be a pair of sets of events satisfying the conditions of Def. 7.4 for the sets of feasible and terminal events, respectively. Then for every non-terminal event $e \in F \setminus T$ the history $H(e)$ has length at most $2|S|$.*

Proof. Let e be a feasible, non-terminal event. We show first that $past(e)$ contains at most $|S|$ events of type 0. Assume the contrary. Then, by the pigeonhole principle two events e' and e'' of $past(e)$ satisfy $St(e') = St(e'')$. Since in the transition system case any two events of $past(e)$ are causally related, we have w.l.o.g. $e'' < e' \le e$, and so e' is a terminal of type 0, contradicting that e is feasible and a non-terminal. Similarly, $past(e)$ contains at most $|S|$ events of type 1, because otherwise two of them, say $e'' < e' \le e$, satisfy $St(e') = St(e'')$, and so e' is a terminal of type (1b). Since events of type 2 are terminals, we have that $past(e)$ contains at most $2|S|$ events, and so all non-terminals have a history of at most this length. □

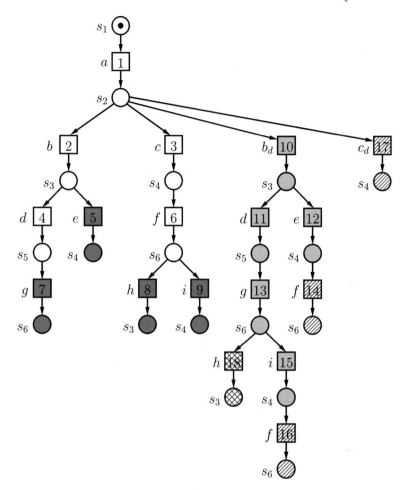

Fig. 7.2. The final prefix of the livelock problem instance of Fig. 7.1

Proposition 7.7. *Let $\prec$ be an arbitrary strategy. The search scheme of Def. 7.4 is well-defined. Moreover, the $\prec$-final prefix is finite.*

Proof. Let (F_1, T_1) and (F_2, T_2) be two pairs of sets of events satisfying the conditions of Def. 7.4 on the feasible and terminal events. By Lemma 7.6, and since there are only finitely many histories of length at most $2|S| + 1$, the sets F_1 and F_2 are finite. We prove $F_1 = F_2$, which also implies $T_1 = T_2$. Assume $F_1 \neq F_2$, and let e be a $\prec$-minimal event satisfying $e \in (F_1 \setminus F_2) \cup (F_2 \setminus F_1)$ (this event exists because F_1 and F_2 are finite). Assume w.l.o.g. that $e \in F_1 \setminus F_2$. Since $e \notin F_2$ there is an event $e' < e$ such that $e' \in T_2$, and since $e' \in F_1$ we have $e' \in T_2 \setminus T_1$. As element of T_2, the event e' must be a terminal of type 0, 1, or 2. If e' is of type 2, then $e' \in F_2$, because terminals are feasible, and $e' \notin F_1$ (otherwise, since all feasible events of type 2 are terminals, we would have $e \in T_1$). So $e' \in F_2 \setminus F_1$. Since $e' < e$ and $\prec$ refines the causal order, we have $e' \prec e$, contradicting the $\prec$-minimality of e. If e' is of type 0 or 1, then e' has a companion $e'' \prec e'$ satisfying $e'' \in F_2$. Moreover, we have $e'' \notin F_1$ (otherwise we would have $e \in T_1$). So $e'' \in F_2 \setminus F_1$, contradicting the $\prec$-minimality of e.

Since the $\prec$-final prefix contains the feasible events, and these are finitely many, the prefix is finite. $\qquad\square$

Proposition 7.8. *The search scheme of Def. 7.4 is sound for every strategy.*

Proof. If the final prefix is successful, then, whatever the strategy, it has a terminal of type (1b). Let e be this terminal, and let e' be its companion. Since $e' < e$, there is a computation c satisfying $H(e')c = H(e)$. Moreover, since e and e' are of type 1, c contains only invisible transitions. Since $St(e') = St(e)$, the computation c can be iterated infinitely often, and so the history $H(e')\, c^\omega$ is a livelock. $\qquad\square$

For the completeness proof we need the following lemma.

Lemma 7.9. *For every executable transition t of $\mathcal{A}$ and for every strategy $\prec$, the $\prec$-final prefix of Def. 7.4 contains at least one event of type 0 labeled by t.*

Proof. If t is executable in $\mathcal{A}$, then the d-unfolding contains at least one event of type 0 labeled by t. Call such an event a *t-witness*. Assume that no t-witness is feasible. Then every t-witness e_w has a spoiler, i.e., an unsuccessful terminal $e_s < e_w$. Since e_w is of type 0, so is e_s. We can now choose a minimal t-witness e_m exactly as in the proof of Thm. 4.11 on p. 46, and derive a contradiction. So some t-witness is feasible, and so it belongs to the $\prec$-final prefix. $\qquad\square$

Theorem 7.10. *The search scheme of Def. 7.4 is complete for every strategy.*

Proof. Assume that $\mathcal{A}$ has a livelock, but the final prefix contains no successful terminals. We derive a contradiction following the general scheme of the proof of Thm. 4.11 on p. 46.

Witnesses. We call an event e of type 1 a *pre-witness* if it is of type 1, the event $d(e)$ is feasible, and $\#_I(e) > |S| + 1$. A pre-witness e is a *witness* if no pre-witness e' satisfies $d(e') \prec d(e)$.

Let an event be a *root event* (a root for short) if it is of type 0 and it is labeled by a transition that is the root of a livelock. We make the following two observations.

(a) $\mathcal{A}$ has a livelock if and only if its d-unfolding contains a witness.

Assume that $\mathcal{A}$ has at least one livelock $h\,t\,c$, where c is an infinite computation containing only invisible transitions. We prove first that the d-unfolding contains a pre-witness. By Lemma 7.9, the final prefix contains at least one event e of type 0 labeled by t. Let e_d be the duplicate of e. Since e is labeled by t and $h\,t\,c$ is a history of $\mathcal{A}$, the computation c starts at the state $St(e)$. Since c is infinite and contains only invisible transitions, infinitely many causal successors of e in the d-unfolding are labeled by invisible transitions, and, since e_d is the duplicate of e, the same holds for e_d. So for every number k there is a causal successor e_k of e_d such that the number of events between e_d and e_k is at least k. In particular, there is a successor e' of e_d satisfying $\#_I(e') > |S| + 1$. Then e' is a pre-witness because $d(e') = e_d$ and since e is feasible, so is e_d. Now we prove that the d-unfolding also contains a witness. Observe that, since the set of feasible events is finite (Prop. 7.7), the set $\{d(e) \mid e$ is a pre-witness$\}$ is finite. So this set has a $\prec$-minimal element, say d. Any pre-witness e satisfying $d(e) = d$ is a witness.

For the other direction, let e be a witness. Then there are at least $|S| + 1$ events e' satisfying $d(e) < e' < e$. By the pigeonhole principle, two of them, say $e_1 < e_2$, satisfy $St(e_1) = St(e_2)$. Let l be the computation satisfying $H(e_2) = H(e_1)\,l$. The history $H(e_1)\,l^\omega$ is a livelock.

(b) If e is a witness, then some predecessor of e is a terminal.

We have just seen that for every witness e there exist events e_1, e_2 such that $d(e) < e_1 < e_2 < e$ and $St(e_1) = St(e_2)$. So we have $d(e_1) = d(e_2) = d(e)$. If e_2 is feasible, then it is a terminal of type (1b). If e_2 is not feasible, then, by the definition of feasibility, some predecessor of e_2 is a terminal.

Since $\mathcal{A}$ has a livelock, the unfolding of $\mathcal{A}$ contains witnesses by (a). By (b), for each witness e_w there is a terminal $e_s < e_w$, and since the final prefix is unsuccessful, e_s is unsuccessful. We call e_s the *spoiler* of e_w. Notice that, since $d(e_w)$ is feasible by the definition of a witness and since e_s is a terminal, we have $d(e_w) \leq e_s$. We prove that e_s satisfies (1c) by excluding all other possibilities.

(1) e_s is not of type 0.

By the definition of event of type 1, the event $d(e_w)$ is of type 1. Since $d(e_w) \leq e_s$ and the successors of an event of type 1 must be of type 1 or type 2, e_s is not of type 0.

(2) e_s is not of type (1a).

Since $d(e_w) \leq e_s < e_w$, we have $d(e_s) = d(e_w)$. Since $d(e_s)$ is a root, from $St(d(e_s))$ we can execute an infinite computation of invisible transitions. Now, let e' be the companion of e_s. Since e' is of type 1, the event $d(e')$ exists. Moreover, the events e'' satisfying $d(e') < e'' \leq e'$ cannot be visible, because otherwise they would be of type 2 and so terminals, contradicting the fact that e' is a feasible event. So they are all invisible. Since $St(e') = St(e_s)$, we can execute an infinite sequence of invisible events starting from $St(e')$, and therefore we can do the same from $St(d(e'))$. So some successor of $d(e')$, say e'_m, is a pre-witness. But then $d(e'_m) = d(e') \prec d(e_s) = d(e_m)$, contradicting the fact that $d(e_w)$ is $\prec$-minimal among pre-witnesses.

(3) e_s is not of type (1b).

Obvious, because e_s is unsuccessful.

(4) e_s is not of type 2.

Obvious, because $e_s < e_w$, and e_w is of type 1.

Minimal witnesses. Define the order $\ll$ as in the proof of Thm. 4.11 on p. 46. Let e_m be a $\ll$-minimal witness, and let e_s be its spoiler. Since e_s is of type (1c), it has a companion $e' \prec e_s$ such that $St(e') = St(e_s)$, $d(e') = d(e_s)$, and $\#_I(e') \geq \#_I(e_s)$. Let c_s be the computation satisfying $H(e_m) = H(e_s) c_s$. Since $St(e') = St(e_s)$, the sequence $H(e') c_s$ is also a history. Since $\#_I(e') \geq \#_I(e_s)$, the event e'_m satisfying $H(e'_m) = H(e') c_s$ is also a pre-witness. Since $d(e'_m) = d(e') = d(e_s) = d(e_m)$, the event e'_m is a witness.

Contradiction. The contradiction is derived exactly as in the proof of Thm. 4.11 on p. 46.   □

As usual, if $\prec$ is a total order then we get a polynomial bound for the size of the final prefix. If we restrict ourselves to strategies satisfying the following mild condition, then the bound is quadratic.

Definition 7.11. *A strategy $\prec$ is a* livelock strategy *if it satisfies the following condition for every two type 1 events e, e': if $e \prec e'$, then $d(e) \prec d(e')$ or $d(e) = d(e')$.*

The intuition behind this definition is particularly clear for a total livelock strategy $\prec$. Assume e_1 and e_2 are duplicates and $e_1 \prec e_2$ holds, i.e., the strategy gives priority to e_1 over e_2. Let e'_1 and e'_2 be any two events of type 1 such that $e_1 < e'_1$ and $e_2 < e'_2$. Then, since $\prec$ is a total livelock strategy and $d(e'_1) = e_1, d(e'_2) = e_2$, we have $e'_1 \prec e'_2$. So, loosely speaking, when a duplicate e_1 is added, a livelock strategy gives priority to exploring its successors: no successors of another duplicate $e_2 \succ e_1$ can be explored before the search finishes the exploration of the successors of e_1.

Theorem 7.12. *If $\prec$ is a total livelock strategy, then the $\prec$-final prefix of Def. 7.4 contains at most $|S|^2 + |S|$ non-terminal events.*

Proof. The final prefix has at most $|S|$ non-terminal events of type 0, because otherwise two type 0 events e, e' satisfy $St(e) = St(e')$, and since $\prec$ is a total order one of them is a terminal.

We have seen in the proof of Lemma 7.6 that the history of a non-terminal event of type 1 contains at most $|S|$ events of type 1. Therefore, for every non-terminal event e of type 1 we have $\#_I(e) \leq |S|$. We prove that for any state $s \in S$ there are at most $|S|$ non-terminal events such that $St(e) = s$. Assume the contrary, and let $e_1, \dots, e_{|S|+1}$ be pairwise different non-terminal events such that $St(e_i) = s$ for all $1 \leq i \leq |S| + 1$. Consider two cases:

- There are $e_j \neq e_k$ of type 1 such that $d(e_j) \neq d(e_k)$.

  Since $\prec$ is total, we can assume w.l.o.g. that $e_j \prec e_k$ holds. Since $\prec$ is a livelock strategy, we have $d(e_j) \prec d(e_k)$, and so e_k is a terminal of type (1a), a contradiction.

- All of $e_1, \ldots, e_{|S|+1}$ are type 1 events satisfying $d(e_1) = \ldots = d(e_{|S|+1})$. Then, since $\#_I(e_i) \leq |S|$ for all $1 \leq i \leq |S|+1$, by the pigeonhole principle there are two non-terminal events $e_j \neq e_k$ such that $\#_I(e_j) = \#_I(e_k)$. Since $\prec$ is a total order we have that either $e_j \prec e_k$ or $e_k \prec e_j$. So either e_j or e_k is a terminal of type (1c), a contradiction.

Since for each state $s \in S$ there are at most $|S|$ non-terminal events of type 1 such that $St(e) = s$, the final prefix contains at most $|S|^2$ non-terminal events of type 1.

Because all type 2 events are terminals, there are in total at most $|S|^2 + |S|$ non-terminal events. □

7.2 Search Scheme for Products

We fix a product $\mathbf{A} = \langle \mathcal{A}_1, \ldots, \mathcal{A}_n, \mathbf{T} \rangle$ of transition systems, where $\mathcal{A}_i = \langle S_i, T_i, \alpha_i, \beta_i, is_i \rangle$. We partition the set $\mathbf{T}$ of global transitions into a set $\mathbf{V}$ of *visible* and a set $\mathbf{I} = \mathbf{T} \setminus \mathbf{V}$ of *invisible* transitions. We also fix a set $\mathbf{L} \subseteq \mathbf{V}$ of *livelock monitors*.

The livelock problem consists of deciding whether $\mathbf{A}$ has an infinite global history of the form $\mathbf{h \, t \, c}$, where $\mathbf{h} \in \mathbf{T}^*$, $\mathbf{t} \in \mathbf{L}$, and $\mathbf{c} \in \mathbf{I}^\omega$, i.e., $\mathbf{c}$ only contains invisible global transitions. We call this history a *livelock with root* $\mathbf{t}$.

For our application to the model checking problem of LTL we do not need to solve the livelock problem for arbitrary instances. It suffices to solve it for instances satisfying the following useful constraint.

> **Visibility constraint:** Some component of the product participates in all visible global transitions.

In particular, this implies that in the unfolding of $\mathbf{A}$ any two $\mathbf{V}$-events are either causally related or in conflict. In the LTL model checking approach of Chap. 8 the component taking part in all visible actions is the one also responsible for detecting executions of the system that violate the temporal formula being model checked.

In order to generalize the search scheme of Def. 7.4, our first task is to define the d-unfolding of $\mathbf{A}$. Recall that the d-unfolding of a transition system $\mathcal{A}$ actually models the behavior of a nondeterministic program that simulates the execution of $\mathcal{A}$ but has two possible modes of operation.

In the transition system case the d-unfolding was obtained by duplicating events labeled with L-transitions. So our first attempt could be to duplicate events labeled with $\mathbf{L}$-transitions. Intuitively, this corresponds to having a nondeterministic program for each component of $\mathbf{A}$, each with its own variable and flag. The addition of a duplicate event e_d models that all the components participating in the transition labeling the event e enter the livelock mode. However, this can lead to a problem. Imagine a system whose components can be partitioned into two groups, say G_1 and G_2, such that no component of G_1 participates in any invisible transition and no component of G_2 participates in any livelock monitor. Then, none of the nondeterministic programs can detect any livelock. The programs for the components of G_1 can enter the livelock mode, but never execute any invisible transition; the programs for the components of G_2 can execute invisible transitions, but never enter the livelock mode. So we can have products that exhibit a livelock, but where the final prefix generated by the naive generalization of Def. 7.4 is unsuccessful.

Example 7.13. Consider the product in Fig. 7.3(a), where we take $\mathbf{T} = \{\langle a, \epsilon \rangle, \langle \epsilon, b \rangle, \langle \epsilon, c \rangle, \langle \epsilon, d \rangle\}$. For clarity, we use $\mathbf{a}$, $\mathbf{b}$, $\mathbf{c}$, $\mathbf{d}$ instead of $\langle a, \epsilon \rangle$, $\langle \epsilon, b \rangle$, $\langle \epsilon, c \rangle$, $\langle \epsilon, d \rangle$ in what follows. Notice that the first component does not participate in any invisible transition and the second one does not participate in any livelock monitor. The global history $\mathbf{a}\,\mathbf{b}\,(\mathbf{c}\,\mathbf{d})^\omega$ is a livelock. Figure 7.3(b) shows the final prefix obtained by the naive generalization of Def. 7.4. Intuitively, when event 5 is added the program of the first component enters the livelock mode. Event 4, shown in dark grey, is a terminal of type 0 having event 2 as companion. Since terminals of type 0 are unsuccessful, the final prefix is unsuccessful.

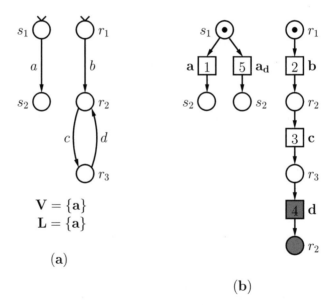

(a)

(b)

Fig. 7.3. An instance of the livelock problem (a) and a failed attempt at a final prefix (b)

To solve this problem we assume that *every component participates in the duplicate events.* In Ex. 7.13, when we add event 5, the duplicate of event 1, we synchronize with the other component. Figure 7.4(**b**) shows the new prefix. Non-terminal events of type 1 are shown in light grey, and terminal

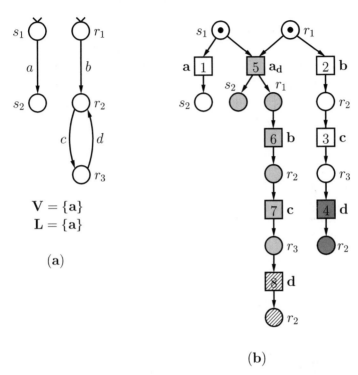

Fig. 7.4. An instance of the livelock problem (**a**) and a correct final prefix revealing a livelock (**b**)

events of type 1 are line-patterned. Event 8 is a successful terminal with 6 as companion.

We define the d-unfolding as follows:

Definition 7.14. *Let e be an event of the unfolding of $\mathbf{A}$ labeled by a global transition $\mathbf{t} = \langle t_1, \ldots, t_n \rangle$. For every component $\mathcal{A}_i$, let e_i be the largest i-event (w.r.t. the causal order $<$) such that $e_i < e$, and let p_i be either the unique i-place of $e_i^{\bullet}$, or the place is_i if there are no i-events $e_i < e$. The duplicate of e is a new event e_d, also labeled by $\mathbf{t}$, such that $^{\bullet}e = \{p_1, \ldots, p_n\}$, and $e^{\bullet} = \{p_1', \ldots, p_n'\}$, where p_i' is a new place for every $i \in \{1, \ldots, n\}$. If $t_i = \epsilon$, then p_i' carries the same label as p_i. If $t_i \neq \epsilon$, then p_i' carries the label $\beta(t_i)$.*

Example 7.15. In the final prefix of Fig. 7.4(**b**) event 5 is the duplicate of event 1. In this case the places p_1 and p_2 of Def. 7.14 are the initial states s_1 and r_1, i.e., the two places at the top of the figure.

Notice that we have $\mathbf{St}(e) = \mathbf{St}(e_d)$. We can see e_d as adding a new "branch" to the prefix from the global state $\mathbf{St}(e)$.

We can now generalize Def. 7.4. The definition of type 0, type 1, and type 2 events does not change at all. By $\#_\mathbf{I}(e)$ we denote the number of events e'' such that $d(e) < e'' \le e$; all of them are labeled by global transitions of $\mathbf{I}$.

Definition 7.16. *Let $\prec$ be a strategy on $[\mathbf{T}^*]$. An event e of the d-unfolding of $\mathbf{A}$ is feasible if no event $e' < e$ is a terminal.*

A feasible event e of type 0 is a terminal if there is a feasible event $e' \prec e$ of type 0, the companion of e, such that $\mathbf{St}(e') = \mathbf{St}(e)$.

A feasible event e of type 1 is a terminal if there is a feasible event $e' \prec e$ of type 1, the companion of e, such that $\mathbf{St}(e') = \mathbf{St}(e)$ and

- *(1a) $d(e') \prec d(e)$; or*
- *(1b) $d(e') = d(e)$ and $e' < e$; or*
- *(1c) $d(e') = d(e)$ and $\#_\mathbf{I}(e') \ge \#_\mathbf{I}(e)$.*

A feasible event of type 2 is always a terminal.

A terminal is successful if it satisfies (1b). The $\prec$-final prefix is the prefix of the unfolding of $\mathbf{A}$ containing the feasible events.

Well-definedness and soundness of the search scheme are proved as in the transition system case.

Lemma 7.17. *Let $\prec$ be an arbitrary strategy, and let (F, T) be a pair of sets of events satisfying the conditions of Def. 7.16 for the sets of feasible and terminal events, respectively. Then for every non-terminal feasible event $e \in F \setminus T$, every component $H_i(e)$ of the history $\mathbf{H}(e)$ has length at most $2K$, where K is the number of reachable states of $\mathbf{A}$.*

Proof. Let e be an arbitrary non-terminal feasible event. Use the same argument as in the proof of Lemma 7.6 (replacing St by $\mathbf{St}$) to prove that for each $i \in \{1, \ldots, n\}$ the history $H_i(e)$ contains at most K events of type 0 and at most K events of type 1. □

Proposition 7.18. *The search scheme of Def. 7.16 is well-defined for every strategy $\prec$. Moreover, the $\prec$-final prefix is finite.*

Proof. Analogous to the proof of Prop. 7.7. □

Proposition 7.19. *The search scheme of Def. 7.16 is sound for every strategy.*

Proof. Analogous to the proof of Prop. 7.8.   □

So far we have not made use of the visibility constraint we mentioned at the beginning of the section. The following slight modification of Ex. 7.13 shows that the scheme of Def. 7.16 is not complete for systems that do not satisfy this constraint.

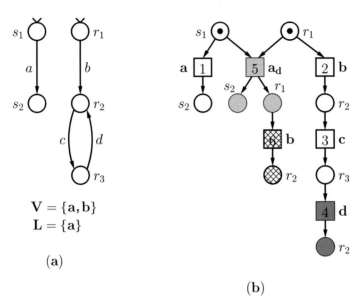

(a)

(b)

Fig. 7.5. Another instance of the livelock problem (a) and the role of the visibility constraint (b)

Example 7.20. Consider again the product of Fig. 7.3(a), but change the set of visible transitions from {**a**} to {**a, b**}, as shown in Fig. 7.5(a). This product does not satisfy the visibility constraint, because neither of the two components participates in both **a** and **b**.

The global history $\mathbf{b\,a\,(c\,d)}^\omega$ is a livelock with root **a**. In Fig. 7.5(b) we show the final prefix obtained by Def. 7.16. The terminals are events 4 and 6. Event 4 is, as before, a terminal of type 0. Event 6, which was invisible in Ex. 7.13, is now visible, and so, since event 5 is a duplicate, it becomes a terminal of type 2. Since terminals of type 0 and 2 are unsuccessful, the final prefix is unsuccessful.

To understand why the search procedure fails, observe that in the case of a transition system, given a livelock $h\,t\,c$ with t as root there is an event e labeled by t such that the infinite computation c starts at $St(e)$. So it is correct to search for infinite invisible computations that start from $St(e)$, and this is the purpose of the duplicate e_d.

In the case of a product, given a livelock $\mathbf{h}\,\mathbf{t}\,\mathbf{c}$ with root $\mathbf{t}$ there may be no event e labeled by $\mathbf{t}$ such that the global computation $\mathbf{c}$ starts at $\mathbf{St}(e)$. In Ex. 7.20, the only candidate for e is event 1, but the computation $(\mathbf{c}\,\mathbf{d})^{\omega}$ starts at $\langle s_2, r_2 \rangle$, while $\mathbf{St}(1) = \langle s_2, r_1 \rangle$. So it may be wrong to search for infinite invisible computations that start from $\mathbf{St}(e)$, which is the purpose of e_d. All these computations may contain visible transitions corresponding to events that are *concurrent* to e.

However, if the product satisfies the visibility constraint, then we are on the safe side. In such a product, since e is visible, no visible event can be concurrent to e. Therefore, the events concurrent to e correspond to invisible transitions that extend the computation $\mathbf{c}$ without changing its property of containing only invisible transitions.

Definition 7.21. *A livelock $\mathbf{h}\,\mathbf{t}\,\mathbf{c}$ of $\mathbf{A}$ with root $\mathbf{t}$ is good if the d-unfolding contains an event e such that $\mathbf{h}\,\mathbf{t}$ is a realization of $past(e)$.*

An event e of the unfolding of $\mathbf{A}$ is a root event if it is of type 0 and $\mathbf{A}$ has a livelock $\mathbf{h}\,\mathbf{t}\,\mathbf{c}$ with root $\mathbf{t}$ such that e is labeled by $\mathbf{t}$, and $\mathbf{St}(e)$ is the global state reached after the execution of $\mathbf{h}\,\mathbf{t}$.

We can prove the following lemmata, which will replace Lemma 7.9 in the completeness proof.

Lemma 7.22. *Let $\mathbf{A}$ be a product satisfying the visibility constraint. If $\mathbf{A}$ has a livelock, then it also has a good livelock.*

Proof. Assume $\mathbf{A}$ has a livelock $\mathbf{h}\,\mathbf{t}\,\mathbf{c}$. Then, by the same argument as in Lemma 7.9, the d-unfolding contains a configuration C such that $\mathbf{h}\,\mathbf{t}$ is a realization of C. Let e be the event of C corresponding to the occurrence of $\mathbf{t}$, and $\mathbf{h}'\,\mathbf{t}\,\mathbf{c}'$ be the realization of C in which $\mathbf{h}'\,\mathbf{t}$ is a realization of $past(e)$. In this realization, the transitions of $\mathbf{h}'\,\mathbf{t}$ correspond to the events $e' \in C$ satisfying $e' \leq e$, while the transitions of $\mathbf{c}'$ correspond to the events $e' \in C$ satisfying $e'\ co\ e$. So no component that participates in $\mathbf{t}$ participates in the transitions of $\mathbf{c}'$. By the visibility constraint, the transitions of $\mathbf{c}'$ are invisible, and so $\mathbf{h}'\,\mathbf{t}\,\mathbf{c}'$ is a livelock with root $\mathbf{t}$. Since $\mathbf{h}'\,\mathbf{t}$ is a realization of the configuration $past(e)$, the livelock is good. □

Lemma 7.23. *Let $\prec$ be an adequate strategy. If the product $\mathbf{A}$ has at least one livelock, then the $\prec$-final prefix of Def. 7.16 contains at least one root event.*

Proof. Assume $\mathbf{A}$ has a livelock. By Lemma 7.22 it has a good livelock $\mathbf{h}\,\mathbf{t}\,\mathbf{c}$. So the d-unfolding contains an event e of type 0 labeled by $\mathbf{t}$ such that $\mathbf{h}\,\mathbf{t}$ is a realization of $past(e)$. It follows that $\mathbf{St}(e)$ is the state reached after the execution of $\mathbf{h}\,\mathbf{t}$, and so the d-unfolding contains at least one root event e. Let e_m be a $\prec$-minimal root event (e_m exists because $\prec$ is well-founded). Assume that e_m is not feasible. Then, some event $e_s < e_m$ is a terminal and, since e_m

is of type 0, e_s is also of type 0. Let e' be the companion of e_s. As in the proof of Thm. 4.43 on p. 62, and using the fact that $\prec$ is preserved by extensions, we can construct another root event e'_m satisfying $e'_m \prec e_m$, contradicting the minimality of e_m. So e_m is feasible, and so it belongs to the $\prec$-minimal prefix. □

We can finally prove the completeness result.

Theorem 7.24. *The search procedure of Def. 7.16 is complete for every adequate strategy.*

Proof. Let $\prec$ be an arbitrary adequate strategy. Assume that **A** has a livelock, but the final prefix contains no successful terminals. We derive a contradiction following the general scheme of the proof of Thm. 4.11 on p. 46.

Witnesses. We call an event e of type 1 a *pre-witness* if it is of type 1, the event $d(e)$ is feasible, and $\#_I(e) > nK+1$, where K is the number of reachable global states of **A**. A pre-witness e is a *witness* if there is no pre-witness $e' \neq e$ such that $d(e') \prec d(e)$.

We make the following two observations:

(a) **A** has a livelock if and only if its d-unfolding contains a witness.
   Assume that **A** has a livelock. By Lemma 7.23, the final prefix contains at least one root event. Let e be a root event of the final prefix, and let e_d be its duplicate (notice that, by definition, root events are labeled by transitions of **L**). Since $\mathbf{St}(e_d) = \mathbf{St}(e)$, there is a livelock $\mathbf{h\,t\,c}$ with root $\mathbf{t}$ such that $\mathbf{St}(e_d)$ coincides with the global state reached after the execution of $\mathbf{h\,t}$. It follows that the computation $\mathbf{c}$ can occur from $\mathbf{St}(e_d)$. So there is a causal successor $e' > e_d$ satisfying $\#_I(e') > nK + 1$. Since $d(e') = e_d$, the event e' is a pre-witness. To prove that the d-unfolding also contains a witness, observe that the set of feasible events is finite, and so the set $\{d(e) \mid e \text{ is a pre-witness}\}$ is also finite. So this set has at least one $\prec$-minimal event $e'' = d(e_w)$ for some pre-witness e_w, making e_w also a witness.
   For the other direction, let e be a witness. Then there are at least $nK + 1$ events e' satisfying $d(e) < e' < e$. By the pigeonhole principle there is a component, say the ith, such that there are at least $K + 1$ i-events between $d(e)$ and e. All these events are causally ordered and so, again by the pigeonhole principle, two of them, say $e_1 < e_2$, satisfy $\mathbf{St}(e_1) = \mathbf{St}(e_2)$. Let $[\mathbf{c}]$ be any computation trace satisfying $\mathbf{H}(e_2) = \mathbf{H}(e_1)[\mathbf{c}]$. Then any realization of the configuration $past(d(e))$ followed by $\mathbf{c}^\omega$ is a livelock.
(b) If e is a witness, then some predecessor of e is a terminal. The proof is as in Thm. 7.10, just observing that $\#_I(e) > nK + 1$ implies that for some component, say the ith, there are at least $K+1$ i-events between $d(e)$ and e.

By (a), and since **A** has a livelock, the unfolding of **A** contains witnesses. By (b), and since the final prefix is unsuccessful, for each witness e_w there is an unsuccessful terminal $e_s < e_w$. We call e_s the *spoiler* of e_w. We prove that e_s has type (1c) exactly as in Thm. 7.10 (replacing, as usual, histories by distributed histories).

Minimal witnesses. As in the proof of Thm. 4.43 on p. 62, let e_m be a $\prec$-minimal witness, and let e_s be its spoiler. Since e_s has type (1c), it has a companion $e' \prec e_s$ such that $d(e') = d(e_s)$, $\mathbf{St}(e') = \mathbf{St}(e_s)$, and $\#_I(e') \geq \#_I(e_s)$. Let $[\mathbf{c_s}]$ be a computation trace satisfying $\mathbf{H}(e_m) = \mathbf{H}(e_s)[\mathbf{c_s}]$. Since $\mathbf{St}(e') = \mathbf{St}(e_s)$, $\mathbf{H}(e')[\mathbf{c_s}]$ is also a history trace. Since $\#_I(e') \geq \#_I(e_s)$, the event e'_m satisfying $\mathbf{H}(e'_m) = \mathbf{H}(e')[\mathbf{c_s}]$ is also a pre-witness. Since $d(e'_m) = d(e') = d(e_s) = d(e_m)$, the event e'_m is a witness.

Contradiction. As in the proof of Thm. 4.43 on p. 62. $\qquad\square$

As for transition systems, we obtain a quadratic bound on the number of non-terminal events for total livelock strategies.

Theorem 7.25. *If $\prec$ is a total livelock strategy, then the $\prec$-final prefix of Def. 7.16 contains at most $nK^2 + K$ non-terminal events.*

Proof. The proof is very similar to that of Thm. 7.12. The final prefix has at most K non-terminal events of type 0, because otherwise two type 0 events e, e' satisfy $\mathbf{St}(e) = \mathbf{St}(e')$, and since $\prec$ is a total order one of them is a terminal.

We have seen in the proof of Lemma 7.17 that for every non-terminal event e of type 1 in the final prefix and for every component $\mathcal{A}_i$ the configuration $past(e)$ contains at most K i-events of type 1. It follows that $past(e)$ contains at most nK events of type 1, and so $\#_I(e) \leq nK$. We prove that for any global state $\mathbf{s}$ the final prefix contains at most nK non-terminal events such that $\mathbf{St}(e) = \mathbf{s}$. Assuming the contrary, let $e_1, \ldots, e_{nK+1}$ be pairwise different non-terminal events such that $\mathbf{St}(e_i) = \mathbf{s}$ for all $1 \leq i \leq nK + 1$. Consider two cases:

- There are $e_j \neq e_k$ of type 1 such that $d(e_j) \neq d(e_k)$.
  Since $\prec$ is total, we can assume w.l.o.g. that $e_j \prec e_k$ holds. Since $\prec$ is a livelock strategy, we have $d(e_j) \prec d(e_k)$, and so e_k is a terminal of type (1a), a contradiction.
- All of $e_1, \ldots, e_{nK+1}$ are type 1 events satisfying $d(e_1) = \ldots = d(e_{K+1})$.
  Then, since $\#_I(e_i) \leq nK$ for all $1 \leq i \leq nK+1$, by the pigeonhole principle there are two non-terminal events $e_j \neq e_k$ such that $\#_I(e_j) = \#_I(e_k)$. Since $\prec$ is a total order we have either $e_j \prec e_k$ or $e_k \prec e_j$. So either e_j or e_k is a (1c)-terminal, a contradiction.

Since for each global state there are at most nK non-terminal events e of type 1 such that $\mathbf{St}(e) = \mathbf{s}$, the final prefix contains at most nK^2 non-terminal events of type 1.

Because all type 2 events are terminals, there are in total at most $nK^2 + K$ non-terminal events. $\qquad\square$

Bibliographical Notes

In the literature livelocks are also called divergences. The livelock problem for products was studied by the authors in [35, 36], and the contents of this chapter are an extended and modified version of these references. The approach is heavily based on ideas of Valmari in tester-based verification [117]. See also more recent work by Helovuo, Valmari, Hansen, and Penczek in tester-based verification [62, 55, 54].

The nondeterministic algorithm for guessing when to move from main mode to livelock detection mode bears close resemblance to the liveness-to-safety reduction by Biere, Artho, and Schuppan [14].

8

Model Checking LTL

In this chapter we present the main result of this work, a search procedure for model checking products of transition systems against specifications written in Linear Temporal Logic (LTL).[1] The chapter is divided in several sections.

In Sects. 8.1 and 8.2 we recall the syntax and semantics of LTL, show how to interpret LTL on products, and define the model checking problem.

In Sect. 8.3 we introduce the concept of *Büchi tester for an LTL property*. Loosely speaking, a tester of a product is a new component added to the product in order to observe and register the occurrences of (some) global transitions. A tester may "recognize" a history of the product based on the occurrences it has observed. The tester for an LTL property is designed to recognize the histories that violate the property. We show that every LTL property has a Büchi tester.

Section 8.4 presents a first approach to the model checking problem, in which the Büchi tester is synchronized with the product in a very tight way: Every global transition of the product is synchronized with at least one transition of the tester. This is the classical approach due to Vardi and Wolper, and we observe that it is not suitable for the unfolding method. Since the tester is a sequential transition system, its synchronization with the product yields a new product in which no two global transitions can ever occur concurrently. As a result our search procedures generate final prefixes which are at least as large as the transition system of the new product, and so unfolding techniques have no advantage over the classical approach.

In Sect. 8.5 a second approach is presented in which, intuitively, the tester is far more loosely coupled with the product: It only observes those occurrences of global transitions which are relevant for the LTL property being checked. Since these are typically only a small number, the new product can retain much of the concurrency present in the original one.

---

[1] To be precise, the net unfolding approach can be more efficient than traditional methods only for the so-called stuttering-invariant subset of LTL; see Sect. 8.5 for details.

8.1 Linear Temporal Logic

The set of formulas of Linear Temporal Logic (LTL) over a given nonempty set AP of *atomic propositions* is inductively defined as follows:

- every atomic proposition is an LTL formula,
- if ψ_1 is an LTL formula, then $\neg\psi_1$ and $\mathbf{X}\,\psi_1$ are LTL formulas; and
- if ψ_1, ψ_2 are LTL formulas, then $\psi_1 \vee \psi_2$ and $\psi_1 \,\mathbf{U}\, \psi_2$ are LTL formulas.

Formulas are interpreted over infinite words whose letters are sets of atomic propositions, i.e., infinite words over the alphabet 2^{AP}. Intuitively, atomic propositions correspond to the basic assertions about which we wish to reason, and the ith letter of a word corresponds to the assertions that hold at the ith time instant. Given a formula ψ and a word $\pi = x_0 x_1 x_2 \ldots$, where $x_i \in 2^{AP}$ for every $i \geq 0$, we denote by $\pi \models \psi$ that π satisfies ψ. The satisfaction relation $\models$ is inductively defined as follows, where p denotes an element of AP and π^i denotes the suffix $x_i x_{i+1} x_{i+2} \ldots$ of π:

$$
\begin{aligned}
&\pi \models p && \text{if } p \in x_0, \\
&\pi \models \neg\psi_1 && \text{if } \pi \not\models \psi_1, \\
&\pi \models \psi_1 \vee \psi_2 && \text{if } \pi \models \psi_1 \text{ or } \pi \models \psi_2, \\
&\pi \models \mathbf{X}\,\psi_1 && \text{if } \pi^1 \models \psi_1, \text{ and} \\
&\pi \models \psi_1 \,\mathbf{U}\, \psi_2 && \text{if } \exists n \geq 0 \text{ such that } \pi^n \models \psi_2 \text{ and } \pi^i \models \psi_1 \text{ for all } 0 \leq i < n.
\end{aligned}
$$

As usual, we read $\mathbf{X}\,\psi$ as "next ψ" and $\psi_1 \,\mathbf{U}\, \psi_2$ as "ψ_1 until ψ_2". Loosely speaking, $\mathbf{X}\,\psi$ holds if ψ holds at the next time instant, and $\psi_1 \,\mathbf{U}\, \psi_2$ holds if eventually ψ_2 holds and ψ_1 holds until then.

We employ the usual shorthands for LTL formulas: $true = \neg p \vee p$ for an arbitrary $p \in AP$, $false = \neg true$, $\psi_1 \wedge \psi_2 = \neg(\neg\psi_1 \vee \neg\psi_2)$, $\psi_1 \Rightarrow \psi_2 = \neg\psi_1 \vee \psi_2$, $\psi_1 \,\mathbf{R}\, \psi_2 = \neg(\neg\psi_1 \,\mathbf{U}\, \neg\psi_2)$, $\mathbf{F}\,\psi_1 = true \,\mathbf{U}\, \psi_1$, and $\mathbf{G}\,\psi_1 = false \,\mathbf{R}\, \psi_1$.

Example 8.1. $\mathbf{G}\,(p \Rightarrow \mathbf{X}\,\neg p)$ and $\mathbf{F}\,(p \wedge \mathbf{X}\,p)$ are LTL formulas over the set $\{p\}$ of atomic propositions. Loosely speaking, they assert "if p holds at a time instant then it does not hold at the next one" and "there exist two consecutive time instants at which p holds", respectively. Let $(\{p\}\,\emptyset)^\omega$ and $\emptyset\,\emptyset\,\{p\}\,\{p\}\,(\emptyset)^\omega$ denote the infinite sequences $\{p\}\,\emptyset\,\{p\}\,\emptyset\,\{p\}\,\emptyset \ldots$, and $\emptyset\,\emptyset\,\{p\}\,\{p\}\,\emptyset\,\emptyset\,\emptyset \ldots$, respectively. We have

$$
\begin{aligned}
(\{p\}\,\emptyset)^\omega &\models \mathbf{G}\,(p \Rightarrow \mathbf{X}\,\neg p) && \emptyset\,\emptyset\,\{p\}\,\{p\}\,(\emptyset)^\omega \not\models \mathbf{G}\,(p \Rightarrow \mathbf{X}\,\neg p) \\
(\{p\}\,\emptyset)^\omega &\not\models \mathbf{F}\,(p \wedge \mathbf{X}\,p) && \emptyset\,\emptyset\,\{p\}\,\{p\}\,(\emptyset)^\omega \models \mathbf{F}\,(p \wedge \mathbf{X}\,p)
\end{aligned}
$$

In fact, as the reader has probably observed, the second formula is equivalent to the negation of the first.

8.2 Interpreting LTL on Products

Let $\mathbf{A} = \langle \mathcal{A}_1, \ldots, \mathcal{A}_n, \mathbf{T} \rangle$ be a product, where $\mathcal{A}_i = \langle S_i, T_i, \alpha_i, \beta_i, is_i \rangle$. The basic assertions we are interested in are of the form "the current local state of the ith component is s_j", and so we choose $AP = \bigcup_{i=1}^{n} S_i$ as the set of atomic propositions.

Given an infinite global history $\mathbf{h} = \mathbf{t_1 t_2 t_3} \ldots$ of $\mathbf{A}$, there is a unique sequence $\mathbf{s_0 s_1 s_2} \ldots$ of global states such that $\mathbf{s_0} = \mathbf{is}$ and $\langle \mathbf{s}_i, \mathbf{t}_{i+1}, \mathbf{s}_{i+1} \rangle$ is a step of $\mathbf{A}$ for every $i \geq 0$ (this is the sequence of global states visited by $\mathbf{A}$ along the execution of $\mathbf{h}$). We define the infinite sequence $\pi(\mathbf{h})$ of sets of atomic propositions as follows: for every $i \geq 0$, the ith element of $\pi(\mathbf{h})$ is the set of local states of the global state $\mathbf{s}_i$ (i.e., the set of local states of the components at the ith time instant). Observe that, by the definition of step, if $\mathcal{S}_i$ and $\mathcal{S}_{i+1}$ are the ith and $(i+1)$th elements of $\pi(\mathbf{h})$, then we have $\mathcal{S}_{i+1} = (\mathcal{S}_i \setminus {}^\bullet \mathbf{t}_i) \cup \mathbf{t}_i^\bullet$.

Example 8.2. Consider the product of Fig. 8.1. We consider LTL over the set of atomic propositions $AP = \{t_1, t_2, u_1, u_2\}$. The sequence $\mathbf{h} = \mathbf{a}\,\mathbf{b}\,\mathbf{c}\,(\mathbf{a}\mathbf{b})^\omega$ is an infinite history. The sequence of global states visited along its execution is $\langle t_1, u_1 \rangle \langle t_1, u_2 \rangle \langle t_1, u_1 \rangle (\langle t_2, u_1 \rangle \langle t_2, u_2 \rangle)^\omega$, and we have $\pi(\mathbf{h}) = \{t_1, u_1\} \{t_1, u_2\} \{t_1, u_1\} (\{t_2, u_1\} \{t_2, u_2\})^\omega$.

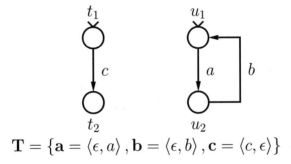

$$\mathbf{T} = \{\mathbf{a} = \langle \epsilon, a \rangle, \mathbf{b} = \langle \epsilon, b \rangle, \mathbf{c} = \langle c, \epsilon \rangle\}$$

Fig. 8.1. A running example for LTL model checking

We can now interpret an LTL formula ψ on $\pi(\mathbf{h})$. We say that $\mathbf{h}$ satisfies ψ if $\pi(\mathbf{h}) \models \psi$, and write $\mathbf{h} \models \psi$. We say that $\mathbf{A}$ satisfies ψ, and write $\mathbf{A} \models \psi$, if every infinite history of $\mathbf{A}$ satisfies ψ. So, loosely speaking, a product satisfies a property if all its infinite histories satisfy it.[2] The *model checking problem* consists of deciding, given $\mathbf{A}$ and ψ, whether $\mathbf{A} \models \psi$ holds.

Example 8.3. Consider the setting of Ex. 8.2 and the formulas

$$\mathbf{G}\,(u_1 \Rightarrow \mathbf{X}\,\neg u_1) \qquad \text{and} \qquad \mathbf{F}\,(u_1 \wedge \mathbf{X}\,u_1).$$

Since $\pi(\mathbf{h})$ contains $\{t_1, u_1\} \{t_2, u_1\}$ as subword, we have

---

[2] Note that, by this definition, in the rest of this book finite histories ending in a deadlock state are not among the infinite histories of $\mathbf{A}$.

$$\pi(\mathbf{h}) \not\models \mathbf{G}\,(u_1 \Rightarrow \mathbf{X}\,\neg u_1) \qquad \text{and} \qquad \pi(\mathbf{h}) \models \mathbf{F}\,(u_1 \wedge \mathbf{X}\,u_1)\,.$$

So, by definition, we have

$$\mathbf{h} \not\models \mathbf{G}\,(u_1 \Rightarrow \mathbf{X}\,\neg u_1) \qquad \text{and} \qquad \mathbf{h} \models \mathbf{F}\,(u_1 \wedge \mathbf{X}\,u_1)\,.$$

The reader can easily check that the history $(\mathbf{a}\,\mathbf{b})^\omega$ violates $\mathbf{F}\,(u_1 \wedge \mathbf{X}\,u_1)$. So both properties are violated by at least one history; hence

$$\mathbf{A} \not\models \mathbf{G}\,(u_1 \Rightarrow \mathbf{X}\,\neg u_1) \qquad \text{and} \qquad \mathbf{A} \not\models \mathbf{F}\,(u_1 \wedge \mathbf{X}\,u_1)\,.$$

Notice that this is the case even though each of the properties is equivalent to the negation of the other. In general, $\mathbf{A} \models \psi$ implies $\mathbf{A} \not\models \neg\psi$, but the converse does not hold.

8.2.1 Extending the Interpretation

So far we know how to interpret a formula ψ on the infinite histories of the product $\mathbf{A}$, but it is convenient to extend the interpretation to what we call the ψ-*histories* of $\mathbf{A}$. The reason is that in order to solve the model checking problem we will later construct an automaton accepting exactly these histories.

Let AP_ψ be the set of atomic propositions that appear in ψ. A ψ-*state* is a tuple $\mathbf{r} = \langle r_1, \ldots, r_n \rangle$ such that for every $i \in \{1, \ldots, n\}$ either $r_i \in S_i \cap AP_\psi$ or $s_i = \bot$, where $\bot$ is an special symbol. Given a global state $\mathbf{s} = \langle s_1, \ldots, s_n \rangle$, we assign to it a ψ-state $\mathbf{s}_\psi = \langle s_{1\psi}, \ldots, s_{n\psi} \rangle$ as follows. For every $i \in \{1, \ldots, n\}$,

$$s_{i\psi} = \begin{cases} s_i & \text{if } s_i \in AP_\psi, \text{ and} \\ \bot & \text{otherwise.} \end{cases}$$

So, intuitively, $\mathbf{s}_\psi$ is the information on the global state $\mathbf{s}$ available to an observer that can only see the local states of AP_ψ.

A tuple $\langle \mathbf{r}, \mathbf{t}, \mathbf{r}' \rangle$, where $\mathbf{r}, \mathbf{r}'$ are ψ-states and $\mathbf{t}$ is a global transition, is a ψ-*step* if there exists a step $\langle \mathbf{s}, \mathbf{t}, \mathbf{s}' \rangle$ such that $\mathbf{r} = \mathbf{s}_\psi$ and $\mathbf{r}' = \mathbf{s}'_\psi$. We define ψ-computations and ψ-histories by taking the definitions of computation and history, respectively, and replacing steps by ψ-steps. A sequence $\mathbf{t}_1 \ldots \mathbf{t}_k$ of global transitions is a ψ-*computation* if there is a sequence $\mathbf{r}_0, \ldots, \mathbf{r}_k$ of ψ-states such that $\langle \mathbf{r}_{i-1}, \mathbf{t}_i, \mathbf{r}_i \rangle$ is a ψ-step for every $i \in \{1, \ldots, k\}$. A ψ-computation is a ψ-*history* if one can choose the sequence $\mathbf{r}_0, \ldots, \mathbf{r}_k$ such that $\mathbf{r}_0 = \mathbf{is}_\psi$. Infinite ψ-computations and infinite ψ-histories are defined analogously. To gain some intuition, imagine that an observer can only see the local states of AP_ψ and the transitions having them as source or target states. A sequence of transitions is a ψ-history if this observer cannot conclude that it is not a history by just observing the marking changes in all the places in AP_ψ.

Example 8.4. Consider again the product of Fig. 8.1, and assume that we have $AP_\psi = \{u_1\}$ (the exact formula ψ is irrelevant for this example). The triple $\langle\langle t_1, u_1\rangle, \mathbf{c}, \langle t_2, u_1\rangle\rangle$ is a step, and $\langle\langle \bot, u_1\rangle, \mathbf{c}, \langle \bot, u_1\rangle\rangle$ is its corresponding ψ-step. It follows that $\mathbf{c}\,\mathbf{c}$ is a ψ-history because of the two ψ-steps

$$\langle\langle \bot, u_1\rangle, \mathbf{c}, \langle \bot, u_1\rangle\rangle \; \langle\langle \bot, u_1\rangle, \mathbf{c}, \langle \bot, u_1\rangle\rangle \; .$$

Observe however that $\mathbf{c}\,\mathbf{c}$ is not a history.

On the other hand, the sequence $\mathbf{a}\,\mathbf{a}$ is not a ψ-history. To see why, assume there are ψ-steps $\langle \mathbf{r}_0, \mathbf{a}, \mathbf{r}_1\rangle$ and $\langle \mathbf{r}_1, \mathbf{a}, \mathbf{r}_2\rangle$ such that $\mathbf{r}_0$ is the initial ψ-state, i.e., $\mathbf{r}_0 = \langle \bot, u_1\rangle$. By the definition of ψ-step we have $\mathbf{r}_1 = \langle \bot, \bot\rangle$. But, since $\mathbf{a}$ can only occur at global states such that the second component is in state u_1, there is no $\mathbf{r}_2$ such that $\langle \mathbf{r}_1, \mathbf{a}, \mathbf{r}_2\rangle$ is a ψ-step.

As in the case of histories, it is easy to see that given an infinite ψ-history $\sigma = \mathbf{t}_1\,\mathbf{t}_2\,\mathbf{t}_3\ldots$ of $\mathbf{A}$, there is a unique sequence $\mathbf{r}_0\,\mathbf{r}_1\,\mathbf{r}_2\ldots$ of ψ-states such that $\mathbf{r}_0 = \mathbf{is}_\psi$ and $\langle \mathbf{r}_{i-1}, \mathbf{t}_i, \mathbf{r}_i\rangle$ is a ψ-step of $\mathbf{A}$ for every $i \geq 1$. We denote this sequence by $\pi_\psi(\sigma)$, and call it *the ψ-sequence of σ*. We say that σ satisfies ψ, denoted by $\sigma \models \psi$, if $\pi_\psi(\sigma) \models \psi$.

8.3 Testers for LTL Properties

Deciding whether *all* infinite histories of a product $\mathbf{A}$ satisfy ψ is equivalent to deciding whether *some* infinite history violates ψ, which in turn is equivalent to deciding if some infinite history satisfies $\neg\psi$. The tester approach to the model checking problem reduces this last question to the simpler one of checking if some history of a new product, which depends on ψ, satisfies a *fixed* property.

The tester approach looks at $\mathbf{A}$ as a device that recognizes a language L_1 of infinite words, namely the ψ-histories corresponding to the infinite histories of $\mathbf{A}$. In a nutshell, it provides the following procedure to check a formula:

- Construct a *tester* recognizing the set L_2 of all ψ-histories satisfying $\neg\psi$.
- Using this tester, construct a new product recognizing the intersection $L_1 \cap L_2$, i.e., the set of ψ-histories of $\mathbf{A}$ violating ψ.
- Check whether $L_1 \cap L_2$ is empty or not.

We will see that the check can be reduced to the repeated executability problem. Then, in Sect. 8.5 we additionally resort to also solving the livelock problem for efficiency reasons. We know how both of these problems can be solved from the previous chapters.

The testers suitable for checking LTL properties are called Büchi testers. A *Büchi tester* of $\mathbf{A}$, or simply a *tester*, is a triple $\mathcal{BT} = (\mathcal{B}, F, \lambda)$, where $\mathcal{B} = (S, T, \alpha, \beta, is)$ is a transition system, $F \subseteq S$ is a set of *accepting states*, and $\lambda\colon T \to \mathbf{T}$ is a *labeling function* that assigns to each transition of $\mathcal{B}$ a global transition of **A**. A tester $\mathcal{BT}$ *recognizes* an infinite sequence $\mathbf{t}_1\,\mathbf{t}_2\,\mathbf{t}_3\ldots \in \mathbf{T}^\omega$ if there is an infinite history $h = u_1\,u_2\,u_3\ldots$ of $\mathcal{B}$ and an accepting state $s \in F$ such that $\mathbf{t}_i = \lambda(u_i)$ for every $i \geq 1$ and h visits the state s infinitely often, i.e., the sequence $\pi(h)$ contains infinitely many occurrences of s. The *language* of $\mathcal{BT}$ is the set of words of $\mathbf{T}^\omega$ recognized by $\mathcal{BT}$.

Example 8.5. Figure 8.2 shows a tester of the product of Fig. 8.1 for the property $\mathbf{F}\,t_2$. The names of the tester transitions have been omitted; we show only the global transitions of the product they are labeled with. The states drawn using two circles are the accepting states, and states drawn with a single circle are the non-accepting states. The tester recognizes the sequence $\mathbf{c}(\mathbf{a}\,\mathbf{b})^\omega$, but not $(\mathbf{a}\,\mathbf{b})^\omega$.

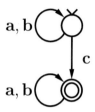

Fig. 8.2. A tester of the product of Fig. 8.1 for $\mathbf{F}\,t_2$

Let ψ be a formula of LTL. A tester $\mathcal{BT}$ *tests the property* ψ or *is a tester for* ψ if it recognizes the infinite ψ-histories of **A** that satisfy ψ.

In the rest of this chapter we show that every LTL formula over AP has a Büchi tester. This is a very well-known topic in the area of model checking, and there exist many different constructions. We sketch a very simple one, without giving a formal proof of correctness. Readers familiar with LTL to Büchi automata translations may wish to jump directly to Sect. 8.4.

8.3.1 Constructing a Tester

The construction proceeds in two steps. First, we construct a *generalized* Büchi tester for ψ, and then transform it into a Büchi tester.

A generalized Büchi tester of **A** is a triple $\mathcal{GT} = \langle \mathcal{B}, \{F_0, \ldots, F_{k-1}\}, \lambda\rangle$, where $\mathcal{B}$ and λ are as for Büchi testers, and $F_0, \ldots, F_{k-1}$ are sets of accepting states. $\mathcal{GT}$ recognizes an infinite sequence $\mathbf{t}_1\,\mathbf{t}_2\,\mathbf{t}_3\ldots \in \mathbf{T}^\omega$ if there is an infinite history $h = u_1\,u_2\,u_3\ldots$ and accepting states $s_0 \in F_0, \ldots, s_{k-1} \in F_{k-1}$ such that $\mathbf{t}_i = \lambda(u_i)$ for every $i \geq 1$ and h visits each of the states $s_0, \ldots, s_{k-1}$ infinitely often. The *language* of $\mathcal{GT}$ is the set of words it recognizes.

From Formulas to Generalized Büchi Testers

The key notion for the construction of the tester is that of *Hintikka sequence* of a ψ-history σ. The Hintikka sequence is an infinite sequence of sets of subformulas of ψ and their negations. Intuitively, the ith set of this sequence contains the subformulas of ψ (and their negations) that hold after the occurrence of the first i transitions of σ.

Before formally defining Hintikka sequences, we need to introduce atoms:

Definition 8.6. *Let ψ be a formula of LTL. The* closure $cl(\psi)$ *of an LTL formula ψ is the set containing all the subformulas of ψ and their negations. An* atom a *of ψ is a propositionally consistent subset of $cl(\psi)$, i.e., a subset satisfying the following two conditions:*

- *For every subformula $\neg\phi$ of ψ: $\phi \in a$ if and only if $\neg\phi \notin a$.*
- *For every subformula $\phi_1 \vee \phi_2$ of ψ: $\phi_1 \vee \phi_2 \in a$ if and only if $\phi_1 \in a$ or $\phi_2 \in a$.*

Notice that if a subset of the closure has a model then it must be an atom.

Example 8.7. The closure of $\psi = t_1 \, \mathbf{U} \, (\neg \mathbf{X} \, u_1)$ is the set

$$cl(\psi) = \{t_1, \neg t_1, u_1, \neg u_1, \mathbf{X} \, u_1, \neg \mathbf{X} \, u_1, \psi, \neg\psi\}.$$

The set $\{t_1, \neg u_1, \mathbf{X} \, u_1, \psi\}$ is an atom, but the set $\{t_1, \neg u_1, \psi\}$ is not: by the first condition in the definition of an atom, either $\mathbf{X} \, u_1$ or $\neg \mathbf{X} \, u_1$ must belong to an atom (but not both).

Definition 8.8. *Let $\sigma = \mathbf{t}_1 \mathbf{t}_2 \mathbf{t}_3 \ldots$ be a ψ-history. For every $i \geq 0$, let a_i be the set of all formulas ϕ in the closure of ψ such that $\mathbf{t}_{i+1} \mathbf{t}_{i+2} \mathbf{t}_{i+3} \ldots \models \phi$. The* Hintikka sequence *of σ, denoted by $hin(\sigma)$, is the infinite sequence $a_0 \, a_1 \, a_2 \ldots$.*

Notice that for every $i \geq 0$ the set a_i of formulas has a model, and so it is an atom. So a Hintikka sequence is a sequence of atoms. Observe also the relation between $\pi_\psi(\sigma)$ and $hin(\sigma)$. Loosely speaking, the ith element of $\pi_\psi(\sigma)$ contains the elements of AP_ψ that hold after the occurrence of the first i transitions of σ. The ith element of $hin(\sigma)$ contains not only those elements, but all the formulas in the closure of ψ that hold at that point.

Example 8.9. Let $\psi = t_1 \, \mathbf{U} \, (\neg \mathbf{X} \, u_1)$, and consider the history $\sigma = \mathbf{a} \, \mathbf{c} \, (\mathbf{b} \, \mathbf{a})^\omega$ of the product of Fig. 8.1. We have

$$\pi(\sigma) = \langle t_1, u_1 \rangle \, \langle t_1, u_2 \rangle \, (\, \langle t_2, u_2 \rangle \, \langle t_2, u_1 \rangle \,)^\omega.$$

In order to obtain the Hintikka sequence, we start with $\pi_\psi(\sigma)$ and transform its elements into subsets of AP_ψ. Abusing notation, we also call the result $\pi_\psi(\sigma)$:

$$\pi_\psi(\sigma) = \langle t_1, u_1 \rangle \, \langle t_1, \bot \rangle \, (\, \langle \bot, \bot \rangle \, \langle \bot, u_1 \rangle \,)^\omega$$

$$= \{t_1, u_1\} \, \{t_1\} \, (\quad \emptyset \quad \{u_1\} \,)^\omega.$$

We now add to each set of atomic propositions the other formulas of the closure of ψ that hold at that point. For instance, we add to $\{t_1, u_1\}$ the formulas ψ' from the closure of ψ such that $\langle t_1, u_1 \rangle \langle t_1, \bot \rangle (\langle \bot, \bot \rangle \langle \bot, u_1 \rangle)^\omega \models \psi'$, and to $\langle t_1, \bot \rangle$ the formulas ψ'' such that $\langle t_1, \bot \rangle (\langle \bot, \bot \rangle \langle \bot, u_1 \rangle)^\omega \models \psi''$. We have

$$hin(\sigma) = \{t_1, u_1, \neg \mathbf{X}\, u_1, \psi\} \qquad \{t_1, \neg u_1, \neg \mathbf{X}\, u_1, \psi\}$$
$$(\{\neg t_1, \neg u_1, \mathbf{X}\, u_1, \neg \psi\} \{\neg t_1, u_1, \neg \mathbf{X}\, u_1, \psi\})^\omega.$$

Notation 4. *In what follows, we continue abusing notation and identifying a ψ-state $\langle r_1, \ldots, r_n \rangle$ with the set $\{r_1, \ldots, r_n\} \setminus \{\bot\}$. With this convention, if $\mathbf{r}_i$ and a_i are the ith elements of $\pi_\psi(\sigma)$ and $hin(\sigma)$, respectively, then we have $\mathbf{r}_i = a_i \cap AP_\psi$.*

Characterizing Hintikka Sequences

We obtain an alternative, more syntactic, characterization of the Hintikka sequences of the ψ-histories that satisfy ψ, i.e., of the set $\{hin(\sigma) \mid \sigma \models \psi\}$.

For this, let σ be a ψ-history such that $\sigma \models \psi$, and let $hin(\sigma) = a_0\, a_1\, a_2 \ldots$. We enumerate properties satisfied by $a_0\, a_1\, a_2 \ldots$ until we reach a point at which the conjunction of these conditions is not only necessary but also sufficient. We mean by this that every other sequence $a_0'\, a_1'\, a_2' \ldots$ satisfying the same conditions must be the Hintikka sequence of some ψ-history σ' satisfying ψ.

By the definition of the Hintikka sequence, the atom a_0 contains all the subformulas ψ' of ψ such that $\sigma \models \psi'$. Since $\sigma \models \psi$, we have that, in particular:

(1) a_0 contains ψ.

Since σ is a ψ-history, the atom a_0 is the one corresponding to the initial ψ-state of $\mathbf{A}$, and so:

(2) $(a_0 \cap AP_\psi) = \mathbf{is}_\psi = (\mathbf{is} \cap AP_\psi)$.

For all $i \geq 0$, the two consecutive atoms $a_i\, a_{i+1}$ of a Hintikka sequence must satisfy additional conditions. The first one handles next operators:

(3) For every formula $\mathbf{X}\, \psi_1$ in the closure of ψ, a_i contains $\mathbf{X}\, \psi_1$ if and only if a_{i+1} contains ψ_1.

The next condition is related to the until operator and is a consequence of the following fundamental equivalence law of LTL:

$$\psi_1 \mathbf{U} \psi_2 \equiv \psi_2 \vee (\psi_1 \wedge \mathbf{X} (\psi_1 \mathbf{U} \psi_2)) \tag{8.1}$$

(where $\equiv$ denotes logical equivalence). Intuitively, this means that $\psi_1 \mathbf{U} \psi_2$ holds now if and only if it is either the case that ψ_2 holds now, or ψ_1 holds now and $\psi_1 \mathbf{U} \psi_2$ holds at the next time instant. It follows that for all $i \geq 0$ every pair $a_i a_{i+1}$ of consecutive atoms of a Hintikka sequence must also satisfy:

(4) For every formula $\psi_1 \mathbf{U} \psi_2$ in the closure of ψ, a_i contains $\psi_1 \mathbf{U} \psi_2$ if and only if either a_i contains ψ_2, or a_i contains ψ_1 and a_{i+1} contains $\psi_1 \mathbf{U} \psi_2$.

Conditions (1)–(4) are not yet sufficient for a sequence to be a Hintikka sequence, as shown by the following example.

Example 8.10. Consider the product of Fig. 8.1 and let $\psi = u_1 \mathbf{U} u_2$. We have $AP_\psi = \{u_1, u_2\}$. The sequence of atoms $(\{u_1, \neg u_2, u_1 \mathbf{U} u_2\})^\omega$ satisfies (1)–(4). However, it is not a Hintikka sequence. The reason is that if an atom of a Hintikka sequence contains the formula $u_1 \mathbf{U} u_2$, then, by the semantics of until formulas, u_2 must hold at some later point, and so some later atom must contain u_2. Loosely speaking the formula $u_1 \mathbf{U} u_2$ "promises" that eventually u_2 will hold, and the sequence above keeps "delaying" the promise for ever.

So we add a new condition:

(5) For every formula $\psi_1 \mathbf{U} \psi_2$ in the closure of ψ and for every $i \geq 0$, if a_i contains $\psi_1 \mathbf{U} \psi_2$ then there is an index $j \geq i$ such that a_j contains ψ_2.

Observe that conditions (1)–(4) are local, while condition (5) is global, i.e., in order to check it we need to examine arbitrarily large "windows" of the sequence of atoms.

We still have a last problem to solve.

Example 8.11. Consider the product of Fig. 8.1 and let $\psi = u_1 \mathbf{U} t_2$. The sequence

$$\{u_1, \neg t_2, u_1 \mathbf{U} t_2\} (\{\neg u_1, t_2, u_1 \mathbf{U} t_2\})^\omega$$

is a sequence of atoms satisfying (1)–(5). However, no ψ-history σ exists such that $\pi_\psi(\sigma)$ is equal to this sequence of atoms. Intuitively, the reason is that no global transition of **A** can "transform" the first atom of the sequence into the second. For that, the global transition should make the second component leave the state u_1, and should also make the first component enter the state t_2. Formally, there should be a global transition **t** such that $\langle \langle \bot, u_1 \rangle, \mathbf{t}, \langle t_2, \bot \rangle \rangle$ is a ψ-step. But no such transition exists.

So every two consecutive atoms a_i, a_{i+1} have to be consistent with some ψ-step, meaning that there is a ψ-step $\langle \mathbf{r}_i, \mathbf{t}_{i+1}, \mathbf{r}_{i+1} \rangle$ consistent with it:

(6) For every $i \geq 0$: there exists a global transition $\mathbf{t}_{i+1}$ such that $\langle \mathbf{r}_i, \mathbf{t}_{i+1}, \mathbf{r}_{i+1} \rangle$ is a ψ-step, where $\mathbf{r}_i = a_i \cap AP_\psi$ and $\mathbf{r}_{i+1} = a_{i+1} \cap AP_\psi$.

We have now gathered enough conditions and present the following result without proof:

Proposition 8.12. *An infinite sequence of atoms is a Hintikka sequence for a formula ψ if and only if it satisfies conditions (1)–(6).*

The Generalized Büchi Tester

We now more formally show how to make from the definition of Hintikka sequences a Büchi tester for a particular product of transition systems **A**. After this we will also show how condition (5) mentioned above is handled with acceptance sets. We define a generalized Büchi tester $\mathcal{GT}_\psi = \langle \mathcal{B}_\psi, \{F_0, \ldots, F_{k-1}\}, \lambda_\psi \rangle$ of a product of transition systems **A** and prove that it tests the formula ψ. We first define the transition system $\mathcal{B}_\psi$ and the labeling function λ_ψ.

- The states of $\mathcal{B}_\psi$ consist of all the atoms together with a special state is_ψ, which is also the initial state of the tester.
- The set of transitions of $\mathcal{B}_\psi$ contains:
  - A transition for every global transition $\mathbf{t}_i$ and every pair $a_i\, a_{i+1}$ of states which together satisfy the conditions (3)–(4), (6). The source and target of the transition are a_i and a_{i+1}, respectively, and the transition is labeled by $\mathbf{t}_i$.
  - To connect the initial state to the rest of the tester: A transition for every global transition $\mathbf{t}_i$ and every pair $a_i\, a_{i+1}$ of states which together satisfy the conditions (3)–(4), (6) and a_i also satisfies (1)–(2). The source and target of the transition are is_ψ and a_{i+1}, respectively, and the transition is labeled by $\mathbf{t}_i$.

It remains to choose sets $F_0, \ldots, F_{k-1}$ of accepting states in such a way that the histories of $\mathcal{B}_\psi$ that visit each of $F_0, \ldots, F_{k-1}$ infinitely often satisfy condition (5). This is not difficult. Let $\psi_0 \,\mathbf{U}\, \psi'_0, \ldots, \psi_{k-1} \,\mathbf{U}\, \psi'_{k-1}$ be the **U**-subformulas of ψ. For every $i \in \{0, \ldots k-1\}$, define F_i as follows:

- F_i contains the states a such that $\psi_i \,\mathbf{U}\, \psi'_i \notin a$ or $\psi'_i \in a$.

Proposition 8.13. *An infinite history $\sigma = \mathbf{t}_1\,\mathbf{t}_2\,\mathbf{t}_3 \ldots$ of **A** satisfies conditions (1)–(6) if and only if it is recognized by $\mathcal{GT}_\psi$.*

Putting together this proposition and Prop. 8.12 we get:

Corollary 8.14. *An infinite history $\sigma = \mathbf{t}_1\,\mathbf{t}_2\,\mathbf{t}_3 \ldots$ of **A** satisfies ψ if and only if $\mathcal{GT}_\psi$ recognizes σ.*

Example 8.15. Figure 8.3 shows the tester of the product of Fig. 8.1 for the formula $\psi = \mathbf{F}\,(u_1 \wedge \mathbf{X}\,u_1)$. Notice that u_1 holds in the initial state. We have $\psi = \mathbf{F}\,(u_1 \wedge \mathbf{X}\,u_1) \equiv (u_1 \vee \neg u_1)\,\mathbf{U}\,(u_1 \wedge \mathbf{X}\,u_1)$. Thus we get $cl(\psi) = \{u_1, \neg u_1, u_1 \vee \neg u_1, \neg(u_1 \vee \neg u_1), \mathbf{X}\,u_1, \neg\mathbf{X}\,u_1, u_1 \wedge \mathbf{X}\,u_1, \neg(u_1 \wedge \mathbf{X}\,u_1), (u_1 \vee \neg u_1)\,\mathbf{U}\,(u_1 \wedge \mathbf{X}\,u_1), \neg((u_1 \vee \neg u_1)\,\mathbf{U}\,(u_1 \wedge \mathbf{X}\,u_1))\}$. By analyzing the formula further, we get that $u_1 \vee \neg u_1$ holds in all atoms, and whether $u_1 \wedge \mathbf{X}\,u_1$ holds in an atom or not is fully determined by whether u_1 and $\mathbf{X}\,u_1$ hold in the same atom. Thus, the contents of each atom is fully determined by whether any of the following three formulas hold or not: $\{u_1, \mathbf{X}\,u_1, (u_1 \vee \neg u_1)\,\mathbf{U}\,(u_1 \wedge \mathbf{X}\,u_1)\}$. We now obtain a tester by restricting our attention to those atoms that are reachable from the initial state of the tester by the transition relation of the tester defined above.

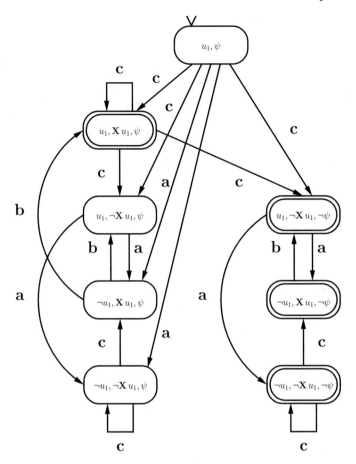

Fig. 8.3. A tester of the product of Fig. 8.1 for $\mathbf{F}(u_1 \wedge \mathbf{X}\, u_1)$

From Generalized Büchi Testers to Büchi Testers

It is easy to see that for every generalized Büchi tester there is a Büchi tester
that recognizes the same language. This is a well known construction (see,
e.g., [26]). Intuitively, the transition system of the Büchi tester consists of k
copies of the transition system of the generalized Büchi tester, one for each
set of accepting states. The transitions are chosen so that the Büchi tester
stays in the ith copy until it hits a state of F_i; when this happens, instead
of moving to a successor state in the ith copy it moves to the corresponding
state in the $(i+1)$th copy modulo k. The accepting states are the states in
the first copy of the set F_0. The Büchi tester so defined satisfies the following
property: between two visits to states of the first copy of F_0 there must be a
visit to the second copy of F_1, to the third copy of F_2, and so forth.

8.4 Model Checking with Testers: A First Attempt

We define a synchronization of a tester and product in which the tester observes all global transitions of the product. We show that this synchronization reduces the model checking problem to the repeated executability problem.

It is convenient to introduce some notation. Given a global transition $\mathbf{t} = \langle t_1, \ldots, t_n \rangle$ of $\mathbf{A}$ and a transition u of a tester $\mathcal{BT}$, we use $\langle \mathbf{t}, u \rangle$ as an abbreviation of the tuple $\langle t_1, \ldots, t_n, u \rangle$. Similarly, given a global state $\mathbf{s} = \langle s_1, \ldots, s_n \rangle$ of $\mathbf{A}$ and a state r of $\mathcal{BT}$, we abbreviate $\langle s_1, \ldots, s_n, r \rangle$ to $\langle \mathbf{s}, r \rangle$.

Definition 8.16. *Let $\mathcal{BT} = (\mathcal{B}, F, \lambda)$ be a tester. The* full synchronization *of* $\mathbf{A}$ *and* $\mathcal{BT}$ *is the product* $\mathbf{A} \| \mathcal{BT} = \langle \mathcal{A}_1, \ldots \mathcal{A}_n, \mathcal{B}, \mathbf{U} \rangle$, *where the synchronization constraint* $\mathbf{U}$ *contains a global transition* $\langle \mathbf{t}, u \rangle$ *for every global transition* $\mathbf{t}$ *of* $\mathbf{A}$ *and every transition* u *of* $\mathcal{BT}$ *such that* $\lambda(u) = \mathbf{t}$.

Given a sequence $\sigma = \langle \mathbf{t}_1, u_1 \rangle \langle \mathbf{t}_2, u_2 \rangle \langle \mathbf{t}_3, u_3 \rangle \ldots$ of transitions of $\mathbf{A} \| \mathcal{BT}$, we call $\sigma_{\mathcal{A}} = \mathbf{t}_1 \mathbf{t}_2 \mathbf{t}_3 \ldots$ the *projection of σ on* $\mathbf{A}$, and $\sigma_{\mathcal{BT}} = u_1 u_2 u_3 \ldots$ the *projection of σ on* $\mathcal{BT}$. It follows immediately from the definition of full synchronization that σ is a history of $\mathbf{A} \| \mathcal{BT}$ if and only if $\sigma_{\mathcal{A}}$ and $\sigma_{\mathcal{BT}}$ are histories of $\mathbf{A}$ and $\mathcal{BT}$, respectively. We say that σ *visits accepting states infinitely often* if there are infinitely many indices $i \geq 1$ such that the target state of the transition u_i is an accepting state of $\mathcal{BT}$.

Proposition 8.17. *Let $\mathcal{BT}_{\neg \psi}$ be a tester for $\neg \psi$. A history of $\mathbf{A}$ violates ψ if and only if it is the projection on $\mathbf{A}$ of an infinite history of $\mathbf{A} \| \mathcal{BT}_{\neg \psi}$ that visits accepting states infinitely often.*

Proof. Recall that a history of $\mathbf{A}$ violates ψ if and only if it satisfies $\neg \psi$, and so if and only if it is recognized by $\mathcal{BT}_{\neg \psi}$. So it suffices to show that a history of $\mathbf{A}$ is recognized by $\mathcal{BT}$ if and only if it is the projection on $\mathbf{A}$ of an infinite history of $\mathbf{A} \| \mathcal{BT}$ that visits accepting states infinitely often.

If $\mathcal{BT}$ recognizes an infinite history $\mathbf{t}_1 \mathbf{t}_2 \ldots$ of $\mathbf{A}$, then there is an infinite history $u_1 u_2 u_3 \ldots$ of $\mathcal{BT}$ such that $\mathbf{t}_i = \lambda(u_i)$ for every $i \geq 1$ and $u_1 u_2 u_3 \ldots$ visits accepting states of $\mathcal{BT}$ infinitely often. By the definition of $\mathbf{A} \| \mathcal{BT}$, we have $\langle \mathbf{t}_i, u_i \rangle \in \mathbf{U}$ for every $i \geq 1$. It follows that the sequence $\langle \mathbf{t}_1, u_1 \rangle \langle \mathbf{t}_2, u_2 \rangle \ldots$ is an infinite history of $\mathbf{A} \| \mathcal{BT}$, that visits accepting states infinitely often.

Conversely, assume that some infinite history $\mathbf{h} = \langle \mathbf{t}_1, u_1 \rangle \langle \mathbf{t}_2, u_2 \rangle \ldots$ of $\mathbf{A} \| \mathcal{BT}$ visits accepting states infinitely often. Since $\mathbf{h}$ is a history of $\mathbf{A} \| \mathcal{BT}$, its projection on $\mathbf{A}$ is a history of $\mathbf{A}$. By the definition of $\mathbf{U}$, we have $\mathbf{t}_i \in \lambda(u_i)$ for every $i \geq 1$, and the target state of u_i is an accepting state of $\mathcal{BT}$ for infinitely many $i \geq 1$. It follows that $\mathcal{BT}$ recognizes $\mathbf{h}$. $\qquad\square$

Example 8.18. Consider the transition system $\mathcal{A}$ shown in Fig. 8.4. Suppose we want to check whether $\mathcal{A}$ satisfies $\psi_1 = \mathbf{F}(u_1 \wedge \mathbf{X} u_1)$, i.e., whether all global histories of $\mathcal{A}$ eventually contain two consecutive time steps in which $\mathcal{A}$ is in state u_1. A Büchi tester $\mathcal{BT}_{\neg\psi_1} = \mathcal{BT}_{\mathbf{G}\,(u_1 \Rightarrow \mathbf{X}\,\neg u_1)}$ is shown in Fig. 8.5. Note that this tester is much simpler than the tester of Fig. 8.3 for two reasons: first of all there are no invisible transitions in Fig 8.4, and secondly the extra initial state has been optimized away while still preserving the language accepted by the tester. The full synchronization of the transition system of Fig. 8.4 and the tester of Fig. 8.5, namely $\mathcal{A} \,\|\, \mathcal{BT}_{\neg\psi_1}$, is in Fig. 8.6. The full synchronization $\mathcal{A} \,\|\, \mathcal{BT}_{\neg\psi_1}$ has an infinite history $(\langle a, t_1\rangle \langle b, t_2\rangle)^{\omega}$, and thus the infinite history $(ab)^{\omega}$ of $\mathcal{A}$ violates ψ.

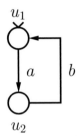

Fig. 8.4. A transition system $\mathcal{A}$ under LTL model checking

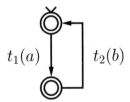

Fig. 8.5. A tester of the transition system of Fig. 8.4 for $\mathbf{G}\,(u_1 \Rightarrow \mathbf{X}\,\neg u_1)$

Proposition 8.17 allows us to reduce the model checking problem to the repeated executability problem. Recall that in the repeated executability problem we check if there exists an infinite history that executes global transitions from a set $\mathbf{R}$ infinitely often. In contrast, in order to apply Prop. 8.17 we have to check if the history visits accepting states infinitely often. To reduce the latter to the former, it suffices to choose the set $\mathbf{R}$ so that it contains the global transitions whose occurrence leads to an accepting state.

Theorem 8.19. *Let $\mathbf{A}$ be a product and let ψ be a property of LTL. Let $\mathcal{BT}_{\neg\psi}$ be a tester for $\neg\psi$. Let $\mathbf{R}$ be the set of global transitions $\langle \mathbf{t}, u\rangle$ of $\mathbf{A} \,\|\, \mathcal{BT}_{\neg\psi}$ such that the target state of u is an accepting state of $\mathcal{BT}_{\neg\psi}$. $\mathbf{A}$ satisfies ψ if and only if the answer to the instance of the repeated executability problem given by $\mathbf{A} \,\|\, \mathcal{BT}_{\neg\psi}$ and $\mathbf{R}$ is negative.*

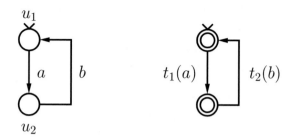

$$\mathbf{U} = \{\mathbf{a} = \langle a, t_1\rangle, \mathbf{b} = \langle b, t_2\rangle\}$$

Fig. 8.6. Full synchronization of the tester of Fig. 8.5 with the transition system of Fig. 8.4

Proof. By Prop. 8.17 $\mathbf{A}$ violates ψ if and only if some infinite history $\mathbf{h}$ of $\mathbf{A} \parallel \mathcal{BT}_{\neg\psi}$ visits accepting states infinitely often. This is the case if and only if the projection of $\mathbf{h}$ on $\mathcal{BT}_{\neg\psi}$ is an infinite history of $\mathcal{BT}_{\neg\psi}$ containing infinitely many transitions whose target state is an accepting state of $\mathcal{BT}_{\neg\psi}$. Finally, this is the case if and only if $\mathbf{h}$ contains infinitely many occurrences of global transitions of $\mathbf{R}$. $\square$

While this approach is perfectly sensible when $\mathcal{A}$ only has one component, it has a serious problem for general products when used with the unfolding method. To understand why, we take a closer look at the definition of full synchronization (Def. 8.16). Recall that $\langle \mathbf{t}, u\rangle$ if and only if $\mathbf{t} \in \mathbf{T}$, $u \neq \epsilon$, and $\mathbf{t} \in \lambda(u)$. In particular, it follows that $\mathcal{BT}_{\neg\psi}$ participates in *all* global transitions of $\mathbf{A} \parallel \mathcal{BT}_{\neg\psi}$. But, in this case, the final prefix of $\mathbf{A} \parallel \mathcal{BT}_{\neg\psi}$ does not contain any pair of concurrent events, and so the unfolding method does not present any advantage over exploring all the global states of the product.

8.5 Stuttering Synchronization

The solution to the problem above is to replace the full synchronization by a "less intrusive" synchronization, in which the tester does not participate in all global transitions. This approach, which is the subject of this section, comes at a price (not very high, as we shall see): it only works for the stuttering-invariant fragment of LTL.

Definition 8.20. *Two infinite words $\pi, \pi' \in (2^{AP})^\omega$ are stuttering equivalent if there are two infinite sequences of positive integers $0 = i_0 < i_1 < i_2 < \dots$ and $0 = j_0 < j_1 < j_2 < \dots$ such that for every $k \geq 0$:*

$$\pi_{(i_k)} = \pi_{(i_k+1)} = \dots = \pi_{(i_{(k+1)}-1)} = \pi'_{(j_k)} = \pi'_{(j_k+1)} = \dots = \pi'_{(j_{(k+1)}-1)} \, .$$

A formula ψ of LTL is stuttering-invariant *if $\pi \models \psi$ implies $\pi' \models \psi$ for every two stuttering equivalent words π, π'.*

Loosely speaking, two stuttering equivalent words can be divided into blocks of letters whose starting points are at indexes $i_0, i_1, i_2, \ldots$ for π and at indexes $j_0, j_1, j_2, \ldots$ for π' such that for every $k \geq 0$ the blocks starting at i_k and j_k consist of repetitions or "stutterings" of the same alphabet letter. A formula is stuttering equivalent if it is "insensitive" to the length of these blocks: a word satisfies the formula if and only if every other word stuttering equivalent to it satisfies the formula.

Example 8.21. Formulas like $\mathbf{F}p$ and $p\,\mathbf{U}\,q$ are stuttering-invariant. Loosely speaking, they promise that something will eventually happen, but do not specify when, which makes them insensitive to stuttering. On the contrary, the formula $\mathbf{X}p$ is not stuttering-invariant, since we have $\emptyset\,(\{p\})^\omega \models \mathbf{X}p$, but $\emptyset\,\emptyset\,(\{p\})^\omega \not\models \mathbf{X}p$.

In the tester approach, full synchronization is essentially unavoidable if we wish to check properties that are not stuttering-invariant. Intuitively, testers for properties that are not stuttering-invariant need to "count" the number of occurrences of global transitions up to a finite number. For instance, in order to decide if the property $(\mathbf{X})^k p$ holds, where $(\mathbf{X})^k$ denotes the concatenation of k "next" operators, the tester has to be able to determine the moment at which $\mathbf{A}$ has executed exactly k global transitions. For this it needs to synchronize with all global transitions of the product that may occur during the first k steps of a computation.

Stuttering-invariant properties play a very prominent role in formal verification. Lamport has famously argued that every sensible LTL specification must be stuttering-invariant (see Bibliographical Notes at the end of this chapter). The reason is that whether a property holds or not should not depend on the "granularity" of the system. It is very difficult to agree on what is a step of a system; what looks like a step at a level of abstraction becomes a series of steps at the next level. Therefore, a property like "the system will react after at most five steps" makes little sense in many situations and should be replaced by "the system will eventually react".

The stuttering-invariant fragment of LTL is the set of LTL formulas that are stuttering-invariant. It is easy to prove by structural induction that $\mathbf{X}$-free formulas are stuttering-invariant. Moreover, Wilke and Peled have proved in [100] that every stuttering-invariant formula is equivalent to some $\mathbf{X}$-free formula. So the stuttering-invariant fragment can be replaced by the fragment of $\mathbf{X}$-free formulas, denoted by LTL-X, without loss of expressive power.

Let us now consider our particular context, in which the set of atomic propositions AP is the set of local states of all components.

Definition 8.22. *A* global transition $\mathbf{t}$ *is* stuttering *w.r.t. ψ (or just stuttering, when ψ is clear from the context) if $AP_\psi \cap {}^\bullet\mathbf{t} = AP_\psi \cap \mathbf{t}^\bullet$, where AP_ψ is the set of atomic propositions that occur in ψ.*

Observe that if $\mathbf{t}$ is stuttering then $\mathcal{S} = (\mathcal{S} \setminus {}^\bullet\mathbf{t}) \cup \mathbf{t}^\bullet$ holds for every $\mathcal{S} \subseteq AP_\psi$. Intuitively, the occurrence of a stuttering transition does not change the values of the atomic propositions that appear in ψ. The *non-stuttering projection* of a sequence σ of global transitions is the sequence obtained by removing all occurrences of stuttering transitions from σ.

The following proposition follows easily from the definitions:

Proposition 8.23. *Let ψ be a stuttering-invariant formula, and let σ, σ' be two infinite sequences of global transitions having the same non-stuttering projection. Then $\sigma \models \psi$ if and only if $\sigma' \models \psi$.*

Proof. Let $\sigma = \mathbf{t}_1 \mathbf{t}_2 \mathbf{t}_3 \ldots$ and $\sigma' = \mathbf{t}_1' \mathbf{t}_2' \mathbf{t}_3' \ldots$. Define an infinite increasing sequence of positive integers as follows. If the non-stuttering projection of σ is an infinite sequence $\mathbf{t}_{i_1} \mathbf{t}_{i_2} \mathbf{t}_{i_3} \ldots$, then take the sequence $0 = i_0 < i_1 < i_2 < i_3 < \ldots$. If it is a finite sequence $\mathbf{t}_{i_1} \mathbf{t}_{i_2} \ldots \mathbf{t}_{i_k}$, then take $0 = i_0 < i_1 < \ldots < i_k < i_{k+1} < i_{k+2} \ldots$ where $i_{k+l} = i_k + l$ for every $l \geq 1$. Define the sequence $0 = j_0 < j_1 < j_2 < j_3 \ldots$ analogously, taking the sequence σ' instead of σ.

Consider the sequences $\pi(\sigma) = \mathcal{S}_0 \mathcal{S}_1 \mathcal{S}_2 \ldots$ and $\pi(\sigma') = \mathcal{S}_0' \mathcal{S}_1' \mathcal{S}_2' \ldots$. We prove by induction on k that

$$\mathcal{S}_{i_k} = \mathcal{S}_{i_k+1} = \ldots = \mathcal{S}_{i_{k+1}-1} = \mathcal{S}_{j_k}' = \mathcal{S}_{j_k+1}' = \ldots = \mathcal{S}_{j_{k+1}-1}'.$$

For the induction basis, let $k = 0$. We have $\mathcal{S}_0 = \mathcal{S}_0'$ by definition of $\pi(\sigma)$ and $\pi(\sigma')$. The chains of equalities $\mathcal{S}_{i_0} = \mathcal{S}_{i_0+1} = \ldots = \mathcal{S}_{i_1-1}$ and $\mathcal{S}_{j_0}' = \mathcal{S}_{j_0+1}' = \ldots = \mathcal{S}_{j_1-1}'$ follow from the fact that that the sequence $\mathbf{t}_1 \ldots \mathbf{t}_{i_1-1}$ only contains stuttering transitions. For the induction step, let $k > 0$. By induction hypothesis we have $\mathcal{S}_{i_k-1} = \mathcal{S}_{j_k-1}'$. We first prove $\mathcal{S}_{i_k} = \mathcal{S}_{j_k}'$. By definition of $\pi(\sigma)$ and $\pi(\sigma')$ we have

$$\mathcal{S}_{i_k} = (\mathcal{S}_{i_k-1} \setminus {}^\bullet\mathbf{t}_{i_k}) \cup \mathbf{t}_{i_k}^\bullet \text{ and } \mathcal{S}_{j_k}' = (\mathcal{S}_{j_k-1}' \setminus {}^\bullet\mathbf{t}_{j_k}) \cup \mathbf{t}_{j_k}^\bullet.$$

Then, since σ and σ' have the same non-stuttering projection, we have $\mathbf{t}_{i_k} = \mathbf{t}_{j_k}$ and so $\mathcal{S}_{i_k} = \mathcal{S}_{j_k}'$. As in the base case, the chains of equalities $\mathcal{S}_{i_k} = \mathcal{S}_{i_k+1} = \ldots = \mathcal{S}_{i_{k+1}-1}$ and $\mathcal{S}_{j_k}' = \mathcal{S}_{j_k+1}' = \ldots = \mathcal{S}_{j_{k+1}-1}'$ follow from the fact that that the sequence $\mathbf{t}_{i_k+1} \ldots \mathbf{t}_{i_{k+1}-1}$ only contains stuttering transitions. $\square$

We are now ready to define a new notion of synchronization between a tester for a stuttering-invariant property and a product.

Definition 8.24. *Let $\mathcal{BT}_\psi = (\mathcal{B}_\psi, F_\psi, \lambda_\psi)$ be a tester for a stuttering-invariant formula ψ. The stuttering synchronization of $\mathbf{A}$ and $\mathcal{BT}_\psi$ is the product $\mathbf{A} \|^s \mathcal{BT}_\psi = \langle \mathcal{A}_1, \ldots \mathcal{A}_n, \mathcal{B}_\psi, \mathbf{U} \rangle$, where the synchronization constraint $\mathbf{U}$ contains:*

- *a transition $\langle \mathbf{t}, u \rangle$ for every non-stuttering transition $\mathbf{t}$ of $\mathbf{A}$ and every transition u of $\mathcal{BT}_\psi$ such that $\mathbf{t} = \lambda(u)$; and*

- *a transition* $\langle \mathbf{t}, \epsilon \rangle$ *for every stuttering transition* $\mathbf{t}$ *of* $\mathbf{A}$.

A transition $\langle \mathbf{t}, u \rangle$ of $\mathbf{A} \,\|^s\, \mathcal{BT}_\psi$ is stuttering if $\mathbf{t}$ is stuttering or, equivalently, if $u = \epsilon$.

Intuitively, the tester in a stuttering synchronization only observes the non-stuttering transitions executed by the product. All others occur "silently", without the knowledge of the tester. This motivates the following definition:

Definition 8.25. *An infinite history of* $\mathbf{A}$ *is* recurrent *if it contains infinitely many occurrences of non-stuttering transitions. An infinite history of the stuttering synchronization* $\mathbf{A} \,\|^s\, \mathcal{BT}_{\neg\psi}$ *is* recurrent *if its projection on* $\mathbf{A}$ *is recurrent or, equivalently, if the tester participates in infinitely many transitions.*

We will now show that Prop. 8.17 still holds for recurrent histories.

Proposition 8.26. *Let* ψ *be a stuttering-invariant formula of LTL and let* $\mathcal{BT}_{\neg\psi}$ *be a tester for* $\neg\psi$. *A recurrent infinite history of* $\mathbf{A}$ *violates* ψ *if and only if it is the projection on* $\mathbf{A}$ *of an infinite history of* $\mathbf{A} \,\|^s\, \mathcal{BT}_{\neg\psi}$ *that visits accepting states infinitely often.*

Proof. ($\Rightarrow$): Let $\mathbf{t}_1 \mathbf{t}_2 \mathbf{t}_3 \ldots$ be a recurrent infinite history of $\mathbf{A}$ that violates ψ. Let $\mathbf{t}_{i_1} \mathbf{t}_{i_2} \mathbf{t}_{i_3} \ldots$ be the sequence obtained by removing all occurrences of stuttering transitions from $\mathbf{t}_1 \mathbf{t}_2 \mathbf{t}_3 \ldots$. By Prop. 8.23, and since ψ is stuttering-invariant, $\mathbf{t}_{i_1} \mathbf{t}_{i_2} \mathbf{t}_{i_3} \ldots$ also violates ψ, and so it is recognized by $\mathcal{BT}_{\neg\psi}$. So there is a history $u_1 u_2 u_3 \ldots$ of $\mathcal{BT}_{\neg\psi}$ that visits accepting states of $\mathcal{BT}_{\neg\psi}$ infinitely often and satisfies $\mathbf{t}_{i_j} = \lambda(u_j)$ for every $j \geq 1$. By the definition of stuttering synchronization, the sequence $\mathbf{c}_1 \mathbf{c}_2 \mathbf{c}_3 \ldots$ given by

$$\mathbf{c}_1 = \langle \mathbf{t}_1, \epsilon \rangle \langle \mathbf{t}_2, \epsilon \rangle \ldots \langle \mathbf{t}_{i_1 - 1}, \epsilon \rangle \langle \mathbf{t}_{i_1}, u_1 \rangle, \text{ and}$$
$$\mathbf{c}_j = \langle \mathbf{t}_{i_j + 1}, \epsilon \rangle \langle \mathbf{t}_{i_j + 2}, \epsilon \rangle \ldots \langle \mathbf{t}_{i_{j+1} - 1}, \epsilon \rangle \langle \mathbf{t}_{i_{j+1}}, u_j \rangle \text{ for every } j > 1,$$

is a sequence of global transitions of $\mathbf{A} \,\|^s\, \mathcal{BT}_{\neg\psi}$. Moreover, since $\mathbf{t}_1 \mathbf{t}_2 \mathbf{t}_3 \ldots$ is a history of $\mathbf{A}$ and $u_1 u_2 u_3 \ldots$ is a history of $\mathcal{BT}_{\neg\psi}$, we have that $\mathbf{c}_1 \mathbf{c}_2 \mathbf{c}_3 \ldots$ is a history of $\mathbf{A} \,\|^s\, \mathcal{BT}_{\neg\psi}$ that visits accepting states infinitely often. Since $\mathbf{t}_1 \mathbf{t}_2 \mathbf{t}_3 \ldots$ is the projection of $\mathbf{c}_1 \mathbf{c}_2 \mathbf{c}_3 \ldots$ on $\mathbf{A}$, we are done.

($\Leftarrow$): Let $\mathbf{h} = \langle \mathbf{t}_1, u_1 \rangle \langle \mathbf{t}_2, u_2 \rangle \langle \mathbf{t}_3, u_3 \rangle \ldots$ be an infinite history of $\mathbf{A} \,\|^s\, \mathcal{BT}_{\neg\psi}$ that visits accepting states infinitely often (here $\mathbf{t}_i$ is a global transition of $\mathbf{A}$, and u_i is a transition of either $\mathcal{BT}$ or ϵ). We prove that $\mathbf{h}_\mathbf{A} = \mathbf{t}_1 \mathbf{t}_2 \mathbf{t}_3 \ldots$ violates ψ.

Let $\langle \mathbf{t}_{i_1}, u_{i_1} \rangle \langle \mathbf{t}_{i_2}, u_{i_2} \rangle \langle \mathbf{t}_{i_3}, u_{i_3} \rangle \ldots$ be the subsequence of $\mathbf{h}$ containing all transitions $\langle \mathbf{t}_i, u_i \rangle$ such that $u_i \neq \epsilon$. By the definition of $\mathbf{A} \,\|^s\, \mathcal{BT}_{\neg\psi}$, the sequence $u_{i_1} u_{i_2} u_{i_3} \ldots$ is a history of $\mathcal{BT}_{\neg\psi}$ (the tester only "moves" when $u_i \neq \epsilon$). Since $\mathbf{h}$ visits accepting states infinitely often, so does $u_{i_1} u_{i_2} u_{i_3} \ldots$. It follows that $\mathcal{BT}_{\neg\psi}$ recognizes the sequence $\mathbf{t}_{i_1} \mathbf{t}_{i_2} \mathbf{t}_{i_3} \ldots$, and so $\mathbf{t}_{i_1} \mathbf{t}_{i_2} \mathbf{t}_{i_3} \ldots$ violates ψ. By the definition of stuttering synchronization, $\mathbf{t}_i$ is non-stuttering if and only if $u_i \neq \epsilon$. So $\mathbf{t}_{i_1} \mathbf{t}_{i_2} \mathbf{t}_{i_3} \ldots$ is the non-stuttering projection of $\mathbf{h}_\mathbf{A}$

and, in particular, $\mathbf{h_A}$ and $\mathbf{t}_{i_1}\mathbf{t}_{i_2}\mathbf{t}_{i_3}\ldots$ are stuttering equivalent. Since ψ is stuttering-invariant, $\mathbf{h_A}$ violates ψ (Prop. 8.23).   □

Consider now the case of non-recurrent histories. If an infinite history $\mathbf{h}'$ of $\mathbf{A} \|^s \mathcal{BT}_{\neg\psi}$ is non-recurrent, then it can be split into a minimal length prefix $\mathbf{h}$ and a suffix $\mathbf{c}$ that starts at the smallest index i such that $\mathbf{c} = \langle\mathbf{t}_i,\epsilon\rangle\,\langle\mathbf{t}_{i+1},\epsilon\rangle\,\langle\mathbf{t}_{i+2},\epsilon\rangle\ldots$ contains only stuttering transitions. Let $\langle\mathbf{s},q\rangle$ be the global state reached by $\mathbf{h}'$ after executing $\mathbf{h}$, i.e., right before the execution of $\langle\mathbf{t}_i,\epsilon\rangle$. The key intuition is that we can detect whether $\mathbf{h}'$ violates ψ by looking at the tester's state q reached after executing $\mathbf{h}$. Prop. 8.28 proves that it suffices to check whether, loosely speaking, $\mathcal{BT}$ with q as initial state recognizes some infinite sequence of $\mathbf{A}$ containing only stuttering transitions. The intuition is that all such sequences are "indistinguishable"; if the tester recognizes any of them it will also recognize $\mathbf{c}$.

Definition 8.27. *A state q of $\mathcal{BT}$ is* stutter-accepting *if some computation starting at q visits accepting states infinitely often and contains only transitions of $\mathcal{BT}$ labeled by stuttering transitions of $\mathbf{A}$.*

Proposition 8.28. *Let ψ be a stuttering-invariant formula of LTL and let $\mathcal{BT}_{\neg\psi}$ be a tester for $\neg\psi$. A non-recurrent infinite history of $\mathbf{A}$ violates ψ if and only if it is the projection on $\mathbf{A}$ of an infinite history $\mathbf{h}' = \mathbf{h}\,\mathbf{c}$ (split into $\mathbf{h}$ and $\mathbf{c}$ as described above) of $\mathbf{A} \|^s \mathcal{BT}_{\neg\psi}$ satisfying the following properties:*

- *the tester's state reached by the occurrence of $\mathbf{h}$ is stutter-accepting; and*
- *$\mathbf{c}$ contains only stuttering transitions.*

Proof. ($\Rightarrow$): Let $\mathbf{t}_1\,\mathbf{t}_2\,\mathbf{t}_3\,\ldots$ be an infinite non-recurrent history of $\mathbf{A}$ that violates ψ. By Prop. 8.17, $\mathbf{t}_1\,\mathbf{t}_2\,\mathbf{t}_3\,\ldots$ is the projection on $\mathbf{A}$ of an infinite history $\langle\mathbf{t}_1,u_1\rangle\,\langle\mathbf{t}_2,u_2\rangle\,\langle\mathbf{t}_3,u_3\rangle\ldots$ of $\mathbf{A}\,\|\,\mathcal{BT}_{\neg\psi}$ (the full synchronization of $\mathbf{A}$ and $\mathcal{BT}_{\neg\psi}$) that visits accepting states infinitely often. Moreover, by the definition of full synchronization we have

$$\lambda(u_1 u_2 u_3 \ldots) = \lambda(u_1)\lambda(u_2)\lambda(u_3)\ldots = \mathbf{t}_1\,\mathbf{t}_2\,\mathbf{t}_3\,\ldots\,.$$

Notice, however, that $\langle\mathbf{t}_1,u_1\rangle\,\langle\mathbf{t}_2,u_2\rangle\,\langle\mathbf{t}_3,u_3\rangle\ldots$ need not be a history of $\mathbf{A}\,\|^s\,\mathcal{BT}_{\neg\psi}$.

Since $\mathbf{t}_1\,\mathbf{t}_2\,\mathbf{t}_3\,\ldots$ is non-recurrent, it has a finite non-stuttering projection $\mathbf{t}_{i_1}\,\mathbf{t}_{i_2}\ldots\mathbf{t}_{i_k}$, and so the following two infinite sequences $\lambda(u_1 u_2 u_3 \ldots)$ and $\lambda(u_{i_1} u_{i_2} \ldots u_{i_k} u_{i_k+1} u_{i_k+2} \ldots)$ are stuttering equivalent. Since $\lambda(u_1 u_2 u_3 \ldots) = \mathbf{t}_1\,\mathbf{t}_2\,\mathbf{t}_3\,\ldots$ and $\mathbf{t}_1\,\mathbf{t}_2\,\mathbf{t}_3\,\ldots$ violates ψ and ψ is stuttering-invariant, the sequence $\lambda(u_{i_1} u_{i_2} \ldots u_{i_k} u_{i_k+1} u_{i_k+2} \ldots)$ violates ψ too, and is recognized by the tester $\mathcal{BT}_{\neg\psi}$. So $\mathcal{BT}_{\neg\psi}$ has a history $v_1 v_2 v_3 \ldots$ that visits accepting states infinitely often and satisfies $\lambda(v_1 v_2 v_3 \ldots) = \lambda(u_{i_1} u_{i_2} \ldots u_{i_k} u_{i_k+1} u_{i_k+2} \ldots)$. Define

$$\mathbf{h} = \langle\mathbf{t}_1,\epsilon\rangle \ldots \langle\mathbf{t}_{i_1-1},\epsilon\rangle\,\langle\mathbf{t}_{i_1},v_1\rangle$$
$$\langle\mathbf{t}_{i_1+1},\epsilon\rangle \ldots \langle\mathbf{t}_{i_2-1},\epsilon\rangle\,\langle\mathbf{t}_{i_2},v_2\rangle$$
$$\ldots$$
$$\langle\mathbf{t}_{i_{(k-1)}+1},\epsilon\rangle \ldots \langle\mathbf{t}_{i_k-1},\epsilon\rangle\,\langle\mathbf{t}_{i_k},v_k\rangle\,, \text{ and}$$
$$\mathbf{c} = \langle\mathbf{t}_{i_k+1},\epsilon\rangle\,\langle\mathbf{t}_{i_k+2},\epsilon\rangle\,\langle\mathbf{t}_{i_k+3},\epsilon\rangle\,\ldots\,.$$

By the definition of stuttering synchronization, $\mathbf{hc}$ is a history of $\mathbf{A} \parallel^s \mathcal{BT}_{\neg\psi}$ and, by construction, $\mathbf{c}$ contains only stuttering transitions. Consider now the state of the tester reached by the execution of $\mathbf{h}_{\mathcal{BT}_{\neg\psi}} = v_1 \ldots v_k$. Since $v_1 v_2 v_3 \ldots$ visits accepting states infinitely often, $\lambda(v_{k+j}) = \mathbf{t}_{i_k+j}$ for every $j > 0$, and since $\mathbf{t}_{i_k+j}$ is stuttering for every $j > 0$, the state is stutter-accepting.

($\Leftarrow$): Let $\mathbf{h} = \langle \mathbf{t}_1, u_1 \rangle \langle \mathbf{t}_2, u_2 \rangle \ldots \langle \mathbf{t}_k, u_k \rangle$ and let $\mathbf{c} = \langle \mathbf{t}_{k+1}, \epsilon \rangle \langle \mathbf{t}_{k+2}, \epsilon \rangle \ldots$ be sequences satisfying the properties. We show that the projection of $\mathbf{hc}$ on $\mathbf{A}$ violates ψ.

Let $\langle \mathbf{s}, q \rangle$ be the state of $\mathbf{A} \parallel^s \mathcal{BT}_{\neg\psi}$ reached after the occurrence of $\mathbf{h}$. Since q is stutter-accepting, some computation $v_1 v_2 v_3 \ldots$ of $\mathcal{BT}_{\neg\psi}$ visits accepting states infinitely often. So $u_1 \ldots u_k v_1 v_2 v_3 \ldots$ is an infinite history of $\mathcal{BT}_{\neg\psi}$ that visits accepting states infinitely often, which implies that $\lambda(u_1 \ldots u_k v_1 v_2 v_3 \ldots)$ violates ψ. Since the projection of $\mathbf{hc}$ on $\mathbf{A}$ is stuttering equivalent to $\lambda(u_1 \ldots u_k v_1 v_2 v_3 \ldots)$, it violates ψ as well. $\qquad\square$

Propositions 8.26 and 8.28 allow us to reduce the model checking problem for stuttering-invariant properties to instances of the repeated executability *and* the livelock problems. Recall that an instance of the livelock problem consists of a product with a distinguished subset $\mathbf{V}$ of visible transitions, and an even more distinguished subset $\mathbf{L}$ of visible transitions called livelock monitors. A livelock is a history $\mathbf{htc}$ such that $\mathbf{t}$ is a livelock monitor and $\mathbf{c}$ is an infinite computation containing only invisible transitions. The reduction declares the non-stuttering transitions visible, and the stuttering transitions invisible. The livelock monitors are defined as the non-stuttering transitions whose occurrence leaves the tester in a stutter-accepting state. In this way, after the occurrence of the livelock monitor the product can execute an infinite computation of stuttering transitions, and the tester can execute an infinite computation that visits accepting states infinitely often and is labeled by stuttering transitions only.

However, we still have to solve a small problem. If the initial state of the tester happens to be stutter-accepting, then in the history $\mathbf{hc}$ the finite history $\mathbf{h}$ may be empty. In this case no livelock monitor leaves the tester in a stutter-accepting state, because the tester is in such a state from the very beginning! This technical problem can be solved by instrumenting $\mathbf{A} \parallel^s \mathcal{BT}_{\neg\psi}$:

Definition 8.29. *The* instrumentation *of* $\mathbf{A} \parallel^s \mathcal{BT}_{\neg\psi}$*, which we denote by* $\mathcal{I}(\mathbf{A} \parallel^s \mathcal{BT}_{\neg\psi})$*, is obtained by*

- *adding to each component* $\mathcal{A}_i$ *of* $\mathbf{A}$ *a new initial state* is_i' *and a new transition* it_i *leading from* is_i' *to the old initial state* is_i*;*
- *adding to* $\mathcal{BT}_\psi$ *a new initial state* $is_{\mathcal{BT}}'$ *and a new transition* $it_{\mathcal{BT}}$ *leading from* $is_{\mathcal{BT}}'$ *to the old initial state* $is_{\mathcal{BT}}$*; and*
- *adding to the synchronization constraint a new transition* $\langle \mathbf{it}, it_{\mathcal{BT}} \rangle$*, where* $\mathbf{it} = \langle it_1, it_2, \ldots, it_n \rangle$*.*

We can now state and prove the desired theorem.

Theorem 8.30. *Let* **A** *be a product and let* ψ *be a stuttering-invariant property of LTL. Let* $\mathcal{BT}_{\neg\psi}$ *be a tester for* $\neg\psi$. *Define:*

- **V** *as the set containing the non-stuttering transitions of* $\mathcal{I}(\mathbf{A} \,\|^s \mathcal{BT}_{\neg\psi})$ *and the transition* $\langle \mathbf{it}, it_{\mathcal{BT}} \rangle$; *and*
- **R** *and* **L** *as the subsets of* **V** *containing those transitions* $\langle \mathbf{t}, u \rangle$ *such that the target state of* u *is, respectively, an accepting state and a stutter-accepting state of* $\mathcal{BT}_{\neg\psi}$.

A *satisfies* ψ *if and only if the answers to*

- *the instance of the repeated executability problem given by* $\mathcal{I}(\mathbf{A} \,\|^s \mathcal{BT}_{\neg\psi})$ *and* **R**; *and*
- *the instance of the livelock problem given by* $\mathcal{I}(\mathbf{A} \,\|^s \mathcal{BT}_{\neg\psi})$, **V**, *and* **L**

are both negative.

Proof. ($\Rightarrow$): We prove the contrapositive. If the answer to the repeated executability problem is positive, then $\mathcal{I}(\mathbf{A} \,\|^s \mathcal{BT}_{\neg\psi})$ has an infinite history containing infinitely many occurrences of transitions of **R**. After removing the first transition from this sequence, we get a history of $\mathbf{A} \,\|^s \mathcal{BT}_{\neg\psi}$. By the definition of **R**, this history visits accepting states infinitely often. By Prop. 8.26, some (recurrent) history of **A** violates ψ.

If the answer to the livelock problem is positive, then $\mathcal{I}(\mathbf{A} \,\|^s \mathcal{BT}_{\neg\psi})$ has an infinite history $\mathbf{h\,t\,c}$ such that $\mathbf{t}$ is a livelock monitor and $\mathbf{c}$ contains only invisible transitions. By the definition of a livelock monitor, the state of the tester reached after the execution of $\mathbf{t}$ is stutter-accepting. By the definition of **V**, the computation $\mathbf{c}$ contains only stuttering transitions. By Prop. 8.28, some (non-recurrent) history of **A** violates ψ.

($\Leftarrow$): We prove the contrapositive. If some recurrent history of **A** violates ψ, then, by Prop. 8.26 and the definition of instrumentation, $\mathcal{I}(\mathbf{A} \,\|^s \mathcal{BT}_{\neg\psi})$ has a history that visits accepting states infinitely often. By the definition of **R**, the answer to the repeated executability problem is positive. If some non-recurrent history of **A** violates ψ, then, by Prop. 8.28, $\mathbf{A} \,\|^s \mathcal{BT}_{\neg\psi}$ has a history $\mathbf{h\,c}$ such that $\mathbf{c}$ contains only stuttering transitions and the state of the tester reached after the occurrence of $\mathbf{h}$ is stutter-accepting. By the definition of the instrumentation, $(\langle \mathbf{it}, it_{\mathcal{BT}} \rangle \, \mathbf{h\,c})$ is a history of $\mathcal{I}(\mathbf{A} \,\|^s \mathcal{BT}_{\neg\psi})$. If $\mathbf{h}$ is non-empty, then its last transition is a livelock monitor. If $\mathbf{h}$ is empty, then the initial state is is stutter-accepting and, by the definition of **L**, the transition $\langle \mathbf{it}, it_{\mathcal{BT}} \rangle$ is a livelock monitor. In both cases, the answer to the livelock problem is positive. $\qquad\square$

Theorem 8.30 reduces the model checking problem for stuttering-invariant formulas to the repeated executability and the livelock problems, for which we have given algorithms in the previous chapters. To see that this is the case, notice that the visibility constraint defined in the beginning of Sect. 7.2

is satisfied, as the tester participates in all visible global transitions of the stuttering synchronization. In order to obtain a model checking algorithm we still have to show how to compute the set of stutter-accepting states of $\mathcal{BT}$. The next proposition shows that this is a simple task.

Proposition 8.31. *The set of stutter-accepting states of $\mathcal{BT}$ can be computed in linear time in the size of product $\mathbf{A} \|^s \mathcal{BT}_{\neg\psi}$.*

Proof. Whether a given transition of $\mathbf{A}$ is stuttering or not can be easily checked by inspecting its source and target states (Def. 8.22), and takes only linear time in the size of $\mathbf{A}$. Let $\mathcal{BT}'$ be the result of removing from $\mathcal{BT}$ all transitions u whose label $\lambda(u)$ is a non-stuttering transition of $\mathbf{A}$. By the definition of stutter-accepting, we have to compute the states q of $\mathcal{BT}'$ such that some computation of $\mathcal{BT}'$ starting at q visits accepting states infinitely often. A way to do this in linear time is to proceed in two steps:

(1) compute the strongly connected components of $\mathcal{BT}'$ that contain at least one accepting state and at least one edge whose both source and destination states belong to the component; and
(2) return the states from which any of these components can be reached by a path of $\mathcal{BT}'$.

The algorithm is clearly correct. Step (1) can be performed in linear time using Tarjan's algorithm (see, e.g., [114]), while step (2) can be performed by means of a backward search starting at the states computed in (1).   □

Example 8.32. Consider the product of transition systems $\mathbf{A}$ in Fig. 8.7. We want to check whether the LTL formula $\psi = \mathbf{F}\,\mathbf{G}\,(\neg u_2)$ holds in $\mathbf{A}$. Since $AP_\psi = \{u_2\}$, a global transition $\mathbf{t}$ is stuttering if $\{u_2\} \cap {}^\bullet\mathbf{t} = \{u_2\} \cap \mathbf{t}^\bullet$ (Def. 8.22). So the stuttering transitions are $\mathbf{a}_1, \mathbf{a}_2, \mathbf{a}_3$, and $\mathbf{b}$.

In order to check ψ we create a Büchi tester $\mathcal{BT}_{\neg\psi} = \mathcal{BT}_{\mathbf{G}\,\mathbf{F}\,(u_2)}$, depicted in Fig. 8.8.[3] In order to further simplify the figure we have used some conventions. By $d(\tau)$ we mean that the tester has four transitions $d(\mathbf{a}_1), d(\mathbf{a}_2), d(\mathbf{a}_3)$, and $d(\mathbf{b})$, labeled with $\mathbf{a}_1, \mathbf{a}_2, \mathbf{a}_3$, and $\mathbf{b}$, respectively. Similarly for $f(\tau)$. The transitions $e(\mathbf{a}_4)$ and $g(\mathbf{a}_4)$ are labeled by $\mathbf{a}_4$. Since the transitions $f(\tau)$ are labeled by stuttering transitions of the product, v_2 is also stutter-accepting The tester accepts all infinite histories of $\mathbf{A}$ which visit infinitely many global states at which u_2 holds.

The stuttering synchronization of $\mathbf{A}$ and $\mathcal{BT}_{\neg\psi}$ is a product $\mathbf{P}$, whose Petri net representation is shown in Fig. 8.9 (some global transitions which can never occur have been removed from $\mathbf{P}$ to reduce clutter). The figure also shows the sets $\mathbf{R}$, $\mathbf{V}$, and $\mathbf{L}$ defined in Thm. 8.30. The set $\mathbf{V}$ contains the transition $\mathbf{i}$ and the non-stuttering transitions of $\mathbf{P}$, i.e., $\mathbf{a}_4$ and $\mathbf{c}$. Since v_2 is

---

[3] This tester is not the tester generated by the procedure described earlier, but an optimized one accepting the same language.

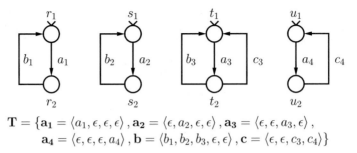

$$\mathbf{T} = \{\mathbf{a_1} = \langle a_1, \epsilon, \epsilon, \epsilon \rangle, \mathbf{a_2} = \langle \epsilon, a_2, \epsilon, \epsilon \rangle, \mathbf{a_3} = \langle \epsilon, \epsilon, a_3, \epsilon \rangle,$$
$$\mathbf{a_4} = \langle \epsilon, \epsilon, \epsilon, a_4 \rangle, \mathbf{b} = \langle b_1, b_2, b_3, \epsilon, \epsilon \rangle, \mathbf{c} = \langle \epsilon, \epsilon, c_3, c_4 \rangle\}$$

Fig. 8.7. A product of transition systems **A** under LTL model checking

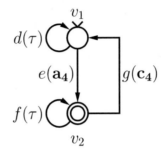

Fig. 8.8. Büchi tester of **A** for $\mathbf{G\,F}\,(u_2)$

the only accepting and stuttering-accepting state of the tester, the sets **R** and **L** coincide, and both contain the transition $\mathbf{a_4}$. Graphically, we signal that $\mathbf{a_4}$ belongs to **R** by drawing it with a double rectangle, and we signal that it belongs to **L** by coloring it light grey.

Notice that the transitions d and f of the tester do not produce any transition in the stuttering synchronization. However, it is because of f that v_2 is stutter-accepting, and that is the reason why $\mathbf{a_4}$ is added to **L**.

Figure 8.10 shows the final prefix for the repeated executability problem using the distributed size-lexicographic search strategy. Event 4 is a successful terminal having event 1 as companion. Terminal and companion correspond to the infinite global history $(\mathbf{a_4a_3c})^\omega$, which constitutes a counterexample to the property ψ.

Similarly, Fig. 8.11 shows the final prefix for the livelock problem using a variant of the distributed size-lexicographic strategy. Also this prefix contains a successful terminal, corresponding to the infinite global history $\mathbf{a_4(a_3a_2a_1b)}^\omega$ of **A**. This is a second counterexample to ψ.

Consider now the family $\mathbf{A_1}, \mathbf{A_2}, \dots$ of products defined as follows. The product $\mathbf{A_n}$ consists of $n-2$ transition systems like the one on the left of Fig. 8.7 and the two transition systems on the right of the same figure. Its global transitions are: $\mathbf{a_1}, \dots, \mathbf{a_n}$, where the ith component of $\mathbf{a_i}$ is a_i, and all other components are equal to ϵ; $\mathbf{b} = \langle b_1, \dots, b_{n-2}, \epsilon, \epsilon \rangle$; and

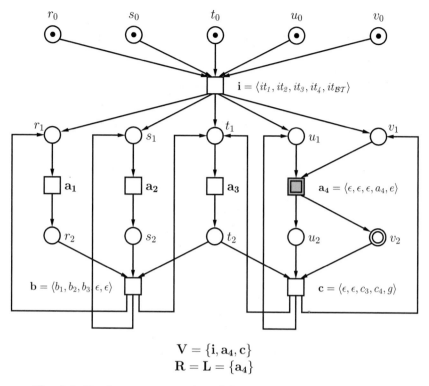

$$V = \{i, a_4, c\}$$
$$R = L = \{a_4\}$$

Fig. 8.9. Petri net representation of the stuttering synchronization **P**

$c = \{\epsilon, \dots, \epsilon, c_{n-1}, c_n\}$. The product of Fig. 8.7 is the element of the family corresponding to $n = 2$. The transitions $a_1, \dots, a_n$ of A_n are concurrent, and so A_n has more than 2^n reachable global states. A model checking approach based on the (naive) exploration of the interleaving semantics can take exponential time. On the other hand it is easy to see that, whatever the strategy, the final prefixes for the repeated reachability and the livelock problems only grow linearly in n.

Bibliographical Notes

Temporal logic was first studied in the area of mathematical logic, most prominently by Arthur Prior; see, e.g., [105]. Linear temporal logic (LTL) was suggested as a formalism for program specification by Pnueli [104]. The idea of using Büchi automata to check LTL specifications was developed by Vardi and Wolper in a series of papers (see [119] for an early reference and [120] for a more polished journal version). Our algorithm for transforming an LTL formula into a Büchi automaton is fairly primitive. Better ones can be found in [46, 44]. Lamport was the first to introduce the idea of invariance under

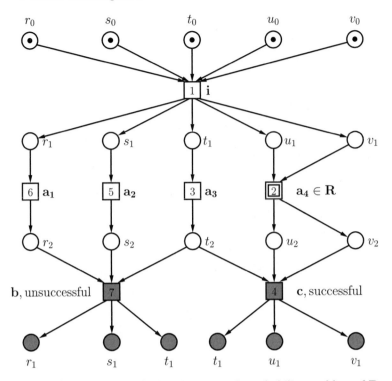

Fig. 8.10. The final prefix for the repeated reachability problem of **P**

stuttering and to explain why it is a vital for temporal logics [79]. Our discussion of stuttering equivalence uses notation adapted from [24].

The reduction of the model checking problem to the repeated executability and livelock problems was introduced in [35] and later refined in [37]. It is heavily based on ideas of Valmari on tester-based verification [117]; see also [62, 55, 82] for more recent work. Part of the motivation for using an approach in which testers are synchronized with the system and the result is unfolded, instead of directly unfolding the system, was the high complexity results obtained by the second author in [59]. The model checking algorithm has been parallelized and extended to high-level Petri nets by Schröter and Khomenko [110].

The design of unfolding-based model checking algorithms is a delicate and error prone task. In [33], the first author introduced an algorithm for a simple branching time logic. Unfortunately, the algorithm contains a flaw, which was later dealt with by Graves [52]. Some years later, another algorithm for LTL-X was presented by Wallner in [122]. Again, it contained a subtle mistake which could lead to an incorrect answer for certain formulas. Due to these experiences, we have presented the proofs of our results in detail.

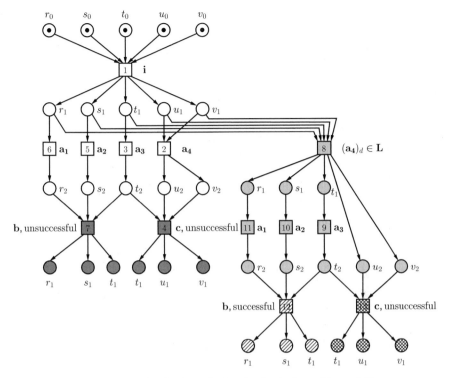

Fig. 8.11. The final prefix for the livelock problem of **P**

9

Summary, Applications, Extensions, and Tools

9.1 Looking Back: A Two-Page Summary of This Book

We have shown that unfoldings can be used as the basis of a model checking algorithm for products of transition systems and properties expressible in Linear Temporal Logic (LTL). In favorable cases (products with a high degree of concurrency) the algorithm only needs to construct very small prefixes of the unfolding, beating other algorithms based on the interleaving representation of the product.

The model checking algorithm has been presented following a bottom-up approach. First, algorithms for basic verification problems (executability, repeated executability, livelock), have been developed. Second, these algorithms have been combined to yield the model checker. In this section, with the benefit of hindsight, we summarize the main ideas behind the model checking algorithm, this time in a top-down fashion.

The model checking algorithm is based on the automata-theoretic approach. Given a property of LTL, we construct a tester (a Büchi automaton) accepting, loosely speaking, the behaviors of the product that violate the property. By fully synchronizing the tester and the product we can reduce the model checking problem to a repeated executability problem. Unfortunately, this synchronization destroys all the concurrency present in the product. Since the unfolding approach has no advantages for products exhibiting no concurrency, this idea does not work.

The way out is to let testers synchronize only with some of the transitions of the product, "destroying" as little concurrency as possible. However, there is collateral damage. First, since testers cannot know how many events occur between two events they have observed, they can only be used to check stuttering-invariant properties, and so we have to restrict ourselves to the fragment LTL-X. Second, since testers do not observe all transition occurrences, identifying runs that violate the property becomes more difficult. Given such a run, there are two possible cases: the tester observes infinitely many events of the run, or it observes only finitely many. In the first case, the tester has all the necessary information to declare a violation, and the model checking problem still reduces to a repeated reachability problem. In the second case, however, the following scenario is possible:

- After synchronizing with the product for the last time, the tester deduces that if the product continues to run forever, then it will violate the property. Loosely speaking after the last synchronization the tester *observes danger*.
- After synchronizing with the tester for the last time, the product (more precisely, some components of the product, not necessarily all) continues to run forever.

In this scenario, neither the tester nor the product has the necessary information to declare a violation. The tester knows there is danger, but, since it never synchronizes with the product again, it ignores that the product runs forever. The product knows it runs forever, but, since it never synchronizes with the tester again, it ignores that the tester has observed danger.

This problem is solved by changing the definition of the unfolding: whenever the tester observes danger, it synchronizes with all the components of the product to tell them the news. Thus, any component running forever can declare the violation. In this case, the model checking problem reduces to a livelock problem.

The repeated executability and livelock problems can be solved by means of search procedures. Search procedures consist of a search scheme and a search strategy. In the case of transition systems, search schemes exist that are sound, complete, and quadratic for all total strategies, where quadratic means that the number of events explored by the search grows at most quadratically in the number of global states of the product. This no longer holds for products. If a scheme is sound and complete for every total strategy, then there are strategies for which it is not quadratic. If a scheme is quadratic for every total strategy, then there are strategies for which it is not complete. However, some schemes are sound, complete, and quadratic for all total *adequate* strategies. We have identified some total adequate strategies.

While it is not directly needed for model checking of LTL-X, we have extensively studied the executability problem. In a nutshell, we have the same situation as for the repeated executability and livelock problems, but replacing quadratic by linear.

9.2 Some Experiments

The material of this book attacks some questions of the theory of concurrency which we think have intrinsic interest. In particular, we have presented some fundamental results about which search strategies lead to correct search procedures. However, at least equally important is whether the theory leads to more efficient verification algorithms in terms of time, space, or both. This question must be answered experimentally, and in fact many of the papers mentioned in the last chapters contain experimental sections [39, 41, 42, 56, 57, 58, 60, 61, 70, 71, 74, 85, 84, 86, 87, 88, 109, 110, 121] in which the performance of the unfolding technique is measured and compared with the performance of other techniques. In particular, [110] compares the performance of PUNF, an implementation of a model checking algorithm similar to the one described in this book, and the Spin model checker.

9.3 Some Applications

The unfolding technique can be seen as a general-purpose approach to the analysis and verification of concurrent systems. As such, it has been applied to analyze (models of) distributed algorithms, communication protocols, hardware and software systems, etc. There are two specific areas in which the unfolding technique seems to be particularly suitable:

- Analysis and synthesis of asynchronous logic circuits.
  Asynchronous circuits have no global clock. It is commonly agreed that they have important advantages, like absence of clock skew problems and low power consumption, but are notoriously difficult to design correctly. Signal transition graphs (STGs) are a popular formalism for specifying asynchronous circuits [25]. They are Petri nets in which the firing of a transition is interpreted as the rising or falling of a signal in the circuit. Not every STG can be implemented as a physical circuit. A central question related to implementability of an STG is whether it contains *state coding conflicts*. In a number of papers, a group at the University of Newcastle consisting of Alex Yakovlev, Maciej Koutny, and Victor Khomenko has developed an unfolding-based toolset which allows us to detect and solve these conflicts [74, 76, 75].
- Monitoring and diagnosis of discrete event systems.
  In the area of telecommunication networks and services, faults are often transient. When a fault occurs, sensors can detect problems caused by it and raise alarms. Alarms are collected by local supervisors having only partial knowledge of the system's structure. In order to repair a fault, it is first necessary to diagnose it. For this one constructs "correlation scenarios" showing which faults are compatible with the observed pattern of alarms. Unfoldings are an ideal tool for this task, since they keep information about causal relationship and spatial distribution. A group at INRIA Rennes led by Albert Benveniste and Claude Jard works on the development of unfolding-based techniques for monitoring and diagnosis of these systems [9, 10, 20].

9.4 Some Extensions

Petri nets and products of transition systems are fundamental and very simple models of concurrency, playing similar roles as finite automata or Turing machines in sequential computation. When modelling real systems it is convenient to add other features, which requires us to extend the definition of the unfolding, as well as the techniques to generate finite prefixes. Several such extensions have been studied in the literature, and we discuss briefly some of them.

- **Bounded Petri nets.**
  In this book we have considered Petri nets in which a place can contain at most one token. (This follows immediately from the fact that we defined markings as *sets* of places.) More generally, one can allow a place to contain a larger number of tokens, a *capacity*. Markings are then defined as *multisets* of places (or, equivalently, as mappings $M: P \to \mathbb{N}$, where P is the set of places). The transition rule must be modified accordingly. When a transition t occurs at a marking M, it no longer leads to the set-marking $M' = (M \setminus {}^\bullet t) \cup t^\bullet$, as defined in the book, but to the multiset-marking $M' = (M - {}^\bullet t) + t^\bullet$, where $+$ and $-$ denote multiset addition and multiset difference, respectively. The definition of the unfolding can be extended to nets with bounded capacity. Complete prefixes for this case have been discussed in numerous papers (see, e.g., [41]).

- **Unbounded Petri nets.**
  Petri nets can be further generalized by allowing a place to contain arbitrarily many tokens. Unbounded Petri nets may have infinitely many reachable markings. It is not difficult to define the unfolding of an unbounded net. However, for unbounded Petri nets the existence of finite complete prefixes is not guaranteed. Some properties of unbounded Petri nets can be checked by means of a clever backwards reachability algorithm based on the theory of well-quasi-orders [1]. In [2], Abdulla, Purushothaman Iyer, and Nylén use the unfolding technique to give a more efficient version of this algorithm for nets with a high degree of concurrency.

- **Petri nets with read arcs.**
  Read arcs are arcs connecting a place to a transition. Intuitively, the transition can only occur if the place carries a token, but its occurrence does not remove the token from the place. Read arcs are useful for modelling systems in which different agents can concurrently read the value of a variable, a register, or any other unit storing information. In [121], Vogler, Semenov, and Yakovlev define the unfolding of a Petri net with read arcs and show how to construct a complete prefix. The algorithm for the detection of terminal events is unfortunately more complicated. However, they also identify a class, called read-persistent nets, for which this additional complexity disappears. The class is of interest for modelling asynchronous circuits

- **High-level Petri nets**.
  In all the Petri net models discussed so far, tokens have no identity. For modelling purposes it is very convenient to allow tokens to carry data. This leads to *high-level* Petri net models, of which the most popular are Jensen's colored Petri nets [68]. The unfolding of a colored Petri net can be constructed by first expanding the colored net into a low-level net of the kind used in this book, and then unfolding this net. However, this procedure may be extremely inefficient: many of the transitions of the expansion (often a large majority) can never occur. These transitions are "dead wood" that delay the construction of the unfolding, but do not contribute to it. In some cases the low-level net can even be too large to fit into the memory of a high-end workstation, even though the unfolding itself is still quite manageable. In [110], Schröter and Khomenko have extended the model checking algorithm of this book to high-level nets. The algorithm constructs the necessary prefixes of the unfolding directly from the high-level Petri net, shortcutting the expansion to a low-level model.
- **Time Petri nets**.
  Time Petri nets are an extension of Petri nets with timing information with the goal of modelling concurrent real-time systems. In time Petri nets, each transition is associated with an earliest and a latest firing delay. Intuitively, each token is assigned a clock which starts to tick when the token is "born" (created by the firing of an input transition of the place the token lives in) and stops when it "dies" (consumed by the firing of an output transition). A transition can fire only if the age of all the tokens it consume lies in the interval determined by the earliest and the latest firing delays.[1] The processes of time Petri nets have been studied by Aura and Lilius in [5]. An algorithm for the construction of a complete prefix has been proposed by Chatain and Jard [22]. Another construction with a discrete-time semantics has been given by Fleischhack and Stehno [43].
- **Networks of timed automata**.
  Timed automata [3] are the most popular formal model of real-time systems. In a sense, networks of timed automata are to time Petri nets what products of transition systems are to Petri nets (there are many other important differences concerning the urgency of actions which are beyond the scope of this paper). Complete prefixes for networks of timed automata have been proposed by Bouyer, Haddad, and Reynier [16], and by Cassez, Chatain, and Jard [19].

---

[1] There are different dialects of time Petri nets in which this condition takes a slightly different form.

9.5 Some Tools

A number of tools concerning different aspects of the unfolding technique (unfolders, checkers) have been implemented. At the time of writing this book, the tools below are available online. We refrain from providing the URLs since these change very often. The tools should be easy to locate with the help of a search engine.

- **PEP**. The PEP tool (Programming Environment based on Petri Nets) is a comprehensive set of modelling, compilation, simulation, and verification components, linked together within a Tcl/Tk-based graphical user interface. The verification component includes an unfolder that generates a finite complete prefix of a given net. PEP 1.0 was developed at the group of Eike Best by a number of people coordinated by Eike Best and Bernd Grahlmann. At the time of writing the current version is PEP 2.0, maintained by Christian Stehno.

- **The Model Checking Kit**. The Model Checking Kit is a collection of programs which allow us to model a finite-state system using a variety of modelling languages, and verify it using a variety of checkers, including deadlock checkers, reachability checkers, and model checkers for the temporal logics CTL and LTL. It has a textual user interface. The Kit includes implementations of several unfolding-based verification algorithms. The tools of the Kit were contributed by different research groups. The Kit itself was designed and implemented by Claus Schröter and Stefan Schwoon.

- **Mole**. Developed by Stefan Schwoon, Mole is an overhaul of a former program by Stefan Römer. Mole constructs a complete prefix of a given Petri net using the search strategy described in [40]. The strategy is similar to the Parikh-lexicographic strategy. Mole is designed to be compatible with the tools in the PEP project and with the Model Checking Kit.

- **Unfsmodels**. A research prototype of an LTL-X model checker based on unfoldings using the approach presented in this book. The search for possible extensions is done using a tool to find stable models of logic programs called **smodels** [96]. Part of the functionality requires other tools, which may be difficult to find. Developed by the second author.

- **PUNF**. PUNF (Petri Net Unfolder) builds a finite and complete prefix of a safe Petri net. It is an efficient parallel implementation, and can be used both as a separate utility and as a part of the PEP tool. The prefixes generated by PUNF can be passed as input to the CLP model checker. Developed by Victor Khomenko.

- **CLP**. CLP (Checker based on Linear Programming) uses a finite complete prefix of a Petri net and can check deadlock-freeness and the reachability of a given marking. It can also check if there exists a reachable marking satisfying the given predicate. CLP can be used both as a separate utility and as a part of the PEP tool. CLP is developed by Victor Khomenko.

References

1. Parosh Aziz Abdulla, Karlis Cerans, Bengt Jonsson, and Yih-Kuen Tsay. Algorithmic analysis of programs with well quasi-ordered domains. *Information and Computation*, 160(1-2):109–127, 2000.
2. Parosh Aziz Abdulla, S. Purushothaman Iyer, and Aletta Nylén. Unfoldings of unbounded Petri nets. In E. Allen Emerson and A. Prasad Sistla, editors, *CAV*, volume 1855 of *Lecture Notes in Computer Science*, pages 495–507. Springer, 2000.
3. Rajeev Alur and David L. Dill. A theory of timed automata. *Theoretical Computer Science*, 126(2):183–235, 1994.
4. André Arnold. *Finite Transition Systems: Semantics of Communicating Systems*. Prentice Hall, 1994.
5. Tuomas Aura and Johan Lilius. A causal semantics for time Petri nets. *Theoretical Computer Science*, 243(1-2):409–447, 2000.
6. Paolo Baldan, Roberto Bruni, and Ugo Montanari. Pre-nets, read arcs and unfolding: A functorial presentation. In Martin Wirsing, Dirk Pattinson, and Rolf Hennicker, editors, *WADT*, volume 2755 of *Lecture Notes in Computer Science*, pages 145–164. Springer, 2002.
7. Paolo Baldan, Andrea Corradini, and Barbara König. Verifying finite-state graph grammars: An unfolding-based approach. In Philippa Gardner and Nobuko Yoshida, editors, *CONCUR*, volume 3170 of *Lecture Notes in Computer Science*, pages 83–98. Springer, 2004.
8. Paolo Baldan, Stefan Haar, and Barbara König. Distributed unfolding of Petri nets. In Luca Aceto and Anna Ingólfsdóttir, editors, *FoSSaCS*, volume 3921 of *Lecture Notes in Computer Science*, pages 126–141. Springer, 2006.
9. Albert Benveniste, Eric Fabre, Claude Jard, and Stefan Haar. Diagnosis of asynchronous discrete event systems, a net unfolding approach. *IEEE Transactions on Automatic Control*, 48(5):714–727, 2003.
10. Albert Benveniste, Stefan Haar, Eric Fabre, and Claude Jard. Distributed monitoring of concurrent and asynchronous systems. In Roberto M. Amadio and Denis Lugiez, editors, *CONCUR*, volume 2761 of *Lecture Notes in Computer Science*, pages 1–26. Springer, 2003.
11. Eike Best and Raymond R. Devillers. Sequential and concurrent behaviour in Petri net theory. *Theoretical Computer Science*, 55(1):87–136, 1987.

158   References

12. Eike Best and Javier Esparza. Model checking of persistent Petri nets. In Egon Börger, Gerhard Jäger, Hans Kleine Büning, and Michael M. Richter, editors, *CSL*, volume 626 of *Lecture Notes in Computer Science*, pages 35–52. Springer, 1991.

13. Eike Best and César Fernández. *Nonsequential Processes*. EATCS Monographs on Theoretical Computer Science. Springer, 1988.

14. Armin Biere, Cyrille Artho, and Viktor Schuppan. Liveness checking as safety checking. *Electronic Notes in Theoretical Computer Science*, 66(2), 2002.

15. Blai Bonet, Patrik Haslum, Sarah Hickmott, and Sylvie Thiébaux. Directed unfolding of Petri nets. In *Workshop on Unfolding and Partial Order Techniques (UFO) in 28th International Conference on Application and Theory of Petri Nets and Other Models of Concurrency*, 2007. To appear.

16. Patricia Bouyer, Serge Haddad, and Pierre-Alain Reynier. Timed unfoldings for networks of timed automata. In Graf and Zhang [50], pages 292–306.

17. Julian C. Bradfield and Colin Stirling. Local model checking for infinite state spaces. *Theoretical Computer Science*, 96(1):157–174, 1992.

18. Luboš Brim and Jiří Barnat. Tutorial: Parallel model checking. In Dragan Bosnacki and Stefan Edelkamp, editors, *SPIN*, volume 4595 of *Lecture Notes in Computer Science*, pages 2–3. Springer, 2007.

19. Franck Cassez, Thomas Chatain, and Claude Jard. Symbolic unfoldings for networks of timed automata. In Graf and Zhang [50], pages 307–321.

20. Thomas Chatain and Claude Jard. Symbolic diagnosis of partially observable concurrent systems. In David de Frutos-Escrig and Manuel Núñez, editors, *FORTE*, volume 3235 of *Lecture Notes in Computer Science*, pages 326–342. Springer, 2004.

21. Thomas Chatain and Claude Jard. Time supervision of concurrent systems using symbolic unfoldings of time Petri nets. In Paul Pettersson and Wang Yi, editors, *FORMATS*, volume 3829 of *Lecture Notes in Computer Science*, pages 196–210. Springer, 2005.

22. Thomas Chatain and Claude Jard. Complete finite prefixes of symbolic unfoldings of safe time Petri nets. In Susanna Donatelli and P. S. Thiagarajan, editors, *ICATPN*, volume 4024 of *Lecture Notes in Computer Science*, pages 125–145. Springer, 2006.

23. Thomas Chatain and Victor Khomenko. On the well-foundedness of adequate orders used for construction of complete unfolding prefixes. *Information Processing Letters*, 104(4):129–136, 2007.

24. Edmund M. Clarke, Orna Grumberg, and Doron Peled. *Model Checking*. The MIT Press, 1st edition, 1999.

25. Jordi Cortadella, Michael Kishinevsky, Alex Kondratyev, Luciano Lavagno, and Alexandre Yakovlev, editors. *Logic Synthesis of Asynchronous Controllers and Interfaces*. Number 8 in Springer Series in Advanced Microelectronics. Springer, 2002.

26. Costas Courcoubetis, Moshe Y. Vardi, Pierre Wolper, and Mihalis Yannakakis. Memory-efficient algorithms for the verification of temporal properties. *Formal Methods in System Design*, 1(2/3):275–288, 1992.

27. Jean-Michel Couvreur. On-the-fly verification of linear temporal logic. In Jeannette M. Wing, Jim Woodcock, and Jim Davies, editors, *World Congress on Formal Methods*, volume 1708 of *Lecture Notes in Computer Science*, pages 253–271. Springer, 1999.

28. Jean-Michel Couvreur, Sébastien Grivet, and Denis Poitrenaud. Designing an LTL model-checker based on unfolding graphs. In Mogens Nielsen and Dan Simpson, editors, *Proc. of ICATPN 2000*, LNCS 1825. Springer, 2000.

29. Jean-Michel Couvreur, Sébastien Grivet, and Denis Poitrenaud. Unfolding of products of symmetrical Petri nets. In José Manuel Colom and Maciej Koutny, editors, *ICATPN*, volume 2075 of *Lecture Notes in Computer Science*, pages 121–143. Springer, 2001.

30. Jörg Desel and Wolfgang Reisig. Place/Transition Petri nets. In Reisig and Rozenberg [106], pages 122–173.

31. Volker Diekert and Grzegorz Rozenberg, editors. *The Book of Traces*. World Scientific Publishing Co., Inc., 1995.

32. Joost Engelfriet. Branching processes of Petri nets. *Acta Informatica*, 28:575–591, 1991.

33. Javier Esparza. Model checking using net unfoldings. *Science of Computer Programming*, 23:151–195, 1994.

34. Javier Esparza. Decidability and complexity of Petri net problems - An introduction. In Reisig and Rozenberg [106], pages 374–428.

35. Javier Esparza and Keijo Heljanko. A new unfolding approach to LTL model checking. In Ugo Montanari, José D. P. Rolim, and Emo Welzl, editors, *ICALP*, volume 1853 of *Lecture Notes in Computer Science*, pages 475–486. Springer, 2000.

36. Javier Esparza and Keijo Heljanko. A new unfolding approach to LTL model checking. Series A: Research Report 60, Helsinki University of Technology, Laboratory for Theoretical Computer Science, Espoo, Finland, April 2000.

37. Javier Esparza and Keijo Heljanko. Implementing LTL model checking with net unfoldings. In Matthew B. Dwyer, editor, *SPIN*, volume 2057 of *Lecture Notes in Computer Science*, pages 37–56. Springer, 2001.

38. Javier Esparza, Pradeep Kanade, and Stefan Schwoon. A note on depth-first unfoldings. *International Journal on Software Tools for Technology Transfer (STTT)*, 2007. To appear, Online First DOI 10.1007/s10009-007-0030-5.

39. Javier Esparza and Stefan Römer. An unfolding algorithm for synchronous products of transition systems. In Jos C. M. Baeten and Sjouke Mauw, editors, *CONCUR*, volume 1664 of *Lecture Notes in Computer Science*, pages 2–20. Springer, 1999.

40. Javier Esparza, Stefan Römer, and Walter Vogler. An improvement of McMillan's unfolding algorithm. In Tiziana Margaria and Bernhard Steffen, editors, *TACAS*, volume 1055 of *Lecture Notes in Computer Science*, pages 87–106. Springer, 1996.

41. Javier Esparza, Stefan Römer, and Walter Vogler. An improvement of McMillan's unfolding algorithm. *Formal Methods in System Design*, 20(3):285–310, 2002.

42. Javier Esparza and Claus Schröter. Reachability analysis using net unfoldings. In *Proceeding of the Workshop Concurrency, Specification & Programming 2000, volume II of Informatik-Bericht 140*, pages 255–270. Humboldt-Universität zu Berlin, 2000.

43. Hans Fleischhack and Christian Stehno. Computing a finite prefix of a time Petri net. In Javier Esparza and Charles Lakos, editors, *ICATPN*, volume 2360 of *Lecture Notes in Computer Science*, pages 163–181. Springer, 2002.

44. Paul Gastin and Denis Oddoux. Fast LTL to Büchi automata translation. In Gérard Berry, Hubert Comon, and Alain Finkel, editors, *CAV*, volume 2102 of *Lecture Notes in Computer Science*, pages 53–65. Springer, 2001.

45. Jaco Geldenhuys and Antti Valmari. More efficient on-the-fly LTL verification with Tarjan's algorithm. *Theoretical Computer Science*, 345(1):60–82, 2005.

46. Rob Gerth, Doron Peled, Moshe Y. Vardi, and Pierre Wolper. Simple on-the-fly automatic verification of linear temporal logic. In Piotr Dembinski and Marek Sredniawa, editors, *PSTV*, volume 38 of *IFIP Conference Proceedings*, pages 3–18. Chapman & Hall, 1995.

47. Patrice Godefroid. *Partial-Order Methods for the Verification of Concurrent Systems – An Approach to the State-Explosion Problem*. Springer, 1996. Volume 1032 of *Lecture Notes in Computer Science*.

48. Patrice Godefroid and Pierre Wolper. Using partial orders for the efficient verification of deadlock freedom and safety properties. *Formal Methods in System Design*, 2(2):149–164, 1993.

49. Ursula Goltz and Wolfgang Reisig. The non-sequential behaviour of Petri nets. *Information and Control*, 57(2/3):125–147, 1983.

50. Susanne Graf and Wenhui Zhang, editors. *Automated Technology for Verification and Analysis, 4th International Symposium, ATVA 2006, Beijing, China, October 23-26, 2006*, volume 4218 of *Lecture Notes in Computer Science*. Springer, 2006.

51. Bernd Grahlmann. The PEP tool. In Grumberg [53], pages 440–443.

52. Burkhard Graves. Computing reachability properties hidden in finite net unfoldings. In S. Ramesh and G. Sivakumar, editors, *FSTTCS*, volume 1346 of *Lecture Notes in Computer Science*, pages 327–341. Springer, 1997.

53. Orna Grumberg, editor. *Computer Aided Verification, 9th International Conference, CAV '97, Haifa, Israel, June 22-25, 1997, Proceedings*, volume 1254 of *Lecture Notes in Computer Science*. Springer, 1997.

54. Henri Hansen. *Alternatives to Büchi automata*. PhD thesis, Tampere University of Technology, Department of Information Technology, Tampere, Finland, 2007.

55. Henri Hansen, Wojciech Penczek, and Antti Valmari. Stuttering-insensitive automata for on-the-fly detection of livelock properties. *Electronic Notes in Theoretical Computer Science*, 66(2), 2002.

56. Keijo Heljanko. *Deadlock and Reachability Checking with Finite Complete Prefixes*. Licentiate's thesis, Helsinki University of Technology, Department of Computer Science and Engineering, 1999. Also available as: Series A: Research Report 56, Helsinki University of Technology, Department of Computer Science and Engineering, Laboratory for Theoretical Computer Science.

57. Keijo Heljanko. Minimizing finite complete prefixes. In Hans-Dieter Burkhard, Ludwik Czaja, Sinh Hoa Nguyen, and Peter Starke, editors, *Proceedings of the Workshop Concurrency, Specification & Programming 1999*, pages 83–95, Warsaw, Poland, September 1999. Warsaw University.

58. Keijo Heljanko. Using logic programs with stable model semantics to solve deadlock and reachability problems for 1-safe Petri nets. *Fundamenta Informaticae*, 37(3):247–268, 1999.

59. Keijo Heljanko. Model checking with finite complete prefixes is PSPACE-complete. In Palamidessi [97], pages 108–122.

60. Keijo Heljanko. *Combining Symbolic and Partial Order Methods for Model Checking 1-Safe Petri Nets*. Doctoral thesis, Helsinki University of Technology, Department of Computer Science and Engineering, 2002. Also available as: Series A: Research Report 71, Helsinki University of Technology, Department of Computer Science and Engineering, Laboratory for Theoretical Computer Science.

61. Keijo Heljanko, Victor Khomenko, and Maciej Koutny. Parallelisation of the Petri net unfolding algorithm. In Joost-Pieter Katoen and Perdita Stevens, editors, *TACAS*, volume 2280 of *Lecture Notes in Computer Science*, pages 371–385. Springer, 2002.

62. Juhana Helovuo and Antti Valmari. Checking for CFFD-preorder with tester processes. In Susanne Graf and Michael I. Schwartzbach, editors, *TACAS*, volume 1785 of *Lecture Notes in Computer Science*, pages 283–298. Springer, 2000.

63. Graham Higman. Ordering by divisibility in abstract algebras. *Proceedings of the London Mathematical Society*, 3(2):326–336, 1952.

64. C. A. R. Hoare. *Communicating Sequential Processes*. Prentice Hall, 1985.

65. Gerard J. Holzmann. *The Spin Model Checker: Primer and Reference Manual*. Addison-Wesley, 2003.

66. Gerard J. Holzmann, Doron A. Peled, and Mihalis Yannakakis. On nested depth first search. In *2nd SPIN Workshop*, pages 23–32, 1996.

67. Ryszard Janicki and Maciej Koutny. Semantics of inhibitor nets. *Information and Computation*, 123(1):1–16, 1995.

68. Kurt Jensen. *Coloured Petri Nets. Basic Concepts, Analysis Methods and Practical Use, Volumes I-III*. EATCS Monographs in Theoretical Computer Science. Springer, 1997.

69. Victor Khomenko. *Model Checking Based on Prefixes of Petri Net Unfoldings*. PhD thesis, School of Computing Science, Newcastle University, 2003. British Lending Library DSC stock location number: DXN061636.

70. Victor Khomenko and Maciej Koutny. LP deadlock checking using partial order dependencies. In Palamidessi [97], pages 410–425.

71. Victor Khomenko and Maciej Koutny. Towards an efficient algorithm for unfolding Petri nets. In Larsen and Nielsen [81], pages 366–380.

72. Victor Khomenko and Maciej Koutny. Branching processes of high-level Petri nets. In Hubert Garavel and John Hatcliff, editors, *TACAS*, volume 2619 of *Lecture Notes in Computer Science*, pages 458–472. Springer, 2003.

73. Victor Khomenko, Maciej Koutny, and Walter Vogler. Canonical prefixes of Petri net unfoldings. *Acta Informatica*, 40(2):95–118, 2003.

74. Victor Khomenko, Maciej Koutny, and Alexandre Yakovlev. Detecting state encoding conflicts in STG unfoldings using SAT. *Fundamenta Informaticae*, 62(2):221–241, 2004.

75. Victor Khomenko, Maciej Koutny, and Alexandre Yakovlev. Logic synthesis for asynchronous circuits based on STG unfoldings and incremental SAT. *Fundamenta Informaticae*, 70(1-2):49–73, 2006.

76. Victor Khomenko, Agnes Madalinski, and Alexandre Yakovlev. Resolution of encoding conflicts by signal insertion and concurrency reduction based on STG unfoldings. In *ACSD*, pages 57–68. IEEE Computer Society, 2006.

77. H. C. M. Kleijn and Maciej Koutny. Process semantics of general inhibitor nets. *Information and Computation*, 190(1):18–69, 2004.

162   References

78. Barbara König and Vitali Kozioura. AUGUR - A tool for the analysis of graph transformation systems. *Bulletin of the EATCS*, 87:126–137, 2005.
79. Leslie Lamport. What good is temporal logic? In R. E. A. Mason, editor, *Information Processing 83*, pages 657–668. Elsevier, 1983.
80. Rom Langerak and Ed Brinksma. A complete finite prefix for process algebra. In Nicolas Halbwachs and Doron Peled, editors, *CAV*, volume 1633 of *Lecture Notes in Computer Science*, pages 184–195. Springer, 1999.
81. Kim Guldstrand Larsen and Mogens Nielsen, editors. *CONCUR 2001 - Concurrency Theory, 12th International Conference, Aalborg, Denmark, August 20-25, 2001, Proceedings*, volume 2154 of *Lecture Notes in Computer Science*. Springer, 2001.
82. Timo Latvala and Heikki Tauriainen. Improved on-the-fly verification with testers. *Nordic Journal of Computing*, 11(2):148–164, 2004.
83. Yu Lei and S. Purushothaman Iyer. An approach to unfolding asynchronous communication protocols. In John Fitzgerald, Ian J. Hayes, and Andrzej Tarlecki, editors, *FM*, volume 3582 of *Lecture Notes in Computer Science*, pages 334–349. Springer, 2005.
84. Kenneth L. McMillan. Using unfoldings to avoid the state explosion problem in the verification of asynchronous circuits. In Gregor von Bochmann and David K. Probst, editors, *CAV*, volume 663 of *Lecture Notes in Computer Science*, pages 164–177. Springer, 1992.
85. Kenneth L. McMillan. *Symbolic Model Checking*. Kluwer Academic Publishers, 1993.
86. Kenneth L. McMillan. A technique of state space search based on unfolding. *Formal Methods in System Design*, 6(1):45–65, 1995.
87. Kenneth L. McMillan. Trace theoretic verification of asynchronous circuits using unfoldings. In Pierre Wolper, editor, *CAV*, volume 939 of *Lecture Notes in Computer Science*, pages 180–195. Springer, 1995.
88. Stephan Melzer and Stefan Römer. Deadlock checking using net unfoldings. In Grumberg [53], pages 352–363.
89. Stephan Melzer, Stefan Römer, and Javier Esparza. Verification using PEP. In Martin Wirsing and Maurice Nivat, editors, *AMAST*, volume 1101 of *Lecture Notes in Computer Science*, pages 591–594. Springer, 1996.
90. Robin Milner. *Communication and Concurrency*. Prentice Hall, 1989.
91. Peter Niebert, Michaela Huhn, Sarah Zennou, and Denis Lugiez. Local first search - A new paradigm for partial order reductions. In Larsen and Nielsen [81], pages 396–410.
92. Peter Niebert and Hongyang Qu. The implementation of Mazurkiewicz traces in POEM. In Graf and Zhang [50], pages 508–522.
93. Mogens Nielsen, Gordon D. Plotkin, and Glynn Winskel. Petri nets, event structures and domains. *Theoretical Computer Science*, 13(1):85–108, 1981.
94. Mogens Nielsen, Grzegorz Rozenberg, and P. S. Thiagarajan. Behavioural notions for elementary net systems. *Distributed Computing*, 4:45–57, 1990.
95. Mogens Nielsen, Grzegorz Rozenberg, and P. S. Thiagarajan. Transition systems, event structures and unfoldings. *Information and Computation*, 118(2):191–207, 1995.
96. Ilkka Niemelä and Patrik Simons. Smodels - An implementation of the stable model and well-founded semantics for normal logic programs. In Jürgen Dix, Ulrich Furbach, and Anil Nerode, editors, *LPNMR*, volume 1265 of *Lecture Notes in Computer Science*, pages 421–430. Springer, 1997.

97. Catuscia Palamidessi, editor. *CONCUR 2000 - Concurrency Theory, 11th International Conference, University Park, PA, USA, August 22-25, 2000, Proceedings*, volume 1877 of *Lecture Notes in Computer Science*. Springer, 2000.

98. Christos H. Papadimitriou. *Computational Complexity*. Addison-Wesley, 1994.

99. Doron Peled. Combining partial order reductions with on-the-fly model-checking. *Formal Methods in System Design*, 8(1):39–64, 1996.

100. Doron Peled and Thomas Wilke. Stutter-invariant temporal properties are expressible without the next-time operator. *Inf. Process. Lett.*, 63(5):243–246, 1997.

101. Carl Adam Petri. *Kommunikation mit Automaten*. Bonn: Institut für Instrumentelle Mathematik, Schriften des IIM Nr. 2, 1962.

102. Carl Adam Petri. Kommunikation mit automaten. *New York: Griffiss Air Force Base, Technical Report RADC-TR-65-377*, 1:1–Suppl. 1, 1966. English translation.

103. Carl Adam Petri. Non-sequential processes. Technical Report ISF-77-5, Gesellschaft für Mathematik und Datenverarbeitung, 1977.

104. Amir Pnueli. The temporal logic of programs. In *FOCS*, pages 46–57. IEEE, 1977.

105. Arthur Prior. *Past, Present and Future*. Oxford: Clarendon Press, 1967.

106. Wolfgang Reisig and Grzegorz Rozenberg, editors. *Lectures on Petri Nets I: Basic Models, Advances in Petri Nets, the volumes are based on the Advanced Course on Petri Nets, held in Dagstuhl, September 1996*, volume 1491 of *Lecture Notes in Computer Science*. Springer, 1998.

107. Stefan Römer. *Theorie und Praxis der Netzentfaltungen als Basis für die Verifikation nebenläufiger Systeme*. PhD thesis, Technische Universität München, Fakultät für Informatik, München, Germany, 2000.

108. Grzegorz Rozenberg and Joost Engelfriet. Elementary net systems. In Reisig and Rozenberg [106], pages 12–121.

109. Claus Schröter. *Halbordnungs- und Reduktionstechniken für die automatische Verifikation von verteilten Systemen*. PhD thesis, Universität Stuttgart, 2006.

110. Claus Schröter and Victor Khomenko. Parallel LTL-X model checking of high-level Petri nets based on unfoldings. In Rajeev Alur and Doron Peled, editors, *CAV*, volume 3114 of *Lecture Notes in Computer Science*, pages 109–121. Springer, 2004.

111. Claus Schröter, Stefan Schwoon, and Javier Esparza. The model-checking kit. In Wil M. P. van der Aalst and Eike Best, editors, *ICATPN*, volume 2679 of *Lecture Notes in Computer Science*, pages 463–472. Springer, 2003.

112. Stefan Schwoon and Javier Esparza. A note on on-the-fly verification algorithms. In Nicolas Halbwachs and Lenore D. Zuck, editors, *TACAS*, volume 3440 of *Lecture Notes in Computer Science*, pages 174–190. Springer, 2005.

113. Colin Stirling and David Walker. Local model checking in the modal mu-calculus. *Theoretical Computer Science*, 89(1):161–177, 1991.

114. Robert E. Tarjan. Depth-first search and linear graph algorithms. *SIAM Journal of Computing*, 1(2):146–160, 1972.

115. Antti Valmari. Stubborn sets for reduced state space generation. In Grzegorz Rozenberg, editor, *Applications and Theory of Petri Nets*, volume 483 of *Lecture Notes in Computer Science*, pages 491–515. Springer, 1989.

116. Antti Valmari. A stubborn attack on state explosion. In Edmund M. Clarke and Robert P. Kurshan, editors, *CAV*, volume 531 of *Lecture Notes in Computer Science*, pages 156–165. Springer, 1990.

117. Antti Valmari. On-the-fly verification with stubborn sets. In Costas Courcou-betis, editor, *CAV*, volume 697 of *Lecture Notes in Computer Science*, pages 397–408. Springer, 1993.
118. Antti Valmari. The state explosion problem. In Reisig and Rozenberg [106], pages 429–528.
119. Moshe Y. Vardi and Pierre Wolper. An automata-theoretic approach to au-tomatic program verification (preliminary report). In *LICS*, pages 332–344. IEEE Computer Society, 1986.
120. Moshe Y. Vardi and Pierre Wolper. Reasoning about infinite computations. *Information and Computation*, 115(1):1–37, 1994.
121. Walter Vogler, Alexei L. Semenov, and Alexandre Yakovlev. Unfolding and finite prefix for nets with read arcs. In Davide Sangiorgi and Robert de Simone, editors, *CONCUR*, volume 1466 of *Lecture Notes in Computer Science*, pages 501–516. Springer, 1998.
122. Frank Wallner. Model checking LTL using net unfoldings. In Alan J. Hu and Moshe Y. Vardi, editors, *CAV*, volume 1427 of *Lecture Notes in Computer Science*, pages 207–218. Springer, 1998.
123. Glynn Winskel. Event structures. In Wilfried Brauer, Wolfgang Reisig, and Grzegorz Rozenberg, editors, *Advances in Petri Nets*, volume 255 of *Lecture Notes in Computer Science*, pages 325–392. Springer, 1986.
124. Glynn Winskel. An introduction to event structures. In J. W. de Bakker, Willem P. de Roever, and Grzegorz Rozenberg, editors, *REX Workshop*, vol-ume 354 of *Lecture Notes in Computer Science*, pages 364–397. Springer, 1988.
125. Pierre Wolper and Patrice Godefroid. Partial-order methods for temporal ver-ification. In Eike Best, editor, *CONCUR*, volume 715 of *Lecture Notes in Computer Science*, pages 233–246. Springer, 1993.

Index

Monographs in Theoretical Computer Science · An EATCS Series

P. Clote, E. Kranakis
**Boolean Functions
and Computation Models**

L.A. Hemaspaandra, M. Ogihara
**The Complexity Theory
Companion**

C.S. Calude
Information and Randomness
An Algorithmic Perspective
2nd ed.

J. Hromkovič
Theoretical Computer Science
Introduction to Automata,
Computability, Complexity,
Algorithmics, Randomization,
Communication and Cryptography

K. Schneider
Verification of Reactive Systems
Formal Methods and Algorithms

S. Ronchi Della Rocca, L. Paolini
The Parametric Lambda Calculus
A Metamodel for Computation

Y. Bertot, P. Castéran
**Interactive Theorem Proving
and Program Development**
Coq'Art: The Calculus
of Inductive Constructions

L. Libkin
Elements of Finite Model Theory

M. Hutter
Universal Artificial Intelligence
Sequential Decisions
Based on Algorithmic Probability

G. Păun, G. Rozenberg, A. Salomaa
DNA Computing
New Computing Paradigms
2nd corr. printing

W. Kluge
Abstract Computing Machines
A Lambda Calculus Perspective

J. Hromkovič
**Design and Analysis of Randomized
Algorithms**
Introduction to Design Paradigms

J. Hromkovič
**Dissemination of Information
in Communication Networks**
Broadcasting, Gossiping, Leader
Election, and Fault Tolerance

R. Kurki-Suonio
**A Practical Theory of Reactive
Systems**
Incremental Modeling of Dynamic
Behaviors

F. Drewes
Grammatical Picture Generation
A Tree-Based Approach

J. Flum, M. Grohe
Parameterized Complexity Theory

D. Bjørner
Software Engineering 1
Abstraction and Modelling

D. Bjørner
Software Engineering 2
Specification of Systems and
Languages

D. Bjørner
Software Engineering 3
Domains, Requirements, and
Software Design

E. Grädel et al.
**Finite Model Theory
and Its Applications**

W. Fokkink
Modelling Distributed Systems

S. Bandyopadhyay
**Dissemination of Information
in Optical Networks**
From Technology to Algorithms